Barracuda Pilot

Barracuda Pilot

D.L.Hadley

Airlife
England

To Patsie

and

my numerous flying instructors

First published in the UK in 1992
by Airlife Publishing Ltd

British Library Cataloguing in Publication Data
  A catalogue record for this book
  is available from the British Library

ISBN 1 85310 195 8

Printed by Livesey Limited, Shrewsbury.

Airlife Publishing Ltd

101 Longden Road, Shrewsbury, SY3 9EB

Contents

Part One — The Tyro

Part Two — The Squadron Pilot

Preface

This book is a line shoot. I make no apology. Most pilots like to shoot a line but dare not do it very often. To get away with it, it has to be done subtly. The classic 'There was I, upside down, nothing on the clock...' is seldom achieved without derisive laughter, well deserved.

But line shooting is a valuable source of information. It is a way of telling your friends about something dangerous, even though exaggerated, in a way that may prevent them killing themselves if they happen to get into the same spot. The average pilot will enjoy the ribaldry and be happy to endure the embarrassment if a little boasting will earn him a moment's glory, and save somebody else from misfortune.

But that is not why I have written this book, although it may turn out to be a lucky consequence. I have written it purely for the fun of shooting a line. I don't think I have exaggerated very much, but I can hear the ribald laughter already.

Part I

The Tyro

Chapter 1
The Beginning

One bleak winter day in 1940 a strange looking aeroplane stood waiting to take off. Poised on its massive undercarriage like some giant insect from a horror story, its Merlin engine throbbing smoothly, it appeared businesslike and efficient. As the pilot opened the throttle it lumbered forward and after a longish run this prototype of the Royal Navy's newest torpedo bomber, the Fairey Barracuda Mark I, struggled gamely into the air on its maiden flight. It was of course but a trick of fate that one year later, on that very same day, on the other side of the world, the pride of the Japanese Naval Air Service swooped treacherously out of a blue Hawaiian dawn to attack Pearl Harbour, crippling the United States Pacific fleet. December 7 is a date unlikely to be forgotten.

I was a medical student then but with the coming of war in 1939 I had lost heart in my studies. In 1940 the Battle of Britain had made the call of the Wild Blue Yonder irresistible, and in November of that year I had my own first flight, from the aerodrome at Abingdon, as a pupil pilot in a de Havilland Tiger Moth, my instructor a rowing blue and a Wing Commander no less. That day, for me at any rate, was an epic day.

Wing Commander Edwards, Commandant of the Oxford University Air Squadron at the time, and I carrying parachutes, walked across the concrete apron towards the Tiger, where it stood waiting on the grass beyond, its wheels chocked, its wings swaying gently in the wind. As the Wing Commander seemed to me somewhat akin to God my replies to his conversation were scarcely more than 'Yes Sir' and 'No Sir'. The truth was I was awed. Here was a man who could fly. I had not met many, and I could feel the glamour of him.

As we reached the aircraft my nostrils picked up a heady scent, an aroma distilled from a mixture of fuel, aircraft dope and oil. Rising in the sun warmed air it has always meant aeroplanes. We stopped to put on our parachutes. The pilot's parachute, which also formed the cushion of his seat, was heavy. I swung it behind my back, wobbling slightly as the weight caught me off balance, then holding one strap over each shoulder clipped them into the 'quick release box', so named because after a landing by parachute, pressing on the centre plate releases all the straps together to prevent the pilot being dragged over the ground like an unhorsed rider with his foot caught in the stirrup. Pulling the leg loop between my legs I threaded the lap straps through it and clipped them into the box as well. I went to straighten up but I couldn't because the parachute is designed to be strapped tightly to the seated person. The cockpit was only two steps away so shambling awkwardly, crouched like a Gibbon, I reached the aircraft. Securely trussed, I climbed carefully up the side, putting my feet in the proper foot steps as the parachute swung me about crazily making things difficult. Aircraft are fragile in places and I had to take care not to kick a hole in the side. I swung a leg over on to the seat then got the other jammed by the parachute as it came over the side. After a bit of juggling I managed to get my feet on to the floor and the parachute on to the seat as I sat down in triumph. To keep me there, there was another harness, the Sutton harness. This had four very strong webbing and leather straps pierced with brass reinforced holes which fitted over a steel peg attached to the left shoulder strap and all held together with a spring clip. Pull out the clip and the harness falls away; useful when leaving in a hurry. Helped by the mechanic I strapped myself in. Right lap strap as tight as possible over left shoulder strap, next left lap strap then right shoulder strap to finish, all as tight as our combined efforts could make them.

I could not move at all, in fact I could scarcely breathe. The mechanic plugged in the Gosport speaking tube from my helmet to the voice pipe to the front cockpit, in a Tiger Moth the pupil sits behind the pilot, and my mentor came on the air.

'Strapped in all right?'

'Yes Sir, the harness feels rather tight though.'

'Has to be — keeps you in the seat when we fly inverted. It'll ease off in a minute or two. Right then here we go.'

With that he began to start the engine. It might seem odd that the pupil in a Tiger Moth sits in the back cockpit, but this is so that there will be no change in trim as the instructor, whose seat is at the centre of gravity, gets out on the day when the pupil makes his first solo. It was thought too, that it was comforting for the pupil to be able to see the instructor's head, to know that he was alive and working properly and as the Tiger was always flown solo from the back seat the pilot was unlikely to forget when he was alone. My mentor was busy.

'Petrol on, switches off, suck in' he called.

The mechanic on the propeller repeated his words.

'Petrol on, switches off, suck in' and began to turn the propeller. After a few revolutions he called.

'Contact.'

'Contact' repeated my instructor, switching on one of the magnetos. The mechanic gave the propeller blade a sharp pull, twisting his body away as the engine fired and my instructor switched on the other magneto.

The tranquillity was broken. The whole aircraft began to shudder. I could hardly hear for the rush of wind and the noise when my instructor spoke.

'Now we ... it at ... revs to ...'

'I can't hear.'

'We run it at a thousand revs to warm up' he shouted.

The primitive communication system was simply a speaking tube. Each of us had a small trumpet to speak into and the tube from it led straight to the others ears. Speech had to be slow and clear to be heard at all and we used standard phrases so that we should know what was said even if we only half heard it.

'Now to avoid confusion when I hand over to you I shall say you've got her — you will then reply — I've got her — and we know who is flying. We do this every time we change over. When she has warmed up I will check the magnetos'.

We waited a while without talking then he slowly opened the throttle. The unsilenced engine, which up to now had sounded like a powerful motorbike, started to roar. The noise became louder and louder until it was deafening and the whole aircraft shook. It had seemed so fragile as I climbed in, now I thought it would shake itself to pieces before we ever left the ground. The little entry flap on the cockpit, secured by two simple sprung wire bolts rattled furiously. The doped canvas sides of the cockpit slammed in and out. The wings juddered and swayed and one of the mechanics leaned over and held tightly on to the tail to prevent it lifting off the ground. Amid this cacophony, and apparently oblivious to it, my instructor switched off each magneto in turn, the Tiger Moth had two in case one faltered, then opened the throttle to full power to check the maximum revolutions, briefly increasing the shattering roar and vibration even more than seemed possible. At last, everything being to his satisfaction, he closed the throttle and comparative peace returned.

'Seems to be OK.' He waved his arms above his head.

The mechanics pulled the chocks away from in front of the wheels. The Tiger Moth has no brakes.

'Now we will taxi out. Because you can see nothing straight ahead we must taxi on a zig-zag course'.

We swerved drunkenly over the grass to the downwind end of the field. It may seem strange to learn to fly in an aircraft in which it is impossible to look straight ahead, even dangerous perhaps, but in fact it does not matter. Lindberg flew the Atlantic in a closed cabin monoplane with only a small window either side and entirely unable to see ahead because of an enormous fuel tank, not that he was expecting to meet anything, but take off and landing are just as easy looking out to one side. At the downwind end we paused.

Now, vital actions for take off, came the voice of God. Remember TMPFF. Throttle friction nut tight; trim two thirds forward, mixture rich — the lever is wired up on these aircraft — we cannot alter the mixture setting but you will need it when you get to Harvards; Pitch — this would be fine pitch but we have a fixed pitch airscrew; fuel switches to the correct tank — we only have one tank — and enough for the flight — you can see the gauge on the tank above my head; flaps we don't have any but the slats on the leading edge of the top wing are unlocked. Now, have a good look round and see if anyone is coming in to land.

'I can't move.'

'Just move your head. You should be able to twist your head far enough to see your own tail. It means life or death when you get on to operations — you must watch your tail'.

I had another go. The strain was awful.

'It gets better with practice' said God.

'Now, there's the green light' a green Aldis lamp was being flashed at us as he spoke, 'I turn into the wind and open the throttle ...'

His voice disappeared in the insane roar as the aircraft again started to shake and rattle. It waddled forwards a few yards and then as it gathered speed the tail came up. I doubted that it would remain in one piece long enough to fly. As it surged forward over the grass the ride became rougher as the speed increased until we were going at what seemed a fearful rate. Thump, crump, bang, the wheels struck the ground with terrible blows. It seemed to me likely that the undercarriage would be destroyed any second. Then suddenly the motion became smooth. The wind increased to a frightening roar, almost drowning the engine. We were flying. The Tiger was vibrant and alive. I could feel the thrill. Then as I looked over the side at the ground it seemed as if we had stopped. The roaring and rushing were still there and the vibration, but the ground, now rapidly falling away, appeared to be passing underneath at snail's pace. It had never dawned on me until then, but the pilot of a slow flying aircraft feels almost stationary in flight, just as to the watcher on the ground a light aeroplane appears to fly slowly. I had just absorbed this fact when I realised that God was on the air again.

'Did you see that?' Entranced by flight itself I hadn't seen anything.

'No, what?'

'That aircraft crashing.' I was dumbfounded.

'Where?'

'Just back there on the aerodrome. He came in to land as we were taking off and crashed. Didn't you see him?'

How could this man, while fully engaged flying this horrendous rattletrap, be watching somebody else crash? He should have had his mind on what he was doing it seemed to me or we would be ending the same way.

'No Sir, I didn't see him.'

'Stalled too high and broke his undercart. Don't think he hurt himself though.'

'Oh!'

'That was a normal take off by the way'.

Well if he said so he must be right.

'Now, we'll climb up to 3000 feet and I will demonstrate the effects of the controls.'

By now I had got used to the cacophony. The force of the slipstream held the canvas tight against the fuselage so that it did not shake so much in flight as it had on the ground. As we climbed I started to look about. The voice babbled on about pitching, rolling, yawing, stalling, spinning and by the time we had reached 3000 feet and levelled off I was expected to be able to control the thing.

'Now fly straight and level — you've got her.'

'I've got her.' I seized the controls and our aircraft's flight, which had been placid, immediately began to jerk about like a dinghy on a rough sea.

'You are overcorrecting — just gentle pressures are all that is needed.' I persevered. After a while —

'Right I've got her, now I will demonstrate the stall.'

He did. The sickening lurch as the aircraft fell out of the sky, like missing a step on the stairs, was unnerving. He calmly chattered on all the way through. We tried a few more manoeuvres.

'Now take me back to the aerodrome.' I looked about. Things look very different from the air, and nowhere could I see anything which looked even remotely like the aerodrome. In fact I couldn't see anything I could recognise at all. I was flying over a field full of dogs — er no they were cows, they looked so small they had me fooled for a minute.

'Can't you see it?'

'No.'

'Look in front — about 10 o'clock.'

I peered in that direction. Still I couldn't see it. After a while, quite by chance, I spotted one of the hangars, then I saw the airfield, it looked very small. I clumsily skidded the aeroplane round towards it and of course it immediately disappeared from view under the nose. Never mind. I aimed for the road junction near by. As we got nearer he took over again.

'I've got her, now I shall make a normal circuit and land.'

He did so explaining carefully how to join the circuit and fly round in a set pattern to avoid the risk of collision.

' ... now on the downward leg, when the wing tip passes the downward boundary turn 90° to port. Now flying crosswind descend at 500 feet a minute, trim to glide at 65 knots. At 400 feet turn 90° to port again, into wind, and begin your final approach.'

As we glided in it seemed to me that we were going too fast and approaching much too steeply, but how would I know? The ground started to flash past more rapidly the nearer we came to it.

'Begin to level off at thirty feet.'

'How do I know when I'm at thirty feet?'

'As you look at the grass now it looks like a green blur.'

'Yes.'

'When you can see the individual blades of grass you are at thirty feet.'

'I see.'

We continued to plunge down.

'Now a little back pressure on the stick — see the blades of grass. As you get close to the ground ease the stick back gently — try to hold it off — try to hold off as long as you can, that's all you have to do. Don't try to land she'll do that herself.'

Bang — bump — bump, the wheels and the tail skid hit the ground together in a perfect landing followed by a gentle bounce.

'Now keep straight — you have to watch her until she stops rolling or she'll swing off.'

I had not expected the landing to sound so loud or feel a thump. Watched from a distance it always looked so smooth.

'Well — how do you like flying?'
I was almost speechless but not quite.

'Fine, I like it.' I scarcely knew it but I was hooked. Life would never be the same again. As we taxied back I scarcely heard the engine. After the shattering roar I had been listening to for the past hour this was nothing, besides I had not been able to clear my ears on the way down and I was slightly deaf.

We switched off and climbed out. As we walked away I felt immense gratitude to this man. I knew now why I wanted to fly. I could not have explained it or say why if any one had asked me, but I knew.

A few days later we went flying again. Since the earliest days of flying, spinning has been viewed with awe by aviators and non-aviators alike. Some aircraft spin and recover quite easily, some do not, and some — especially large aircraft — no pilot would ever dream of spinning. Training aircraft were designed to be spun and to recover fairly easily. Recovery was something the Tiger could do by itself if allowed to, and high enough. My instructor wasted no time messing about.

It was, explained Wing Commander Edwards, about the worst thing that could happen to a pilot. I agreed that no doubt this was so. It was, he said, important therefore to learn how to get out of one. I agreed with that too. You will find, he said, that you have to go against your natural instincts, this too seemed not unlikely. In a spin the aircraft is stalled and falling out of control. The only way to recover, he said, was to increase speed in what seemed a desperate manoeuvre by making the aircraft dive. I agreed that this certainly seemed a desperate manoeuvre, but in the circumstances I thought that perhaps this did not matter if all was lost. He then explained that as it happened all was not lost but that by increasing speed we restored the airflow over the wings and tail, and the aircraft could then be brought back under control. This seemed to me a better proposition. Height, he said, and speed were the pilot's best friends. Do not believe your old granny, he said, when she tells you that you will be safer if you fly slowly and stay close to the ground. I said I wouldn't.

'So' said my instructor 'we will go up and do a spin'.
We took off and climbed up. He came on the air:

'Accidental spinning results from misuse of the controls. An aeroplane spins only if stalled. We are at 5000 feet now, which is plenty for a Tiger. First we make a 360° turn to see that there is no one underneath. Then we close the throttle, and keeping the nose above the horizon wait for the speed to fall.' He did, and it did.

'Just before the stall apply full rudder and ease back the stick and hold it fully back ...'

The bottom fell out of the world. It was awful. A terrible feeling of falling strapped tightly to this shuddering gyrating thing. A nightmare come to life. As I stared down, the only things I could see were fields whirling round and coming closer every second. I felt fear, and sweat beginning to form. Caught in this dreadful kaleidoscope I was conscious only of a cow grazing contentedly at the hub of the vortex. It looked calm and peaceful. I doubted if I would ever enjoy peace or calm again. The voice of my instructor had been droning on unheard. Now I became dimly aware of it. In calm unhurried tones:

' ... full opposite rudder, ease the stick forward. When the spinning stops centralise the rudder and gentle back pressure on the stick to recover from the dive. Note the loss of height.'

The Tiger came out of its dive smoothly, crushing me further into the seat by centrifugal force. Well, I thought, that's it. I shall never, ever, be able to fly after all. I've had it if that's what I have to do. How can anyone fly? The instructor was babbling on:

'Now we have regained the height we lost, nothing below, we'll do one to the right this time.'

I scarcely had time to realise what he had said before we had lurched into another spin. The same horrible falling, whirling yet this time somehow it did not seem so bad. I could see the same cow below again but felt that I might live to join it safely on the ground after all. We recovered uneventfully.

'Right' said Nemesis 'Now you do one'. We climbed up and circled round to have a look below.

'You've got her, you know what to do, carry on and do a spin to the right.'

This time I enjoyed it. Perhaps everything would be all right and I would make a pilot after all. It was a thrill, like going over the top of a roller coaster then hitting a bend.

Tales are still told of spins to make the hair stand on end and curdle the blood. There is the tale of the pilot of a Halifax bomber who was thrown into a spin by a close burst of anti-aircraft fire. By closing the throttles of both engines on the outside wing and fully opening both engines on the inside wing the combined efforts of himself and his co-pilot who each had both feet on one side of the rudder pedals managed to get it out after losing 12,000 feet. It must have aged them. Tail spins, flat spins, inverted spins, spins in cloud all bring to mind visions of peril. It must be worse diving to earth in an aircraft on fire, as one of my later instructors had done and for which he proudly wore a medal, but the spin has a reputation all its own. It is still the unknown quantity. My training continued.

In war time the length of time that it takes to train a pilot is a big disadvantage. In order to try to reduce this the Air Ministry instituted an experiment in the Oxford University Air Squadron in which prospective pilots were 'taught to fly', initially, in a Link Trainer, in the hope that the time it took to go solo would be reduced. The Link Trainer was the forerunner of the flight simulator. Every aerodrome had one, at least. Invented by Ed Link, a Canadian from Gananoque, it was a full sized cockpit equipped with a full set of instruments operated by computers to give simulated flight readings as the controls were moved. Enclosed in a ridiculous toy aeroplane painted bright blue it had silver painted caricatures of wings about six feet wide and a toy tail. It was mounted on a black cube about three feet across which housed bellows, springs and electric motors which wheezed and whirred as they made the 'aeroplane' rotate and pitch and bank in response to the control movements made by the pilot. There even appeared to be a propeller, but this, in fact, was a ventilating fan to keep the harassed pilot cool. The cockpit was covered with a hood so that the pilot could not see the funny little aeroplane he was flying, but only his instruments, although the hood could be raised or removed for initial training.

The movements made by the Link Trainer turning and the speed being varied as the pilot moved the controls were plotted, through the computer, by a wheeled device known as the 'crab' which inched its way across a glass topped table, faithfully recording in red ink the pilot's every change of course, and speed. The instructor, who sat at the table, with a duplicate set of instruments, gave commands and courses to steer over the 'radio telephone' to the pilot, and in order to keep the pupil alert the instructor had various tricks he could play. By pressing a button he could 'ice up' the airspeed indicator or altimeter so that it remained fixed on one reading. It might be some time before the pilot noticed that something was wrong. Another switch turned on 'rough air'. This caused the Link to lurch about and swerve suddenly off course, or else drift gently round in a way which might go un-noticed.

'Now, keeping the aircraft straight and level close the throttle. Look at the vertical speed indicator, you are losing height at 500 feet a minute but your speed has not changed. Now open the throttle fully. The speed stays the same but you are climbing. This shows you that the throttle controls your height not your speed. Resume the cruising speed setting. Push the stick forward — the speed increases — open the throttle to maintain height. The stick controls the speed, the throttle, height. Remember these two things.'

The Link Trainer in Oxford was surrounded by a circular screen painted to represent various types of countryside and weather. There was a horizon visible on part of the screen but this was obscured in the bad weather section. After a few hours practice on the Link I, and other pupils, had a good idea what the controls did and even what to do to recover from a spin, but from the Air Ministry's point of view the experiment was a failure, as almost nobody was able to fly solo after four hours dual instruction in the air, which was what had been hoped. Real flying was different.

Wing Commander Edwards and I flew together a few more times then my medical studies began to take up too much of my time. In the summer of 1941, after much fruitless effort, happily, I failed my exams. There seemed no point in waiting for the inevitable call-up so I wandered down the Woodstock road to the Naval recruiting office and volunteered for the Fleet Air Arm. A few weeks later I had an interview, and a brief medical examination, and I was in.

I spent the next few months while awaiting my call up trying to pass the exams I had failed, in a desultory sort of way, without much hope and even less enthusiasm, then I had a letter from the Admiralty directing me to report to the Royal Naval Air Station — HMS *Daedalus* — at Lee-on-Solent, and enclosing a travel warrant.

Chapter 2

HMS Daedalus

'All the nice girls love a sailor'

A click from the Tannoy loud speaker on the wall of the hut woke me from a dreamless sleep. The gentle hum coming from it told me that it was about to give forth. I lay in the dark, listening. There were a couple of minor noises then, with no further warning, the blast from a naval bugler playing reveille one foot away from the microphone shattered the peace.

Together with the other eleven occupants of the hut I jerked in a spasm of disbelief then fell back limply to wait for the din to stop. It was day break, 0630 hours as the Navy had it, May 1942, although pitch dark in the hut because of the war time blackout over the windows. Before we could gather our wits the lights were switched on and the raucous voice of a Chief Petty Officer came on the air:

'Wakey, wakey, wakey — rise and shine — show a leg, show a leg, show a leg — the sun is burning your eyeballs out — wakey, wakey, wakey — lash up and stow.'

Again we convulsed and collapsed back under the blankets — naval airmen second class didn't get sheets — to wait for a lull. It came, but was brief. The hum in the loud speaker continued, to be followed by the hiss of a gramophone needle. Then again — at full blast:

'Ai, Ai, Ai,' the strident voice of Carmen Miranda, 'the Brazilian Bomb Shell', singing 'Minnie from Trinidad' at the top of her exotic voice.

All hope of further sleep now vanished and we twelve 'new entries' together with a hundred and forty more in similar huts beside the parade ground of HMS *Daedalus* leaped from our beds and set about washing and shaving, dressing and folding our blankets, before rushing outside to be on parade at 0655 hours, there to be greeted by Chief Petty Officer Kent himself.

Once a month the Navy took in about a hundred and fifty hopeful young men to train as pilots for its aircraft. I had reported to HMS

Daedalus the 'stone frigate' at Lee-on-Solent along with the other hopefuls the day before. Eighteen months later about forty of us would have qualified as squadron pilots. Of those who failed the course some would become observers, some would go to sea.

Outside in the fresh morning air Chief Petty Officer Kent addressed us:

'My Farther was an orficer' — he had been a warrant officer, the highest non-commissioned rank in the Navy and one of those pearls of great price that the Navy produces — 'and one day you'll be orficers, but first you 'ave to learn to be'ave like orficers and learn to take orders — and the first thing you 'ave to learn is 'ow to move like orficers so I'm 'ere to teach you Field Training.'

Field Training was the Navy's name for 'square bashing' or parade ground drill.

We were to be at *Daedalus* for two weeks to be kitted out, medically inspected and injected and generally taught the rudiments of naval life before going to HMS *St Vincent* — another stone frigate, in Gosport — for our preliminary training. Chief Petty Officer Kent then dispatched us to breakfast, enjoining us to:

'Get fell in again 'ere at oh eight 'undred 'ours after tidying the 'uts which I shall inspect.'

Now the naval airman second class was generally regarded as the lowest form of life in the Navy. A position previously held by the stokers despite their vital role at sea. We were however to be dressed like sailors so the next thing on the day's agenda was to visit the clothing store. We were placed under the care of a leading naval airman, a 'Killick' because of the anchor he wore proudly on his left arm. In fact he had only been in the Navy three months. He had just finished his training at *St Vincent* and was waiting to be sent to flying training school. But he had the aura of command. However, he realised the fragility of his position. 'Right — feet together — face that way — go.' A smile lit up his face as he said it. He knew that we scarcely knew the meaning of 'quick march', and it broke the ice. We laughed and set off. The clothing store — better known as the slops — was our destination. Here the 'Pusser's mate' presided. He was a Chief Petty Officer in the supply branch and dished out everything from uniform to flags, catapult wires to cutlery, soap to cheese — sometimes barely distinguishable from each other except that the soap was kept in a canvas bag with the sailors kit.

As we entered this emporium we found ourselves separated from the staff by a long counter on which were piles of clothing and everything else we needed.

'Size?'

'I beg pardon.'

'What size are you?'

'I don't know.'

The supply rating gave me a quizzical look then hurled a pair of trousers at me.

'Try these.'

I did — they were about a foot too long.

'Sorry, these are too big.'

'Right try these.' This pair turned out to be quite a good fit.

'Right move along.' He hurled a second pair of trousers at me.

'Try this.' a matelot's jumper flew through the air. Now the sailor's jumper is not as you might suppose a knitted jersey, we were given one of those as well, but a serge garment, like the trousers, with no stretch in it at all. If you can get into it — it fits. There were about twenty of us in this 'detail' which had been sent to get kit, and very soon we were all firmly wedged half in and half out of our jumpers, bent double trying to see through the neck hole and demanding assistance from friends. We pulled and jerked each other into the things then out of them again after which we were all hot, tousled and panting for breath. Once in, the male form became quite the most desirable thing that any gorgeous young female could want, which accounted for the fact that 'Jack' would happily put up with the inconvenience of getting into and out of it.

The generous hand-out went on until we had, as well as the trousers and jumpers, two 'blue jean collars', two pairs of 'drawers' — the official description for pants, two 'flannels' — shirts, two caps — with ribbons, two black silk 'handkerchiefs' — worn as scarves in perpetual mourning for Admiral the Lord Horatio Nelson, Duke of Bronte, one waist belt, two towels, a pair of shoes, a pair of regulation boots, cleaning brushes, a wooden type made up in our names, for marking clothes, comb, hairbrush, tooth brush, clothes brush — sailors always look clean, knife, knife lanyards, two, soap bag — for soap, a 'ditty box' — nothing to do with songs this was a small suitcase for personal possessions, Admiralty Manual of Seamanship volume one, oilskins, an overcoat and to stow the whole lot in, a kit bag.

Acquiring this bonanza took most of the morning. We then stuggled back to our huts carrying the loot. The afternoon we were to spend marking it and trying it on. We had scarcely arrived back and dumped our gear on the beds when the Tannoy clicked menacingly and the bugler came on the air again. He blew a little tune —

meaningless to us — then: 'Hands to dinner' — ratings don't have lunch. You don't wait for a second invitation in the Navy so off we went.

Now every rating, except boys, was entitled at lunch time to a tot of grog. This consisted of a measure of the Navy's best 100% proof, not out of bond, rum diluted with one third of water and accurately ladled out, supervised by the officer of the watch. However, as we were 'under training' we didn't get it. We had an extra three pence a day in lieu. We had our lunch dry, then returned to our huts.

Nothing in the Navy is left to chance so on page four of the manual of seamanship is a paragraph:

How clothing is marked.

The clothes of all ratings are to be marked. The clothes of men dressed as seamen are to be marked as follows, with a ⅜″ type, block letters :-

Blue clothes — with white paint.

White clothes — with marking ink.

Jerseys and comforters — with red worsted, or on a white tape in ink and sewn over with blue worsted.

Overcoats, jackets and oilskins — across the shoulders inside.

Trousers, drawers and cholera belts — on the inside of the waistband at the back.

Jumpers (except working jumpers) — under the collar.

Working jumpers — on the back close up to the collar seam.

Canvas jacket and overalls — on the back close up to the collar inside.

Flannels — on the tail.

Caps — in the crown.

Cap covers on the band inside.

Towels — at both ends in the centre horizontally.

Handkerchiefs — diagonally across the corner.

Boots and shoes — inside the upper.

Jerseys — on the inside of the bottom tabling.

See that the type is clean and the paint is not too thick.

Note. The marking of class I and class III clothes is to conform as far as possible with that laid down for class II.

All as clear as daylight — except that there was no explanation about the final note. Possibly it was some sort of initiative test.

A room was provided for the marking. There were two tables. On one was a tray lined with felt and soaked in black paint. On the other the same in white. We moved from one to the other anointing our clothes in the regulation way supervised by a petty officer who replenished the trays with paint from time to time and answered our queries. The worsted bits we put off for another day and I don't think they ever got done. The sailors 'make and mend' in our day had degenerated into a smoking and card school for new entry N.A.2s.

Now in the Admiralty Manual of Seamanship there was a photograph of a correctly dressed sailor for us to emulate. A three badge Killick with a long service medal on his chest he appears to be of small stature. Doubtless he fitted the page in the seamanship manual better than a taller man would have. He looks solid, even wooden, so it is a surprise to read on his cap ribbon the name of his ship, HMS *Vivid*. I am sure he was a most worthy man and an outstanding member of the destroyer's crew, but any resemblance between him and 'Jack ashore' was accidental and would have been denied by both. Once the matelot left the liberty boat his sex appeal began to shine like a star of the first magnitude. He had no brass to polish like his brothers in the Army or the Royal Air Force but his willowy body in a form fitting uniform with bell bottom trousers and his cap 'flat aback' was a cynosure which drew many eyes. Standing at the bar he had no rival.

However this was not achieved without tremendous effort. The apparent simplicity of the uniform belied its intricacies. To begin with the flannel, or shirt, was often not a shirt but two pieces of material, front and back, tied together with tapes to stretch it tightly across its owner's chest. The 'V' neck of the jumper could be judiciously, if illegally, extended downward so that it gaped to expose the tightly stretched flannel to seductive advantage. The blue jean collar when issued was a deep navy blue, but vigorous and careful washing followed by pressing in the seamanship manual turned it into a delicate pale blue creation with knife edge creases. It too was tied on with tapes running through a loop at the back in a complicated way.

When you live out of your kit bag you cannot have normally creased trousers so the sailor had 'box creases'. You turned the trousers inside out, folded each leg zig-zag into seven folds then rolled both up together in the top part of the trousers and tied the bundle firmly with twine or cod line. If you look for 'string' to do this job, in the Navy you would look in vain, it is unknown. When unfolded, and ready to wear, the trousers almost stood up by themselves. They had no fly, but a drop-flap front like a trap door. Nelson's black handkerchief, also pressed in the seamanship manual, and folded to form a scarf worn under the collar made the matelot quite the most dazzling being ever made.

We practised getting this outfit on. When tea was 'piped' anyone in uniform had to stay that way or miss tea. This turned out to be awkward for one or two or us.

'Hey you.'

'Me.'

'Yes you, don't you salute when you see an officer? and call me sir.'

'Yes sir, sorry sir' I fled. The rest of the day was our own.

Next morning at 0655 we paraded again, in uniform. Dressing was a considerable struggle and most of us needed a friend to pull down the jumper over his head and then extract the collar, which had to be tied on first, so that it lay outside. Some of the scarves looked a little odd. Chief Petty Officer Kent or his 'oppo' Chief Petty Officer Southwell, inspected us closely as we stood before him.

'Put your cap on straight.' He tweaked a few of the scarves where they were tied with tapes at the point of the 'V' neck. They came undone.

'Tie those properly.'

'Now, this morning you 'ave your medicals. After breakfast you come back and get fell in 'ere then we go to the doctors — Dis-miss.'

We ate our breakfast in silent contemplation of the ordeal to come. We had heard hair raising accounts from previous victims. We returned to our huts to await events. We had all been medically examined before we ever joined, in the recruiting office, but in order to fly, a more searching examination was required.

'Squad 'shun — left turn — quick march.'

We were beginning to learn. We arrived at the Sick Bay.

'Squad — halt — stand at ease.'

We waited patiently as the Killick went inside. After a few moments he came out again.

'When I give the order for you to dismiss you will turn left smartly then fall out and file into the Sick Bay.'

'Squad — 'shun. Dis — miss.'

We trooped inside. Part of the hut was divided into cubicles. We stood in a sort of foyer. A Sick Berth Chief Petty Officer eyed us without enthusiasm.

'Right — strip off — pile your gear on the bench by the wall and get fell in 'ere.'

We paraded nude, standing at ease, though uneasily, in a double line. The Chief walked over to the medical officer seated at a desk.

'Detail ready for inspection sir.'

The MO, a gaunt lugubrious Surgeon Commander eased himself out of his chair and came over to us. He walked slowly along the line holding his hands safely behind his back to avoid any possibility of contamination and scrutinised each new entry carefully in the most intimate way as well as giving each one of us a good overall stare. He walked down the front of each line then along the rear to examine us closely from behind. He completed his inspection in breathtaking silence. The expression on his face suggested that he may have been more accustomed to inspecting the drains. At last he had finished.

'Right' he said 'FFI — carry on.'

'Right' said the Chief 'Put your trousers on then collect up the rest of your gear and come with me.'

'What's FFI mean Killick?'

'Free from infestation — no nits, lice, scabies, fleas etc. etc.'

'Wait here' said the Chief 'you will be called in turn for your medical.' We waited.

'Hadley.'

I went through the door where the voice had come from into a darkened room. At one end sat a benign bespectacled MO in a pool of light. He indicated a chair in the shadow.

'Sit down there. I'm going to examine your eyes.'

He asked a few questions then covered my left eye with a spectacle frame in which he put a black disc.

'See that chart over there — read the bottom line.'

'F A X T D N H U P Z.'

'Good' he covered the other eye.

'Now read the bottom line backwards.'

'Z P U H N D T X A F.'

'Good — now just to the left of the chart is a black box.'

I peered into the gloom.

'What can you see?'

'Nothing — er, well I can just see a faint light.'

'Good, what colour is it?'

'Green.'

'Right — now?'

'Red.'

'Good.'

He picked up an instrument which shone a bright light into my eyes as he peered through it.

'That looks all right. Now go to the doctor in the next room — he wants to look in your ears.'

Half blinded by his efforts I staggered out of his office into the next one and was directed to a chair. This doctor had a large mirror strapped to his head.

'Had any trouble with your ears?'

'No sir.'

'Suffer from colds, coughs, sinus troubles, hay fever?'

'No sir.' We all knew that it was best to answer no to all these questions.

'Right.'

The MO swivelled the mirror down in front of his face then peering through a hole in the middle reflected the beam from a powerful searchlight on to my head. He rammed a cold metal trumpet into my ear and then seizing my ear and heaving on it he peered inside. I had the feeling that he rather expected to see right through to the wall on the other side.

'Hold your nose, keep your mouth shut and blow hard.'

I wondered if perhaps he was not a doctor at all but an escaped lunatic. If so it might be better to humour him until I could get away. He still had that trumpet rammed well into my head and a firm grip on my ear. I did as he asked. My ears popped.

'Good, now turn round while I look in the other one.'

We repeated the performance.

'Now, open your mouth.' He pushed a piece of wood into my throat. I was nearly sick on his lap. Doubtless years of practice had sharpened his reflexes enough for him to leap out of the way in time if necessary.

'Right you'll do — through that door.'

'Ah — come in — sit down.'

The new doctor looked a bit older but no less potty than the previous ones. He proceeded to read out a list of diseases and afflictions. Some of these I had not even heard of and some I thought it was rather vulgar of him to mention.

'Have you had any of those?'

'No sir.'

'Blackouts, fits, giddy attacks?'

'No sir' The MO put the cold end of his stethoscope on my chest.

'Breath in — out — in — out — cough — he peered at my private parts, good' He wrapped a cuff round my arm.

'I'm going to measure your blood pressure. This will feel a bit tight.' I wondered if I would ever use my arm again. Eventually he eased it off.

'Now lie on this couch.' He prodded my abdomen as if he were making bread.

'Now come and sit down again.' He extracted from a jar containing some repulsive antiseptic mixture a mouth piece attached to a rubber tube. At the other end of the tube was a gauge containing a column of mercury. He handed the mouthpiece of this revolting contrivance to me.

'I want you to blow into this tube. Blow the mercury up to that mark and hold it there as long as you can.'

I put it in my mouth — it tasted foul. He started a stop-watch as I began to blow. It was not difficult, the mercury level slowly rose to the mark. After fifteen seconds I realised that this was not quite the 'piece of cake' I had supposed. After thirty seconds I felt I couldn't go on much longer.

'That's right — well done — keep it there now, don't let it fall.' The old fool babbled on. I began to go red in the face. My eyes began to bulge. After forty five seconds I was ready to let go.

'Well done — keep it up' this antique sadist was getting quite excited now. My sight started to go dim, my lungs were now bursting. My fading gaze was fixed on that terrible column of mercury as the stop-watch ticked on. This mad man should be locked up I thought, he's insane, all right, I'll show him. I'll hold the mercury up until I drop dead at his feet. That'll upset him. After fifty eight seconds I could do no more. I was pressing my lips together over the mouth-piece with my hand but the air started to escape together with spit making a wet spluttering noise as it did so. Sixty seconds. I exploded. Gasping for breath I dimly heard his voice.

'Well done — that's all from me, now go next door for your inoculations.'

I gathered up my clothes and my wits and moved on.

In the next room a production line was in operation. With a hundred and fifty new entries every month a system was necessary. On a table a sterilizer bubbled merrily, presided over by a fiendish looking Sick Berth Petty Officer holding a pair of long tongs in each hand. From time to time he delved into the cauldron and came up with parts of a syringe which he deftly fitted together then put on a tray ready for the doctor. The doctor meanwhile was giving an injection. As soon as he had finished:

'Next.' The line moved on one place. He turned round, handed the spent syringe to the Petty Officer, picked up a new one, fitted a needle, drew up a generous portion of some evil looking brew, said to be Tetanus Toxoid and Typhoid serum, and plunged it into the arm of the boy standing half naked before him.

'Next.' The line moved again. He repeated the loading procedure as the used syringe was put into the sterilizer, turned again and stabbed the next victim. 'Next.' This all went quite smoothly until he came to Murchison, a youth about five places in front of me. As he turned to renew his syringe after giving the injection another doctor came over to speak to him. He carried on automatically with his task as he held a conversation with his fellow officer but failed to say the magic word — next. Murchison stood his ground obediently, doubtless thinking that perhaps he had only had half his ration as the MO turned round and gave him a second jab. By now feeling a little faint he continued to stand there, his brain unable to take the necessary action to get him moving. The distracted MO spun round and gave him a third dose whereupon Murchison crashed to the floor in a faint, cutting his lip on the edge of a duck board as he fell.

'Oh Gawd — pick that man up and put him on the bench over there.' Two Sick Berth Attendants obliged. People were always fainting when they had injections. The doctor went over to look at him.

'He'll be all right in a minute. When I've finished this lot I'll put a stitch in his lip.'

He went back to his work. The production line moved into top gear again. The Navy had cleverly left the inoculations until the end of the medical exam. After that we were dismissed to lunch. Some of us had by now lost our appetites. The rest of the day was a 'make and mend'. As the afternoon wore on our arms got stiffer and stiffer and we felt slightly unwell, but by the evening we had recovered enough to toy with a little supper. We took care to shield our arms carefully from the accidental buffets of fate and wondered with curiosity what excitements the next day might have in store for us.

It takes time to convert a simple civilian into a ruthless fighter. As we looked at each other I began to wonder how the Admiralty proposed to bring this miracle about. It seemed to me that some of the boys in my hut would scarcely have made deck chair attendants on a cruise liner. Even in uniform I could not see them as the pilots of strike aircraft. However we were still a long way from that. The next thing the Navy wanted to know was whether we could swim. This seemed to show a lack of confidence, I thought, in chaps whose job was to fly off ships. No doubt it would help them to salvage the mistakes, or at least a few of them. In the old days sailors were not encouraged to swim. The Captain preferred to keep them on board. Some even maintained that swimming was unlucky and I dare say it was. The modern Navy however decided to dispense with such superstition. We were taken to the swimming bath.

'How many of you can swim, put your hands up if you can.'

'Right those who can, dive in and swim a length.'

The water was freezing, I swam the fastest length of my life. The non-swimmers went off for something called 'Land drill'. They were instructed in the rudiments in the hope that they might be able to swim before they were taught to fly. A forlorn hope. Our documents were marked swimmer or non-swimmer in the same way that they were marked grog or temperance but there was no extra pay for swimmers, your life was considered to be sufficient reward.

One piece of equipment we all had was a gas mask. We had had those as civilians, given to us in a cardboard box by a protective government and carried over the shoulder by a piece of string. In the Navy this was exchanged for a more elaborate device consisting of a mask connected to a filter by a corrugated hose pipe. The whole thing kept in a green satchel which we had to carry at all times. From time to time we had practice gas alerts. The warning was sounded on a piece of iron girder being hit by another piece of iron. When this happened we had to put the mask on and then carry on doing whatever we were doing before. This was inclined to upset meals or lectures. However, though irksome it was not taken terribly seriously. So in order to impress us with the real necessity of it we had to visit the gas training hut.

'Squad 'shun, rig gas masks.' We did. The instructor then came round to each of us in turn. He squeezed the tube which led from the mask to the filter until the eyes of the occupant began to glaze over then he let go.

'Is it air tight?'

'Yub ther.' the voice did not come very clearly from inside.

The instructor put on his own mask.

'Nov fallob be indo thid hub.'

We trooped inside. The instructor let off a tear gas bomb. As the hut filled with smoke we blundered about as our eye pieces became steamed up — we had forgotten to rub them with the anti-mist cloth provided in the satchel.

'Nov tab of yov maks.' We removed the masks and the stinging gas made us cough and our eyes stream. We rushed for the door.

'Now clean your eye pieces and stow the masks.' We needed no second bidding. We carried them for the whole war.

Our gentle introduction to life in the Royal Navy continued with lectures on ships and aircraft recognition, basic field training, lectures on tradition, a conducted tour of HMS *Victory*, close hair cuts and alternate evenings 'ashore' when we could sample the pleasures of the 'matelot off duty.' For two weeks life jogged pleasantly along then — HMS *St Vincent*.

Chapter 3

41 Pilots Course – HMS St Vincent

'You 'orrible naval airmen'

'Now you lot, tomorrow at 0655 you get fell in 'ere. Them wot's keen gets fell in previous.'

The voice of Chief Petty Officer Willmot rang out across the parade ground. One time Chief Gunner's Mate in HMS *Nelson*, the Navy's mightiest battleship, he was a real sailor. He chewed tobacco. He was a smallish man and a true product of HMS *Excellent* the famous gunnery training school on Whale Island. The gunners were the elite of the Navy. Saved from retirement by the war the fire still burned brightly. He was fierce and had a heart of gold.

Our real training had begun. We paraded frouzily at 0655 and were sent to do odd jobs like cleaning brass or the heads or the floors. We paraded again; had breakfast; paraded again; went to classes; paraded again; had a stand easy, paraded again; went to more classes; paraded again; went to dinner.

We felt we had been hard at work for two days already and were hungry. In the dining hall were giant steel trays — four feet by two feet and three inches deep in which, like huge paving stones, lay steak and kidney puddings, heaving gently under the relentless force of suppressed steam. The chief cook was carving these into goodly sized bricks which he put on to plates. His assistants added potatoes and gravy. As I said we were hungry and we polished off this fare swiftly. Stewed fruit and custard followed and a mug of tea. Five days a week this was our dinner. On Fridays we had fish and on Sundays a roast, when the ubiquitous steel trays contained equivalent sized slabs of plum duff for pudding. The Navy wanted no weaklings in its ships, and suet pudding was the answer.

After dinner we paraded again; went to more classes; paraded again; had a stand easy; paraded again; had tea; paraded again when half of us were dismissed to various minor duties, wearing 'Night Clothing', which was uniform without the collar, while the other half were off watch and could wear their most tiddly dress to 'go ashore' or do as they pleased 'on board'.

At each parade we fell in and were looked over by CPO Willmot or one of his minions to see that we were properly dressed and behaving like 'Orficers'. He would walk round and inspect us closely.

'Am I 'urting you?' He would ask, standing behind some unfortunate.

'No Chief.'

'I should be, I'm standing on you 'air. Get it cut!'

'Yes Chief.'

We were divided into classes of about twenty and, so that we could learn the power of command, each day one of us was put in charge of the others. We marched everywhere as a squad. HMS *St Vincent* had been a boys training establishment. From the main gate the parade ground stretched for fifty yards. An acre of asphalt bounded by sturdy Victorian buildings. Beneath the parade ground were tunnels, converted on the outbreak of war to air raid shelters. Opposite to the main gate was a ship's mast. A full sized mast, square rigged and fully equipped with crosstrees, yards, shrouds with ratlines for climbing them, futtock ropes and on the top the truck, painted gold. From the ground it looked small but was a solid piece of wood big enough to stand on, which occasionally someone did. We were permitted, even encouraged, to climb it. The Navy still expected its sailors to be able to go aloft to haul or reef sails which it had given up using some sixty years before. No doubt they thought it would be good training for the heights of flying. Seamen were notoriously vague about aircraft. A large steel mesh net was provided at the bottom to catch anyone who fell off. Behind the mast was the main barrack block. On the ground floor, fronted by a wide colonnade, were galley, dining hall and classrooms. The two floors above contained dormitories, wash rooms and heads.

We had been in *St Vincent* about a week and were settled happily into the routine of marching about in squads to attend our classes. Naval Airman Second Class Radnor, marching his class to a period of field training on the parade ground, wheeled them under the colonnade. He planned to wheel them out on to the parade ground at the foot of the mast opposite to which the Chief Petty Officer, whose duty it was to instruct them, was standing, waiting. The squad swung briskly along the colonnade. Radnor at the rear, sized up the situation. His class he knew would do exactly what he ordered them to do — right or wrong. As the leading file approached the arch he had decided to march them through. He bided his time, then:

'Squad — left — wheel.'

The double line immediately began to wheel left under the arch he had chosen. Pleased to see that his judgement was correct he followed for a few steps then wheeled left himself through another of the colonnade's arches on to the parade ground. As he stepped into the sunshine he looked over toward his squad. 'My God they've gone!' Of the squad there was no sign. He dodged back under the colonnade to see the last of them disappear between the columns. He hurried back to the parade ground. There was not a soul in sight except the Chief Petty Officer, who had his back to him.

So far as he knew no one had ever actually lost a squad before. He knew of occasions when schoolboys had confused a squad by shouting commands from the other side of the railings when the squad commander had carelessly taken them too close to the road outside *St Vincent*. Squads had been marched accidentally into brick walls by tongue-tied squad commanders. He had even seen a squad marched into a garage. But actually to lose a squad completely, by vanishing, was unknown.

As he stood there and pondered this enigma, eyed curiously by the Chief Petty Office who had turned to greet him, he wished only that he could repeat the trick so skilfully done by the squad. He was about to march over and confess his helplessness when suddenly the squad began to appear. They emerged, two by two, marching in perfect step from the Air Raid shelter. The penny dropped. He had left wheeled them straight into one of the tunnel entrances hidden from him by the pillars of the colonnade.

'Left — wheel.' he called. Obediently the squad marched to the centre of the parade ground as if nothing unusual had happened.

'Squad — halt.' He marched over to the Chief.

'Nearly lost 'em then lad — right, join class.'

But the class was not to be. As he returned to them the air raid warning siren sounded.

'Down the hatch — take cover — chop, chop!'

The Chief Petty Officer hustled them into the shelter again. Naval Airmen Second Class were valuable. They might be useless but they were valuable. They couldn't do anything to keep the enemy's bombers away so they waited in the air raid shelter while Hitler's Stukas and Heinkels had their fun.

But not so CPO Willmot. He was Chief Gunner's mate from Britain's mightiest battleship. Not for nothing had he spent many years training assiduously to reach this exalted post. Anyone who was anyone knew that to be Chief Gunner's mate in HMS *Nelson* was as high as you could go. There was no one, who did not know that. No one who mattered anyway. The Chief Gunner's mate in HMS *Nelson* was a man to be looked up to. He was the Ace. He had nine sixteen inch guns. Monsters which could hurl nine shells, each weighing a ton, twenty miles every 40 seconds as he had done often enough. Then there was the secondary armament, batteries of six inch guns, bigger than those in a destroyer but pop-guns compared to his sixteen inch. And the anti-aircraft guns, the multiple pom-poms. Each pom-pom had eight barrels and each one fired a hundred and twenty rounds a minute. 'Chicago pianos' they were called, and a frightening rattle they played. All of these had been his. Now old, he must have been forty-six if he was a day, he had been put to train naval airmen to be sailors, so that they knew which end of an aircraft carrier was the bow and which the stern, to do the job he had spent his life learning, only they would use bombs and torpedos.

A few months before 41 course came to *St Vincent*, however, his hour had come during another air raid. I could picture him as he hurried up the stairs to the roof of the barrack block, where there was an old Lewis gun, his mouth open as he gasped for breath, showing the black hole studded here and there with blackened fangs which years of tobacco chewing had given him. Panting he reached the roof and whipped the cover off the Lewis gun, all ready, with a drum of ammunition in place. He swung it round as he scanned the horizon. Over Portsmouth he could see the puffs of bursting anti-aircraft shells, and here and there black dust clouds from exploding bombs. A lone Heinkel was flying over the town. He had come too low as he dropped his bombs and was now twisting and turning through the balloon barrage, trying to escape. As Willmot watched, the pilot swung the aircraft out over the harbour at five hundred feet turning steeply and diving to reach the safety of the sea. If he continued the turn the Heinkel would pass right over *St Vincent*. Willmot watched him come. He cocked the Lewis gun and squinted along the barrel. A Chief Gunner's mate he was. Maybe this was only an old .303 Lewis gun, no longer fit for active service, not the nine sixteen inch guns he knew, but it was his, and he had the enemy in his sights. He squeezed the trigger. The old Lewis spoke. Dugger — Dugger — Dugger. The Heinkel was coming straight towards him at two hundred miles an hour. He could see the flashes and puffs of smoke as the nose gunner fired back at him but the bullets went wide. Three or four seconds he held the plane in his sights then it flashed overhead, shaking the building with the roar of its engines as it passed. He swung the Lewis round and took aim again as the Heinkel roared away. Dugger —

Dugger — Dugger. He kept his finger on the trigger until the drum was empty. The plane flew on. He'd missed! But as dejection began to well within him, he, a chief gunner's mate, a puff of black smoke left the port engine. It swelled to a black cloud tinged with flame. The Heinkel lurched to port and began to lose height. As he watched, it sunk down over the town of Gosport and crossed the coast at fifty feet. Another half mile it flew then plunged into the sea.

A slow smile spread over his face. He had not been Chief Gunner's mate in *Nelson* for nothing. He could still lay a gun. As he came down the stairs the smile turned into a broad black grin which spread across his face as he reached the parade ground. 'I got 'im' was all he said as he tilted his cap on to the back of his head like any matelot and strode over to the Chief Petty Officer's mess for his tot.

A ship at anchor in Spithead had to send its off duty sailors ashore in liberty boats, usually at half hourly intervals. In shore establishments the same rules applied. When the 'liberty boat' was piped those wanting to 'go ashore' paraded at the gate. There they were carefully inspected by the officer of the watch or the Master at Arms. Anyone improperly dressed was picked out of line. When the inspection was completed the liberty men were allowed through the gate. If you missed the 'boat' you had to wait for the next one. The 'sea' was just outside the gate just as surely as it was at the foot of a battleship's accommodation ladder in Spithead.

Ashore a sailor might visit the fleapits in Gosport or cross to Portsmouth on the Gosport ferry for a half-penny, where at least six live theatres provided music hall entertainment and the cheapest seats were a shilling. On our pay of two shillings a day we could just manage this plus fish and chips and a beer. If we stayed on board *St Vincent* we could drink in the canteen and play snooker in the haze of duty-free tobacco. Some even managed to study the manual of seamanship or books on aircraft recognition or navigation.

At *St Vincent* we learnt much. Navigation, meteorology, the morse code, how to make a reef knot a bowline and a clove hitch. The only thing we learnt about aircraft was how to recognise some of them in flight. We did our own dhobying, pulled oars in a naval cutter and had lectures on King's Regulations and Admiralty Instructions. Once, as a treat, a pilot, Sub Lieutenant Rose, DSO one of only two pilots to survive the attack by six Swordfish on Scharnhorst and Gneisenau gave us a talk — an hour of dreams — then we lapsed back into the naval routine. Parades, classes, meals, duties, leave. Sometimes there was a little light relief. One day as we stood rigidly to attention before Chief Willmot a Wren hove in sight. As she walked her bosom moved under her blouse like two jellies. They oscillated independently under the forces of gravity, thrust and inertia, upwards and sideways in accordance with Newton's laws of motion, but in a way that could only have been evaluated by Newton's calculus. She was an attractive girl who worked in the clothing store. As she headed across the parade ground eyes, then heads began to swivel on to her. Willmot had the situation in a glance.

'Eyes front.'

His expression left no doubt that any transgressor would be on the Commander's report. The heels clicked steadily towards him. She handed him a piece of paper without saying a word and then turned round and clicked away fully conscious of the impact she had made as Willmot's gaze burned into her back. I could hear heavy breathing behind me.

'Cor.' A youth we had nicknamed 'Simmers' had been hooked. More susceptible than most he spent much time at the clothing store after that but never actually made any headway with the Wren. Her Father was an Admiral.

As the two months drew to a close we prepared for the examinations. They took place in the last week. Much hard work went on in the last few days as we swotted on magnetic variation and deviation, how many guns had the *Prinz Eugen* or a Dido class cruiser, what was stratus cloud or what was the wing span of a Junkers 88 and the morse code — the dreaded morse code. 'We are not trying to fail you — what we want is for you chaps to get through.' So spoke our instructors and meant it. However, they expected us not to torpedo our own ships or get lost. If we passed we would get our killicks, as acting leading airmen.

We had now been reduced by sickness and other causes to about a hundred and forty odd. For three days we wrote our exam. papers and slaved at night. Except for six of us we all passed. 'Oh joy, oh rapture!' Those who had 'dipped' were plunged into gloom. It only meant going back one month on to the next course but it was the end of the world! Six more miserable Naval Airmen you could not find.

Next day the rest of us drew our killicks from the glamorous Wren in the clothing store, and our flying gear. This was the most exciting thing of all. Leather helmet, goggles, an inner and outer flying suit, fur lined boots, three pairs of gloves, pure silk, wool, and fur lined leather gauntlets to go on top. We sat and gloated over it, tried it all on, fitted the Gosport speaking tubes to the helmet then reluctantly packed it all away in the flying kit bag.

We said goodbye to *St Vincent* and went back to *Daedalus* to await being drafted to flying school. As we piled into the bus, loaded down with kit bags ditty box and so on Chief Willmot came to see us off. He didn't have tears in his eyes but he looked pleased with his handiwork. Most pilots who served in the Fleet Air Arm knew Chief Petty Officer Willmot — and he knew most of them.

Chapter 4
24 EFTS

'He who rides a Tiger cannot dismount'

The flying training of Fleet Air Arm pilots was done by the Royal Air Force. The Navy, even in 1939, regarded aircraft as unseamanlike contraptions which, if at all possible, they would rather manage without. 41 Pilots Course, like Gaul, had been roughly divided into three parts to be trained to fly. Some went to the Royal Air Force station at Elmdon near Birmingham and some, of which I was one, were sent to number 24 Elementary Flying Training School at the Royal Air Force Station Sealand in Cheshire. Twenty went to the United States Naval Academy at Pensacola, Florida, to learn to fly the American way. The Royal Air Force had to admit that it couldn't quite manage the whole pie. On the way to Sealand we managed to acquire an extra pupil. He had been at the Royal Naval Air Station at Arbroath training to be an observer. The Navy insisted on training its own observers, whom it regarded as far more important than pilots, believing as it did that the Royal Air Force didn't really know how to navigate anyway and wouldn't know a sixteen inch gun even if it fell over it, or how to spot the fall of shot from one, something which, in Admiralty eyes, might just make the use of aircraft acceptable.

The new arrival, Clough, was a pleasant lad. He had 'dipped' the observer's course but the Navy thought he might still be useful as a pilot. He always appeared to be under a full head of steam and about to explode. He emitted suppressed hisses and phuts as his emotions were whipped into effervescence by the vicissitudes of life. He seemed destined to tangle with Fate at every turn. He had a gift for misunderstanding what other people were doing which usually led to his own confusion and a fortuitous cock-up of some sort.

We arrived at Sealand in October. The aircraft in which we were to learn to fly were Tiger Moths. We shared the airfield with a squadron of Mosquitos and another of Havoc night fighters. No. 24 EFTS itself was housed in two wooden huts, well away from everyone else, with its Tiger Moths parked on the grass outside. I was posted to 'C'

Flight. I suppose that the Royal Air Force must have been overworked, because the Tiger Moths were serviced by mechanics from the firm of Short Brothers and for some reason which no one ever explained the aircraft handling was done by boys. Where they came from or who they were we never knew. They all looked about twelve or thirteen years old but may have been undersized townies. I supposed that they must be too old for school, or perhaps playing truant, and not old enough to be called up for military service. They swung the propellers and manned the chocks or tails, while we ran up the engines, and did all the menial tasks with enormous zest and willingness.

The Naval presence was provided by a Lieutenant Commander, non-flying, and a Chief and two Petty Officers who ruled the barrack where we lived. The Chief was an ex-pug. He had a cauliflower ear and his nose appeared to have stopped a train. So distorted were his breathing passages that he wheezed perpetually. He was a benevolent soul however. Of the Petty Officers one was another Physical Training Instructor called Morgan who spent most of his life in his singlet doing press-ups and running about and trying to make us do the same. The third member of the trio was a torpedoman, a disgruntled 'revolutionary' whom we knew as 'Bloody-Bloody'. He despised all naval officers as tennis playing layabouts and since we, only acting leading airmen though we were, would one day become naval officers too, he regarded with the same scorn. His duties were to see that we kept the barrack rooms tidy, the ablutions clean, and everything arranged in the proper regulation way. Blankets folded, lockers tidy and kit marked as laid down in the Manual of Seamanship. He also supervised the meals. We ate in Short's canteen instead of the RAF mess, doubtless to prevent us demoralising the RAF, while he stood glumly by as we queued through a self-service buffet. He had made it his duty to hold a bowl of HP sauce which he dispensed with a ladle on anything which passed before him. He was quite impartial about this and it required care not to have it poured over the porridge or jam roll by mistake. At other times he would roam round the barrack block muttering:

'Bloody naval airmen, why can't they bloody keep the bloody place tidy. Bloody tennis that's all they bloody think about'.

He had once found a tennis racket amongst somebody's kit and from then on we were all guilty. When the revolution came it would put an end to all that nonsense. The Lieutenant Commander only appeared from time to time to deliver lectures on 'Naval subjects'. He always wore his hat while lecturing.

As a concession to naval tradition we were divided into port and starboard watches. At the passing out exam at *St Vincent* 'Crasher' Ashby, another pupil, who had been a policeman and I had come near the top of the list so, being thereby more 'senior' were detailed to take charge. I think that the nickname Crasher was simply a sort of rhyming slang word with his name because he had it long before we started flying and, so far as I know, he never crashed anything.

I had the port watch and he had the starboard. The training was divided so that we spent half the time flying and half in the class room. At other times half of us were on duty and the other half off, when we could go into Chester if we liked. The watch system made all this division of activities much easier for the Chief and Petty Officers who then knew at a glance if we were doing what we were supposed to be doing. Aside from this the *St Vincent* exam results were of little consequence. The only thing that would count now was whether we could fly.

We wasted no time on arrival. Flying started at once. The air is chilly in October in England and the Tiger Moths had open cockpits. At a height of several thousand feet it was even chillier than on the ground, intensified by the ninety mile an hour gale that the propeller hurled past our heads. To keep our brains and bodies functioning we had to wrap up warm. First we put on rugger stockings over our socks and tucked our bell bottoms into the tops. Next came a thick knitted jersey over the top of our uniform followed by a sort of tailored eiderdown called the inner flying suit. Then we put on a scarf. Some individual preference was tolerated here with regard to the design — stripes, spots and so on — and this was followed by the outer flying suit, a proofed duck overall with fur collar and fur lined pockets, then sheepskin boots, leather helmet, goggles and three pairs of gloves. The final garment, over everything else and tied between the legs, was a Mae West life jacket — in case we came down in the Mersey.

It was at this point that 'men dressed as seamen' found themselves at a disadvantage. The naval uniform had been designed in the reign of Queen Victoria when the only flying machines were balloons. The drop-flap front of the bell-bottoms worked at right angles to the twentieth century zip fasteners on the flying suits. Once encased in his flying gear a man had to 'wait' until he had had his flight if he did not want to repeat the lengthy formalities of getting ready for it.

The only other piece of equipment needed was a parachute. Picking up my parachute I headed for the Tiger Moth where my instructor joined me. A pleasant greying old man of at least twenty nine he was Flight Sergeant Tate. My earlier brief period of instruction, in the Oxford University Air Squadron, had been two years before, so we revised the effect of controls, climbing, gliding and stalling, turns and spins. The next day he handed me over to Flying Officer Dean who was to be my principal instructor, apart from checks at intervals during the course by Flight Lieutenant Arnold, the Commanding Officer of 'C' flight. The first two weeks of EFTS were devoted to going solo.

Towards the end of our time at Elementary Flying Training School would come the Chief Flying Instructor's test. This was a passing out exam. to make sure that we were fit to go on to advanced trainers. A faltering pupil was given a CFI test earlier and there was a steady attrition rate all through our time at Sealand of pupils who would never make it to the end of the course.

But the biggest test, the make or, for about a quarter to a third of us the break, would be the first solo, and we did not have for ever to do it. Everyone knew this of course, both instructors and pupils, and during the first two weeks tension was high and mounting. Each instructor started with four pupils. Weather permitting we each had an hour or so dual instruction a day. After about eight or ten hours a man was expected to be good enough to go solo, although some took a little longer.

We pupils were a mixed bunch, students, policemen, clerks, mechanics and the like but so were the instructors. Some of them, like Flight Lieutenant Vic Arnold, were old stagers. He had joined the RAF about 1922, qualified to fly as a sergeant pilot and flown just about every aeroplane the RAF had ever had since then. He wore an old fur lined Irvine jacket which he came to work in, on a motor bike, flew in it, then went home in it in the evening. For all I knew he had his pyjamas on underneath for I never saw him in anything else but no doubt he wore uniform like the rest of us. He used to check all of us pupils from time to time to see how we were getting on and how the instructors were getting on too.

The others were either ex-civil pilots considered too old for operations or new young pilots just off course themselves and, being good pilots, were held back for a few months and trained as instructors before going on to operations. These young ones usually hated it, and some were inclined to vent their annoyance on the pupils. There were also one or two ex-operational pilots 'having a rest' but instructing didn't do much for their nervous systems either, and they too might be a bit tetchy.

After that first flight, Air Experience it was called, instruction began in earnest. Take off was easy. You just had to open the throttle and keep straight. The Tiger took itself off with no help from anybody, and from time to time accidentally did so unmanned if someone started the engine of an empty aircraft with no wheel chocks in place, although this was exceedingly unpopular whenever it happened. Landing was the problem. Now it is equally true that if the Tiger Moth had been set to glide at 65 knots and left alone it would have made a very good landing on its own as well, but of course we were there to learn how to do it and it never got the chance. Landing needs judgement of height, speed and distance all together and it took time to get it right. Some never would, and as time went by and the first solo got nearer anxiety and apprehension grew.

'A good approach is the Father and Mother of a good landing' our instructors told us and spent the next ten hours teaching us how it should be done.

> Take off — climb at 65 knots to 500 feet — make a 90° climbing turn to port — climb to 1000 feet — level off — turn 90° down wind — fly downwind until the wing tip passes the downwind end of the airfield — turn 90° to port close the throttle and trim to glide at 65 knots, losing height at 500 feet a minute — at 400 feet do a gliding turn 90° to port — make a gliding approach and land. A piece of cake — only it wasn't.

For one thing sharing the airfield with Mosquitos made things a little tricky. They were very fast, and although both the air and the field might be quite clear when a Tiger was about to take off, by the time the pilot had reached 500 feet and was about to turn left a Mosquito could leave its dispersal point, taxi out and take off, and be up on the Tiger's port wing tip. To land they made a fairly long low approach but they were hard to spot from above and many a Tiger pilot was surprised to see one shoot in under his nose just as he was making his final glide to the field.

At the downwind end of the field was a little armoured car painted in black and white checks so that a pilot might see it without any difficulty. This also made it very obvious to any German pilot who came over, so it had a machine gun fixed to its tail and was thereby known as the scorpion. The scorpion housed an aircraftman equipped with a couple of Aldis signalling lamps, one green and one red, a Very Pistol, a stock of ammunition and, if he was lucky, a thermos of hot coffee. One of the poor blighters — erks they were called — sat there all day giving permission for pilots to take off or land. Usually he used the Aldis lamp but if the pilot was so preoccupied that he failed to see the red light when it was unsafe to land for some reason, a warning shot was fired across his bows from the Very Pistol. A pilot might even ignore this, so intense was his concentration, then everybody ducked and hoped.

So, we took off flew round and landed. Took off flew round and landed. We didn't stay on the ground but as soon as it was clear that the landing was all right we opened the throttle and went round again for another. The same applied if it wasn't all right. If when we got to about ten feet it was obvious that it was a 'right pigs ear' with the aircraft half stalled, going sideways and the instructor, his knuckles white, offering up prayers for deliverance and bawling obsceneties through the Gosport tubes, we jammed open the throttle and hoped that we might pull out of the mess before some part of the Tiger hit the ground. In fact it was this point which the poor man really wanted to know about because if we didn't open up and go round again he had to do it for us, and they used to get very nervous wondering just how long they could wait before:

'Right, I've got her — what the bloody hell are you playing at you nit, didn't you know you were levelling out too high?' So off we went round again.

'Right now steady — steady *too fast* I've got her.' And round again we went. As we droned round the circuit the instructor tried to explain in clear wind blown syllables what we had been doing wrong, interspersed with such comments as:

'Wake up man, you hold *off* bank in a climbing turn — as I was saying, when you start your glide move the trimmer *back* so that she glides at 65 knots then you won't come in too fast — where the hell are you going now, turn on to the downwind leg and *throttle back* we're up to 1300 feet — we should be at 1000.'
We flew on. Then we came in yet again.

'Good — good, keep it like that — back a bit — a bit more — *not too much — you've stalled*! keep the stick right back.'

We hit the ground with a sickening crash and bounced up about twelve feet.

'*Keep the stick still* you're not stirring porridge, *Hold it back*!'

The Tiger paused in its upward lunge and started down again.

'I've got her.'

As the Tiger fell back to mother earth he gently put on a bit of throttle to cushion the blow and we landed softly.

'Right, I think that's enough for today. Taxi back to the huts.'
I was glad to oblige.

'Watch out!' A Mosquito, looking enormous, loomed up on the grass in front of us.

'Wait for him to go. If you taxi behind him as he takes off he'll blow us over.'

We watched him go in a smooth roar of power which took him out of sight.

'Well that wasn't too bad. Just remember to trim and don't waggle the stick about so much, you'll do all right.'

My instructor was a kindly man and understood a pupil's problems.

The other pupils and instructors chaffed each other in much the same way. Clough came in one day red in the face and seething visibly.

'That man's an absolute bastard, he'll fail me if he can I know it.'

'Oh I don't think so. What happened?' I asked.

'He was tearing me off a strip so I put the end of the Gosport tube out in the slip stream; that shut him up.'

'What did he say to that!'

'He clutched his head.' Clough laughed 'Then, after a bit, I can't hear what you're saying — I've got her.'

'We had lovely silence all the way back. After we landed he tore me off another strip. He said to be careful to keep the mouth piece away from the slipstream.'

For a week we watched each other bouncing around like tennis balls as we tried to land, alternately convulsed with laughter and horror at the exploits, and all the time the first solo came nearer. To counter the boredom of repeated 'circuits and bumps' we were taken off to practise climbing and gliding turns — both needed in the circuit — and stalls. We also had to show that we knew how to recover from a spin, before going solo.

After that, circuits and bumps seemed tame, but the first solo — that would be different. As the days sped by and we didn't seem to get much better a growing cloud hung over 41 pilots course.

'Don't worry' said our teachers 'It'll come, you'll get it', but we were full of doubt. We tried to encourage each other but it was inevitable that before long the instructor would say either:

'Sorry old man, you'll never make a pilot,' or else:

'All right — take her round yourself.'

Then it happened. I had done a couple of mediocre landings and was feeling faintly miserable about the whole business when:

'Right, now have a solo check with Pilot Officer Lightbody and if he says you are OK you can go.'

Flying Officer Dean climbed out of the cockpit. I waited with the engine running. After a few minutes Pilot Officer Lightbody climbed in.

For the next thirty five minutes we did take off, landing, turns, stall, spin, then another take off and landing.

'All right' he said 'take her up yourself. Make a circuit and landing. I don't mind how many attempts you make. If it's not right go round again. I'll secure the straps in the front seat so that they don't get caught round the stick.' He leant over and did so. 'Off you go. Good luck.'

So, at last, I was on my own as I taxied round to the scorpion. On the way I pondered the task in hand. I had about nine and a half hours flying and about two dozen landings behind me.

No one can learn to land in so short a time. After ten hours most pupils will make a reasonably good landing sometimes. The rest of the time the attempts to land are so bad that to continue with them would be to crash, so the pilot opens the throttle and flies round again for another go. At the time of his first solo all that the pupil has learnt, or so his instructor hopes, is to know when the landing is going to be hopeless and to go round again. Eventually he will get one right if he does not run out of fuel first.

I was the first pupil on 41 course to be sent solo and I was not brimming with confidence. There was only one thing for it. If I did not feel very confident I would have to pretend. Thus I argued as I trundled over the grass to the scorpion:

'This is not my first solo at all. I've been flying for years. Just a routine flight. Just take off in my usual expert fashion and come in for a three point landing. A piece of cake.' Vital actions for take off — friction nut, trim, mixture, pitch, fuel, flaps. There, that was the green light from the scorpion — turn into wind — line up the nose on the tree beyond the far boundary then ease the throttle fully open.

The chuckling noise from the engine changed to the now familiar vibrant shattering roar. I could feel the aeroplane come alive and we were on our way:

Keep straight — bit of rudder — not too much — don't snake — ah, tail coming up, that's right — crikey we're off! Of course, no instructor to lug into the air the old Tiger is much lighter now, takes off much quicker. O boy what a fantastic climb. Oh yes — still flat out aren't we — ease the throttle back a bit, and back with the trim to climb at 65. Ah relax, *relax*! What am I saying we're already at 500 feet. Climbing turn to port, *look round!* — forgot didn't you? nobody to remind you now, lucky there was no Mosquito there to bite you, not too much bank, hold off a bit, steady after turning 90° and continue climb to 1000 feet — level off. What a view, can see much better without that wretched head in the front seat. Turn to port again, downwind leg, now much faster with wind behind, beginning to enjoy this now. Let's shout a few rude remarks down the Gosport tube — sod off — He can't hear your thoughts now. Oh dear down wind leg didn't take long. 'When the downwind end of the airfield is level with the wing tip — turn to port and start your approach.' What next? Oh yes close the throttle, trim back to glide at 65, that's right. At 400 feet look round, no one else on the approach. Those Mossies come from nowhere. Turn to port into wind and start final approach. Don't forget a little extra bank in a gliding turn, that's it and a bit faster — up to 70 knots. Now straighten up, back to 65, we are coming in now. No aircraft in the way on the ground or taking off. Have I judged it right? yes, the boundary fence does not appear to be moving up into the airfield or down away out of it — I should touch down just beyond the scorpion. He's giving me the green light now. That's it — steady — I can see the individual blades of grass now. Begin to flare out — gentle pressure on the stick now ease back — ease back — she's too high! Damn, I've cocked it up — full throttle! check the swing! quick she's reared up — trim forward — keep her straight! keep her level! Climb away — phew! what did I do wrong? It *seemed* all right.

It's all right flying along like this but now I've got to do it all again. Suppose I never get it right? I could bale out. Bale out! what are you thinking of — people don't bale out on their first solo. Oh lor, Hobson's choice — just have to have another go. Once you take off you are flying and you have to keep on flying until you land, or run out of fuel, or bale out, or crash or ... He who rides a Tiger cannot dismount. Oh Lor, oh well here goes — it can't get any worse.

By now the downwind boundary was abeam again:

Turn 90° to port, trim to 65, keep her steady, 400 feet, turn into wind, steady, steady, over the boundary fence now, nicely, down, down, keep her at 65, begin holding off now, that's it, bit too high though, down a bit, too late! she's stalling! crump! Hells bells — hope the wheels are OK. What a bounce! Full throttle! Round again! That was awful!

My mouth was feeling a little dry. This was beginning to be a bit worrying:

Perhaps I am not ready for my first solo after all. I'm stuck with it now though. I've got to get it down somehow. What did I do wrong? Held off too high again — why? The first time was not quite so bad as the second but why? Ah, I forgot, no instructor, doesn't sink quite so fast. I should have tried to stay down though — what was I told? 'If you bounce a bit too high *don't move anything* — not forward nor back nor anything — just hold it exactly where it is and wait. It will come down again. If it seems very high just a little throttle to ease the bounce just before you touch, but not too much or you only make it worse.'

All right here we go again — coming in on final. Nice and steady 65. Hold it like that, we're coming in to land just beyond the scorpion again. Hold it — hold it — steady now — just a little gentle pressure to flare out, stick hardly moves back at all — that's it — individual blades of grass — keep it like that — flying level now — keep straight! Beginning to sink — ease back — a bit more — nose coming up now — can't see ahead any more — look out to port — *keep straight* — ease back, sinking faster now — stick coming back easily, Damn! stalled it too soon again — falling — falling — where the hell's the ground? Bang — up again, right — hold it this time, don't *move anything*. Beginning to come down again — Bump! Thump! we're down! *Keep straight* — watch out — keep her straight to the end of the run — she's stopping — she's stopped. That's it, you did it. Take a bow. Good, have a look round then taxi back.

Well that was really something, a red letter day in anybody's life, I had joined the elite. A man is entitled to feel proud after making his first solo and I did.

During our second week at Sealand and into the third those who were going to go solo did so. Some just couldn't do it and after a chat with their instructors decided that although they still wanted to fly they would never be able to pilot a plane and went to re-muster as observers. Most pilots on their first solo made more than one attempt at a landing before finally getting down, a few did it first time.

Green was a nice lad and being in the starboard watch he was flying while we in the port watch were doing ground subjects. One afternoon as we left the classroom on our way to tea there was a lone Tiger still buzzing round. It was Green. He had taken off about an hour and a half before on his first solo. As we watched he came in for his ninth landing. It didn't look all that bad but he opened up and went round again. He had of course collected quite an audience, not the least interested spectator being his instructor who by this time was looking considerably agitated. Green had the airfield to himself as he came in for the tenth time, even the Mosquito pilots had turned out to watch, having finished their flying for the day. The tenth landing was much like the ninth and off he roared for number eleven. It was now obvious that he simply did not recognise a good landing when he did one. As he came in for number twelve we began to wonder when it would dawn on him to try and stay down regardless, as by now it was beginning to get dark, but his brain had seized and there was no way to tell him what to do. When the luckless boy opened up to go round for the fourteenth time fate took a hand. His fuel tank ran dry. He landed heavily and broke the port undercarriage leg. Concluding that flying was not for him he went to sea.

I found Simmers sitting glumly in a corner one day during this period. After failing to woo the Admiral's daughter in the *St Vincent* clothing store he had been downcast, but soon after arriving at Sealand he took up with a landgirl. These buxom girls had been recruited to do their national service on the farms. They wore thick green jerseys and riding breeches held up with strong leather belts, thick woollen socks stuffed into Wellington boots and felt hats. But underneath this forbidding clobber some were quite nubile as Simmers had noticed.

Thinking to cheer him up I said:

'Don't worry old boy, I'm sure you'll go solo quite soon.'

'I'm not bothered about that' he said — he was a north country lad —

'It's 'ow to get past a land girl's belt that worries me.'

Up till now he had only met girls in skirts and he found the breeches and belt of the land girl to be an impregnable defence. I left him to plan his strategy.

When war broke out Marden had been in a stockbroker's office. His instructor, 'Hutch' was a petulant young man who had been picked off his operational training course, much to his disgust, to do some instructing before he went to a front line squadron. None of his pupils in the previous course to ours had gone solo and he and Marden, a forthright chap, struck sparks. Hutch was a good pilot but impatient and his weapon was sarcasm. One day when they taxied in, the tension between them was almost making steam rise from the cockpits. Hutch climbed out, picked up his parachute and stormed off. Marden, ashen faced, came over to us.

'That man's a swine!'

'What did he do?'

'I think he's going to fail me.'

'What happened!'

He didn't like the way I was making a turn so he grabbed the stick, without saying anything, and put on more bank then let go.

This annoyed me so I seized the stick and shoved it as hard as I could from side to side and banged his knees — then let go so no one was flying it. Then we went into a spiral dive. He grabbed the stick again and pulled it straight and level then started to tear me off a strip for not telling him I had let go and he had control. I told him if he was going to grab the stick when I was flying he could damn well keep it and I would report him to the CO and get another instructor. This made him absolutely livid. He told me not to be insolent. Nobody — he said — could ever teach me to fly, I had more chance of growing feathers than flying. I told him he was a supercilious twit not fit to be an instructor. Right, he said that does it, and we came home in silence. I expect he's telling the 'Old Vic' about me now.

'Marden come in here.' The voice came from the Flight Commander's office. After about ten minutes Marden came out smiling.

'I'm getting another instructor.'

We were delighted, but it didn't do any good. Marden just couldn't get it right. Three days later he departed to join the observers school at Arbroath. And so it went on. At the end of about five weeks we had been whittled down to about 40 as the last pilot to solo made his flight and the last one to fail his CFI test went off to other things. Disappointed they undoubtedly were, but finding that they couldn't quite do it themselves seemed to give them more confidence in those who could and they went, happy to train as observers. Those who had opted for observer training in the first place were often more intellectual than we were, and good at maths; navigation and signalling gave them more satisfaction. Most of them preferred to be chauffeured around anyway as they plied their trade and had little ambition to pilot themselves.

So our initiation came to an end and we began to improve our grasp of this flying business as our instructors taught us more and more of what they knew.

Chapter 5

If at First You Don't Succeed, Fly, Fly Again

The first solo was, of course, only the beginning. For months we had thought of little else. Our whole lives had been vectored to this triumph. We had not looked ahead because until we had done it there *was* no future. Now two things immediately became obvious. The first, a whole new vista of flying opened before us. The other thing was much more pertinent; we would have to go through the whole damn business again every time we took off solo. Still we had done it once, we could always do it again — maybe — unless the first time had been beginner's luck — a fluke. Thinking back on my own efforts at landing I was a little troubled by this thought. Of course we all took the greatest care with our landings and gradually confidence began to replace anxiety, but after one or two good landings a man was liable to become blasé. The vast majority of our landings were not very good — if safe — more or less — but the occasional good ones gave us hope. It was after about three or four weeks that carelessness began to creep in with the occasional blood curdling bounce, fraught with the menace of imminent structural damage, which jolted us back to reality.

During this time our long suffering instructors taught us steep turns, stall turns, side slips, loops, rolls, rolls off the top and, thrown in as a joker, forced landing:

'I am closing the throttle now. Pick a field and make a forced landing approach.'

Usually it was towards the end of a lesson, flying happily back to the aerodrome dreaming of a pint of beer. It came as a shock in an otherwise tranquil scene. As the power was cut the nose dropped at once and the Tiger began to lose precious height rapidly until muggins remembered to trim it back to 65 knots then start to look for a field. He was at a disadvantage here because the sadist in the front cockpit had already selected a field before he started this caper. As the pupil looked wildly around, the entire surface of the Earth appeared to be covered with trees, quarries, houses, very small fields, very large fields full of cows, railway lines, factories and a host of other things like high tension wires and swamps — all quite unsuitable to land on. The field picked out of this jumble by the 'all seeing eye' in the front seat was now rapidly falling astern barely glimpsed by the pupil as it slid past. Vaguely aware that there was somewhere to land he turned hopefully and headed towards where he thought he had seen it.

It was at this precise moment that he realised that he had no idea which way the wind was blowing. He should have of course, we were supposed to notice these things, but how could you position yourself just off the downwind end at 1000 feet if you didn't know that? He was trying, not very successfully, to estimate his drift when he saw some smoke. Providence had come to his aid — his cup was running over. Carefully judging his height and distance he headed for the vital spot in the sky from which to make his approach only to realise when it was too late that the smoke was not coming from a bonfire but from a train doing about sixty miles an hour. Hopelessly committed to the wrong approach he hoped the instructor *might not have* noticed the wind direction.

'Well you made a balls of that — I've got her.'

He climbed up to 2000 feet and demonstrated how it should be done.

Low flying, however, was something we all enjoyed. It stirred the blood as nothing else could. Strictly forbidden of course except when authorised, and only then in specified low flying areas, there were terrible penalties for wrong doers. A bit of unauthorised beating up of the countryside, if detected, could land a man in jail and would undoubtedly ground him, perhaps for ever. In the Luftwaffe pilots had even been shot for it, although we didn't think our side ever went that far.

But the temptation was enormous. A bit of hedge hopping at 90 knots was thrilling enough to make us chance it, usually without being found out. But come back with a twig in the undercarriage and you were in trouble. I don't think that there was a single pilot who did not at some time drop down out of sight somewhere, he hoped, and skim the ground flat out.

One of the less popular things was instrument flying, known throughout the world as IF. In a cloud, on a dark night or a dull misty day, when visibility was bad, you could only fly using the blind flying instruments. The gyro compass to tell you which way you were going and the airspeed indicator and altimeter to tell you how fast and how high. There was also an artificial horizon and a turn and bank indicator to tell you whether you were still right way up and a rate of climb and descent indicator. In the air we practised this either by flying in cloud or if there was none the pupil pulled a canvas hood over his cockpit, so that he could not see outside, while the instructor sat gloomily in front wondering when the halfwit in the back would realise that he was in a spiral dive and do something about it.

However to help us achieve excellence in this art there was of course the Link Trainer, which we endured, while the instructor operated the 'radio beams' used for instrument landings. We all had to spend hours, and after a while it seemed boring hours, playing with this toy aeroplane yet it must have saved hundreds of lives by teaching pilots, in complete safety, almost all they needed to know about IF. It seemed endless, and in fact we all spent about thirty hours in the Link during training, you could not escape. When it got too boring we did a sky writing exercise — working out a set of courses to steer to make the crab write rude words. Even that palled in time. Our colleagues at Pensacola did none of this. The weather was so good that if ever a small cloud appeared people came from miles around to see it. None of them had the slightest idea what 'weather' was. Neither in those days did the United States Army Air Corps.

One day five B. 17s — the famous Flying Fortresses — appeared overhead. They had flown all the way from the USA and had been supposed to land at Prestwick. The first five ever of hundreds more to come over. However, much to their surprise, the place was socked in. Never having seen a mist before, let alone try to fly in one, especially with granite mountains in it, they were diverted to Sealand where the sun was shining. It hadn't occurred to anyone either that they had never before used a grass airfield. Peering down they viewed this prospective disaster area without relish and flew round in contemplative circles until their leader, a gallant man of many flying hours, thought he had better have a go. He peeled off and came round in a wide approach, set himself up smoothly and made a perfect landing. Encouraged by this, number two peeled off and headed for the ground. He too made a good landing but overshot. He finished his run near the boundary fence. Number three came in a bit quicker with his tail up and we could see that he was headed for the boundary fence too, at a good speed. Seeing this himself he slammed on the brakes but of course you can't stop thirty tons of Flying Fortress so easily. The field was wet and he straight away started to slide. As he slewed into a ground loop his wheels threw up a cascade of mud. He too finished up at the boundary fence but going sideways. The crews in the other two Forts watched these goings on from on high then, after some more thoughtful circling, sagely flew off to find on bigger field. Boeings would have been proud of the way their little number performed the first time it touched British soil I think.

Eventually there came a time when we had to try out all that stuff on navigation which had been dinned into us. When the appointed day arrived we sat down with a 'course and speed calculator' and a map, and, bearing in mind magnetic variation and deviation, wind speed and direction, worked out a course which would take us to a town a few miles away and another course to bring us home. Naturally it was not as simple as it sounds. Now you might expect that map reading from an aeroplane would be easy. After all from 2000 feet the ground looked like a map anyway. Surely once you had the map the right way round, then, there was everything laid out below you, just like the map. The catch was — your actual ground wasn't the same colour as the map and didn't have the names written on it. In fact it looked very little like the map. So it was not surprising that a man might get lost. In the palmy days of peace a lost pilot could always dive down and look at the names on the railway stations, but to confuse the Germans these, and all the signposts as well, had been removed when war broke out. It didn't, so far as I know, confuse a single German, but the entire population of Great Britain for six years had no idea where it was whenever it went anywhere. And if it dared to ask was in grave danger of being suspected of being a spy. All this made cross-country flying a gamble. So I was not surprised to see a tense look on Clough's face as he walked out to his aircraft. He took off and set off southward.

For the first fifteen minutes all went well. As he came up to the first landmark where he had to alter course he reached for his map to check his position. Unfortunately he had forgotten to transfer it to his boot when he strapped himself in and it was still in his pocket. The genius who designed the flying suit had overlooked the fact that all the pockets would be held firmly shut by the harness. The realisation of this caused Clough's amperage to begin stewing up as he struggled first to release the Sutton harness then the parachute harness to retrieve the cursed map. At last, triumphantly grasping his map he started to refasten first the parachute harness then the Sutton harness — not so easy in a bucking Tiger Moth while at the same time using one hand to fly it. As he struggled and fumed while the tension inside him rose the slip stream suddenly whipped the map out of his gloved hand. It flew back to wrap his head like a parcel, cutting off his view, then it blew over the side. By now fizzing like a cracked insulator on an electricity pylon in the rain he managed to finish fastening his straps. He had, of course, flown well past his landmark and had not the least idea where he was, so, turning round he headed in what he thought was the direction of Sealand. Half an hour later he had to admit he was lost, and without a map.

Looking round he could see not a single feature he recognised. There was however a large town some miles ahead. It must be Manchester he thought, although it might in fact be any of several other large towns in the district. However, we had been told when lost to head North West until we saw the coast which anyone could recognise. And fly home from there, which he did.

Another of our pilots, I think either Belcher or Gibson, finding himself a little unsure of his whereabouts yet close to a large town felt sure that there must be an aerodrome somewhere near by, and very soon he saw one. If he landed and wandered casually about he might be able to find a notice board or something to tell him, without actually asking anyone, where he was. He made his circuit and put the Tiger down in a reasonable sort of way. He taxied over to some hangars then as an erk ran out with some chocks he pulled up and stopped the engine and got out.

'Good morning Sir, will you be taking off again or are you staying the night?'

The aircraftman had mistaken him for an RAF officer. That was good. If he kept his flying suit on no one would know any different.

'No, I just have to go over to the control tower. I'll be off again in about ten minutes. By the way what do they call this place now?'

'Ringway Sir.' the erk looked puzzled 'What did they used to call it Sir?'

'Oh I don't know, but they keep changing the names of these places.'

He hurried off before the erk could go any deeper into the subject. Reaching the control tower he climbed the stairs and went into the control room.

'I'm on a cross-country from Sealand, did they signal to tell you I was coming?'

'No Sir.'

'Oh well I expect they forgot. Any change in the weather likely?'

'Well it's closing in, are you going to be here long?'

'No, just have to pick up some spares and I'm off.'

'Right — I'll give you a green when you are ready.'

He sauntered back to his aeroplane. He knew his way home from here. As he climbed into the cockpit the erk dutifully helped him to do up the straps, then went round to the propeller.

'Switches off suck in.'

'Switches off suck in Sir.' The erk pulled it through.

'Contact.'

'Contact.' He switched on the magneto. The erk swung the propeller. The engine fired and he was on his way. When he landed back at Sealand he told nothing of this but the telephone had been ringing.

The CO called him into the office. A little while later he came out and told us what had happened.

'What did the CO say?'

'He tore me off a strip, but I think he forgave me — didn't damage the Tiger.'

He got away with it. Another time I saw Pickard *practising* IF. A Tiger flew past me with the hood over the back cockpit and the *front seat empty*.

'Well' he said 'It seemed a good chance to do a bit of IF.'

'But you might have had a collision.'

'Oh no, I wasn't in cloud — anyone could see me.'

The crust of the man.

One day we were idly sitting round waiting to fly when a squadron of Swordfish flew in from a carrier going to Liverpool. Some of us would be flying these machines ourselves so we watched with interest. No long approaches for these boys. They had been flying from the carrier for months, and knew their 'Stringbags' like nobody's business. They swept in from 300 feet in a closely packed stream one after the other in smooth curving approaches and smacked down in three point landings. As they did so we noticed that each plane had two or three bicycles tied to the struts between the wings. As soon as they had taxied round to the hangars they untied the bikes and pedalled off to the mess as hard as they could go.

'I have to go to Ringway — you can come with me and do some map reading.' As Flight Lieutenant Vic Arnold said this to me I glanced at the sky. It was a cloudy day and a bit misty as well, not a map reading sort of day, but he never missed the opportunity to teach us something. We took off and with the 'Old Vic' in control climbed through a hole in the cloud. It was only a hundred feet thick and above was bright sunshine and almost unbroken cloud in all directions, looking like a quilt. So much for map reading. We roared along only a few feet above it sometimes rushing through a bit sticking up above the rest. The sensation of speed was terrific. Flying at 90 knots at 3000 feet on a clear day the pilot feels that he is almost motionless in space. Only the roar of the wind and the engine give any sensation of speed. Flying above the cloud the speed can be *seen*. It is like flying very low over the ground. You can feel the excitement as you go tearing along.

'There's Ringway.' There was nothing but cloud to see anywhere.

'Where?'

'Over there — see that aeroplane climbing out of the cloud — that's Ringway.'

I hadn't noticed it but this pilot had no doubt about where he was. Probably had X-ray eyes. He plunged down through the cloud again, which enveloped us in a moist greyness, and after what seemed a very long time in total obscurity we emerged right over the aerodrome boundary in visibility of about 100 yards and landed.

There was nothing to see except grass and fog and a few huts but obviously my pilot had been here before.

'We're at the wrong end.' was this extraordinary pilot's next remark. He promptly opened the throttle and took off again, then landed almost at once about three hundred yards further on near the control tower. I suppose he knew that no one but he would be flying when visibility was nil. Perhaps it had not been so thick when the pilot we saw coming out of the cloud had taken off.

'Shan't be long' said the Old Vic and throwing back his straps jumped out and made for the tower.

Meanwhile an erk with chocks emerged from the murk to look after our needs. He couldn't have seen us so he must have heard the engine. We chatted as I waited for Vic.

'Do you know' said the erk 'Two nights ago, in weather like this, a Wimpy coming home from a raid came down near here.'

'No' I said 'I didn't.'

Couldn't see a thing so he just came on down until he landed in some water. He'd come down where he thought the Dee was so as to miss the high ground and did a nice ditching. The crew all piled into the dinghy and sat there shivering in the cold night air hoping that in the morning the fog would lift and someone would rescue them. Well in the morning when the fog lifted, they found they weren't in the Dee at all. They'd come down in a large pond. They only had to paddle fifty yards to reach the bank. The silly clots could have been in bed.

Vic returned. He climbed back in and we took off again into the fog. Climbing smoothly up through the cloud he emerged into the blue sky and set off back to Sealand, found a hole with uncanny skill, dived through and there was Sealand below. Whoever would believe flying was like this. A pilot of the old school was Vic. He just knew. Flying Officer Dean, my principal instructor, was a quiet, pleasant man. He never lost his temper with his pupils and I think I might never have gone solo with anyone else. I should have gone to pieces if I had been bullied. F/O Dean was good. Yet somehow I felt that the old Vic was a born pilot, he flew with the feel of a bird.

Although flying accidents were only to be expected when huge numbers of people were being taught to fly we had very few, which was a credit to our instructors. However there was one kind of accident which was entirely due to carelessness and that was a taxying accident. As the Tiger had no brakes taxying needed a lot of skill and care, especially if it was windy. The wings were wide and it was difficult to judge whether the tips would miss anything, especially if you were zig-zagging as well so that you could see ahead. We were supposed to taxi at walking speed. Some people walk pretty fast.

If we flew in the morning we did ground subjects in the afternoon, and vice versa, following the dictum that when learning to fly at least as much study time was needed on the ground as in the air, a fact not always appreciated by starry eyed types like ourselves. One of the things we were supposed to know was how the engine worked. Actually, so long as it did was really what we cared about, nevertheless a flight sergeant from the workshops carefully explained that if we knew how it worked it would be easier for us to keep it going and that in any case it was not really difficult to understand. 'Suck — squeeze — bang — blow' was how he described the four stoke firing cycle and we understood. We also had lectures on the inevitable 'Naval subjects' from the hatted Lieutenant Commander who probably had his hat glued to his head. He may have removed it to go to bed but as none of us ever saw him without it we assumed that he had been scalped by the scythe of time and hadn't quite got over it. The morse code we had every day. Da — di — da — da — on buzzers screwed to our desks in the classroom. We had to achieve twelve words a minute or fail the course. It was a hard grind, still if others could do it so could we. It seemed likely, however, that in action we should be shot down before we could tap out even 'help!'

There was still plenty of exciting flying to do though. Crosswind take off and landing was one little thing. The exercise itself was quite exciting as the aircraft crabbed over the ground and you had to be careful not to stick a wing in, but there was also the chance of meeting some nit-wit doing a normal landing and so intent on his own affairs that he had not seen the red light from the scorpion warning him to go round again because you were about to cross his path, and delighted with himself, until a Tiger at full throttle roared over his head. Or should he wake up a little sooner and see disaster approaching then both would probably be at full throttle and miss each other by an even narrower margin. It set the nerves tingling.

Starting the engine in flight we only did a few times. We always did this over the aerodrome partly in case it didn't and partly I think because the engine seldom stopped in flight anyway, unless some instructor stopped it. We had to dive very steeply to get it going again. Nothing happened during the dive. The propeller only started to revolve as you pulled out. Something to do with gravity I believe, but a bit disconcerting.

During the last two weeks of the course there was *night flying*. It always took place during the hours when everyone else was relaxing after the day's work. Sealand had no built-in lights for night flying. Our 'flare path' was made from a dozen 'Glim Lamps', just about as glim as they sound, arranged in a more or less straight line into wind. The only other light was a 'Glide path Indicator', set to shine along the approach. Coming in to land we could see green if our approach was correct, red if too low and orange if too high. There was nothing else. The entire aerodrome, as for that matter the rest of Great Britain was 'blacked out'. We had navigation lights on the aircraft but they were not switched on in case a German aircraft saw them. We had to flash them in the famous 'Morse Code' to get permission to land that was all. There was, too, the glow from the exhaust. It wasn't until we flew at night that we realised that the exhaust pipe became red hot and a foot long flame came from the end.

Flying at night somehow seemed unreal. There was all the noise, all the risk and all the paraphernalia to wear — a November night was even colder than the day in an open cockpit. Once airborn the pilot seemed isolated — cut off. If it was very dark, if there was no moon, all we could see when in the air was a row of glim lamps, if we were not too far away, and *nothing else*. We flew in an inky pool. We knew we were at 1000 feet because the altimeter said so. We knew it was 65 knots because the air speed indicator said so yet you couldn't even see the ground when you landed on it, only the glim lamps, and not always all of them if the clown who landed just before you had mowed one or two down. We had to learn to land all over again.

Now just come in on a steady glide trimmed to 65 knots and watch the glide path indicator, keep your hand on the throttle and adjust your rate of descent to stay in the green. Line the aircraft up on the flare path — when you reach it level off and just let the aircraft sink slowly down and 'feel for the ground' when you touch close the throttle, keep straight, and wait.

Strange to say landing at night was easier than in the day time and the air was smoother. There was a little mobile canteen which served mugs of hot cocoa to keep us alive between flights. This proved to be a pleasant diversion for us all but especially Simmers who struck up a friendship with the Waaf who poured it out and which in his view compensated for the otherwise utter disruption of his social life.

The last big hurdle was the CFI test. The chief flying instructor, or one of his assistants, had to give each pupil a thorough test to decide after about 60 hours whether the pupil was fit to continue. This was no sinecure, it was quite possible to fail, and one or two on each course did. It lasted about three-quarters of an hour and was searching. Instrument flying — straight and level — climbing — turns on to compass courses — taking off — landing — spinning — low flying for 10 minutes, important for a naval pilot — steep turns — climbing turns — forced landing — aerobatics. There was no pause for breath and at the end a man felt like a wet rag. On this we were graded average, above average or below average or, very occasionally, excellent. At the end of the EFTS 40 of us had survived. Not everybody could take the CFI test on the last day, the tests were spread over about a week and at the end of the week we went on leave, firmly convinced that we were now pilots, with little or nothing between us and the enemy, except a bit more training.

A week later we all turned up at a transit camp at Wilmslow, in Cheshire, where we were joined by the survivors from the other EFTS at Elmdon, to await transport to Canada for the rest of our training. A transit camp is a dismal place entirely composed of vast numbers of people coming and going and like refugees, no one has the slightest idea how long they will be there and usually no idea where they are going. Some of them probably didn't even know where they had come from. There was an exceedingly bored resident staff who spent their entire lives issuing travel warrants, kit for all parts of the world and meals three times a day and nothing else. We stayed there but four days, during which only Simmers managed to score with one of the Waafs, then suddenly bunged into a train, we arrived in Liverpool to board the troopship to take us to Canada.

Chapter 6
A Life on the Ocean Wave

The Royal Mail Steamer *Andes* was a superb ship. At the outbreak of war she had been whipped off the South American run, on which she carried two or three hundred passengers in extravagant luxury to Brazil, and back. She was converted from a first class floating hotel, filled with gorgeous cabins and magnificent public rooms, into a troopship. She was modern and fast and equipped with 4.5 inch naval guns in case she met the enemy. However being modern and fast and equipped with 4.5 inch naval guns the enemy never came anywhere near her and she used to cross the Atlantic on her own, instead of in convoy as more scruffy ships did, zig-zagging at high speed all the way across and stuffed to the gunwales with aircrews under training. It was hoped that she would elude the enemy, and she did.

Being sailors, however inferior, it was slightly humiliating that our first experience of life on the ocean wave should be as passengers in a ship run by the RAF. Of course the plush accommodation in RMS *Andes* had been modified somewhat to accommodate rather more than her usual complement. Crammed in amongst ant-like hordes of leading aircraftmen, all learning to fly as we were, 41 pilots course found it had been assigned to the ball room — to live. The ball room was a glorious room, two decks high, surmounted by a large dome. Bunks had been constructed in tiers all round the sides. In the middle of the parquet dance floor the dockyard had gone to town. They had built two huge edifices four bunks long, four bunks wide and four bunks high. The top reached into the dome where the ends of the upper construction timbers had knocked holes as this vast multi-bed had swayed about in the North Atlantic swell. I found I had been allocated a bunk, one in, from the end and, one in, from the side on the lowest tier. This seemed reasonably satisfactory as should the occupants of the upper bunks vomit, as seemed possible, the spray would be unlikely to reach me.

Meals of course were taken in the tourist class dining room but, because of the overcrowding, there had to be four sittings at each of the three daily meals. The ships plumbing, too, was totally inadequate to cope with us. The officers travelling in the ship naturally went first class and had all the cabins and the plumbing that went with them. For the likes of us other arrangements had been made. We had not been on board long when Geoff Elms came to see me. We had been at the University together, although we hadn't met there. While he did arts, I was doing medicine. With a clerical collar Geoff Elms would have passed for a curate anywhere. He had a pleasant face and a dead pan sense of humour which frequently sucked in his hearers.

'Hey Doc' I had been Doc from the day I joined because of my previous activities, 'Have you seen the bog?'

'No Geoff.'

'It's mediaeval. Where the swimming pool used to be on the aft deck they've build a giant privy made of wood and corrugated iron. At least a 48 holer it's like a conference hall.'

'Good Lord.'

'And there's another built on the fo'castle. It looks a bit exposed to me. If we take it green over the bows I reckon it will be washed away or at the very least wet the feet of the faithful at their devotions.'

I went to have a look. It was already congested in the stern privy. It could only kindly be described as utilitarian. There was a six inch gap between the walls and the deck to allow water to escape and slots here and there to let in fresh air. There were no lights of course which would have attracted U-boats at night. Even in the daytime the interior was dim. And boy, was it cold!

'My God — it's awful' one look at the place and I felt inhibited. But what was a chap to do? I couldn't last out until we reached Canada.

'What do you reckon we ought to do Doc?'

'I don't know about you but I'm going to use the officer's lavatories.'

'You'll probably be court martialled.'

'I'll make damn sure I'm not caught.'

After all once inside with the door locked who was to know. I would just have to be careful.

One thing I learned on this ship was — never travel anywhere without a plug. Most of the wash basins, even in the officers quarters, did not have them and I had to plug the hole with my face flannel, but the water still leaked out. One day I found a basin with a plug in it, which I naturally stole, and had no problems from then on. Sometimes however the water supply dried up. The ship's stills had not been designed to cope with our numbers so from time to time there was a pause in the supply while the stills tried to catch up with demand.

Rumour had it that there were females aboard, we didn't know for sure. If there were any they must have been reserved exclusively for the officers. None ever appeared on the weather decks where we took our ease from time to time when the ball room became uninhabitable because of the cigarette smoke. But this was not really surprising. It was exceedingly cold outside and apart from a greenish grey sea and a grey sky there was nothing to look at except the creosoted walls of the 48 holer. We spent most of our time lying in our bunks smoking, reading or playing cards. Meal times came as a welcome break when we joined a long queue to obtain our victuals.

'For exercise — for exercise — man your lifeboat stations.' When the pipe came we had to muster at the appropriate point on deck. We, of course as all people at sea in wartime, wore lift belts all the time. The life belt was the famous Admiralty blue sausage. Inflated and worn round the waist it was guaranteed to hold the head of an unconscious man under water until he drowned, although keeping his stomach fairly dry.

For ten days we endured. It was so cold that there must have been icebergs, but if there were we passed them at night for we never saw any. At dawn on Christmas Day we steamed into the harbour at Halifax, Nova Scotia. The sea was calm and grey. The land was covered with snow and there were lights. We hadn't seen lights for three years. We tied up alongside and waited. Anyone who has ever travelled will know that as soon as you arrive the formalities begin. Passports, customs, the works. Rather than let us ashore, where we might wander off and get lost, the officials came on board. We had no passports of course so they stamped our pay-books. If you have a rubber stamp it must go on something. Then the customs had a go at us. What they thought that acting leading naval airmen, on three shillings and sixpence a day, and carrying only their kit were likely to be smuggling into Canada in the middle of war, coming from a severely rationed place like Britain where people were sending food parcels to, we had no idea. Nevertheless they searched our kit diligently. Then came the doctors to see that we were not importing anything catching. After that we were allowed ashore — not to go anywhere but to board a train. At this point we did see some women leaving the ship, so they had been there after all, yet even Simmers hadn't found them. The boy was definitely slipping.

The train didn't actually get going until the evening, so that all we saw of Canada was the snow beside the railway lines. We rumbled all through the night dozing uncomfortably in exceedingly stuffy carriages and in the morning were disgorged at Monkton in New Brunswick, a dry state.

We were taken in trucks to the Royal Canadian Air Force Station to wait. Monkton was actually an airfield where the RAF trained a lot of its bomber pilots. We never saw the airfield. The part we occupied appeared to be a transit camp for aircrews destined for other parts of Canada. We arrived somewhat hungry on the morning of Boxing Day. Almost everybody seemed to be on holiday, and that led to our first spot of trouble.

Personnel in the Navy always lived in ships, if not actually afloat then in ships ashore. That meant that we always behaved in a civilised manner. We might sleep, on occasions, in hammocks but we always had proper plumbing and ate in proper mess halls off plates with the cutlery provided by the Admiralty. The RAF on the other hand tended to model their lives more on the style of the Army. They usually lived in barracks but from time to time branched out into tents or even ruined buildings or billets or holes in the ground. For this reason the airman, like the soldier, was issued with his own personal knife fork and spoon, which he wore in his uniform and produced, like a conjurer, whenever or wherever it was time to eat. The only implement issued to the sailor was the 'pusser's dagger' and that was a large pocket knife with marline spike intended for cutting and splicing ropes, not eating mince or fish and chips.

So when we arrived at Monkton along with 1000 hungry airmen all properly equipped with a knife fork and spoon, 41 pilots course hit the canteen to find itself deprived. We had not needed 'eating irons' on board ship or even at Sealand where Short's canteen was fully supplied with cutlery, nor of course at *St Vincent*. As soon as the horror of the situation dawned, 41 pilots course turned to *me*. I had been the designated leader at Sealand, where no leadership was required, and also on board ship which entailed no duties or privileges whatsoever. But now a spokesman — a champion — was required to go for Goliath. 41 pilots course was hungry and ready for blood if necessary. If it wasn't Goliath's it might be mine.

'Doc, you've got to do something.'

'Yes Doc, go and see the Sergeant, tell him we need knives and forks.'

I approached the mess Sergeant.

'Excuse me Sergeant, the Navy do not issue cutlery to ratings, could we draw some from the RAF?'

'Not today son, it's Boxing Day, the store's closed.'

'Couldn't it be opened?'

'No, the storekeeper's on leave.'

'Isn't there another key, couldn't someone else issue us cutlery?'

'I doubt it.'

'But we have no knives and forks, how do we eat until the store opens?'

'Couldn't you borrow some?'

Now it is a firm rule in the Services that lending and borrowing is not allowed. In fact it is a crime and carries a penalty, because it makes stealing too easy. If somebody else's property is found in your kit it is assumed to be stolen, and you are charged.

'Sergeant, you know as well as I do that borrowing is not allowed, besides we don't know any airmen to borrow off, and in any case at meal times they will be using them themselves. Can't you get us some from the store?'

'No. Even if I could get the key I couldn't issue them, the storekeeper would have to do that, and he's not here.'

'Well what do you suggest?'

The Sergeant shrugged. He wasn't unduly bothered. The store would be open tomorrow.

'You'll have to do the best you can and report to the store tomorrow.'

So that was that. We would have to use our fingers or the pusser's dagger, and this was easier said than done. Our first meal on Canadian shores was fried bacon and egg, and just as I was about to pick it up the cook added a pancake and a dollop of maple syrup. Born and brought up in England I was appalled. I demanded an extra plate and slid off the bacon and egg to convert it into a two course meal. The cook, a Canadian, thought I was crazy, but still smarting from the cutlery fiasco I was in no mood to see his point of view. With the aid of a piece of bread and the marline spike I managed to consume most of the meal.

The only reason we were at Monkton at all was because the course ahead of us at 31 Service Flying Training School at Kingston Ontario had not quite finished, so for two weeks we had to kick our heels. There did not seem to be much to do in Monkton and there were no bars. As well as cutlery we also drew from the stores Canadian overshoes. These were essential and everybody wore them over their shoes to go out. It was so cold outside that the snow squeaked when you walked on it and we never went out, even to the dining hall, without overshoes, overcoat and a balaclava helmet or we should have had frost bitten ears. We wandered aimlessly round Monkton chatting with the locals but there were no sights to see. After two weeks we were again put on a train and after another uncomfortable night arrived at Kingston.

The trains were stuffy but they were romantic. Enormous engines with bells and cowcatchers, they had a wonderful two tone whistle which stirred memories of cowboys and mounties and the wild west. The pudgy greasy drivers in striped baggy hats smiled at us as they went past. Again we saw very little of Canada from the train. What we did see was flat and covered with snow.

Chapter 7

Oh Canada, all White with Snow

'What's underneath I'd like to know'

The town of Kingston stands on the North shore of Lake Ontario just at the beginning of the St Lawrence river. It is very close to that part of the river which in summer is a holiday place known as 'The Thousand Islands.' The islands all have little chalets where, during the summer, Canadians and Americans boated and fished and fought with mosquitos which were said to be of enormous size, equipped with armour piercing stings and which never hunted in packs of less than about two hundred. Fortunately they were now all frozen solid, along with the lake. A little way down the river the 'International Bridge' joined Canada to the USA at the town of Syracuse. It was heavily patrolled by eagle eyed policemen who, while really keeping a look-out for escaped German prisoners of war, or so it was said, took the numbers of any aircraft which tried to fly underneath it and reported them to the Royal Canadian Air Force.

31 Service Flying Training School was located at the Royal Canadian Air Force Station. It was staffed by the RAF exclusively to train Naval pilots. We moved into a well insulated wooden barrack block with double glazed windows and heated by steam which came in thick, lagged, pipes from a large boiler lurking somewhere in the camp. The rooms contained steel double bunks and a wall locker for each of us and that was all. We ate in a mess hall.

'Who's in charge here?' Following my efforts at Monkton, and before that at Sealand, they all pointed at me and chorused:

'Doc'

The Flight Sergeant who had asked the question turned to me.

'What's your name?'

'Hadley, Flight.'

'Right — get your men to stow their kit then go to the mess for lunch. After lunch parade in that hangar' — he pointed to one near the control tower — 'at 1400 hours, I'll be there'.

Lunch was good. The Canadians believed that if the inner man was satisfied the outer man would get on all right. After lunch we assembled in the hangar. When the Sergeant appeared we hastily got into two ranks, except that whenever I tried to find a place to line up with the others the line closed up solid and I was left out in front.

'Atten — shun' called the Sergeant and I was marooned, like an off-shore island, as the ranks came rigidly to attention behind me.

'Right Hadley', mine was the only name he knew, 'march your men round to the crew room where the instructors are waiting'.

'Squad right turn — by the right — quick march,' and off we went. We reached the crew room.

'Squad — halt — stand at — ease' I went inside to report.

'41 Pilots Course reporting Sir.'

'Right, wheel 'em in.' I did so.

'Now settle down chaps and I'll give you the gen.'

Flight Lieutenant Harvey was a calm experienced instructor in his early thirties who had been instructing on Harvards for several years. He picked up a pile of small blue booklets and handed them round.

> These are the pilot's notes for the Harvard II, I want you to study them this evening. Tomorrow I expect you to understand the fuel system and have learnt the starting procedure. The Harvard II is the standard advanced trainer for ourselves and the Americans — they call it the AT 6 or Texan. There was a Harvard I, but it was found that it did not always come out of a spin. You may have heard of it. After a while this began to bother the authorities somewhat and the design was modified to become the Harvard II which spins perfectly safely. It is a good aeroplane — easy to fly and will do all you ask it. It has one vice. It tends to ground loop at the end of the landing run. After you've touched down be sure to keep straight until you stop or she'll whip round at the last minute just when you think you are out of trouble.
>
> There are a lot of features which you will find new after the Tiger Moth. The main difference is the retractable undercarriage, and it is a monoplane of course. It has a closed cockpit, brakes, flaps, a constant speed propeller, a rudder trim as well as the elevator trim and *two* fuel tanks. There are other differences too, but we will deal with them when we get to them. Now come into the hangar and we'll have a look at one.

We followed him into the hangar. Here were the Harvards. This was what we had come 3000 miles to fly. We had not seen them before, except in pictures. We walked up to one. This aeroplane was as different from the Tiger Moth as chalk from cheese. It was big, solid, painted bright yellow all over and tough. If you kicked a Tiger Moth you would make a hole in it; if you kicked a Harvard you would break your foot. It must have weighed several tons. It looked much too solid to fly at all. The big radial engine gave it a purposeful look. The pupil sat in the front seat, just behind it. It had no struts or wires to spoil its beautiful lines. We walked round it in awe as Flight Lieutenant Harvey described the features. There were about a dozen aircraft in the hangar and as other instructors appeared we dissolved into little clumps round each one. We took it in turns to climb into the cockpit and examine the controls.

The cockpit was crammed full of dials, levers and switches and a number of strange shaped boxes each with their own dials and levers. These turned out to be camera switches, signalling switches, the gyro gun-sight, radios, bomb release buttons, radio beam approach equipment, and the stick had a fighter pilot's spade grip handle with a gun firing button on it. Flying this was going to be a full time job.

When we arrived in Kingston we found that we had once more acquired an extra pupil, Turton. He had been to Pensacola. The Americans had a reputation for being rather tough instructors and the Admiralty sometimes sent the failed Pensacola pilots on to Kingston for a second chance if they thought that a man had been unjustly failed. Turton had failed his Chandelles. The Chandelle was a first world war manoeuvre, pretty to watch, but considered by the RAF to be useless as a combat manoeuvre as anyone who had tried it was more than likely to be shot down. However the Americans were very fond of it and the Pensacola pilots' log books were always full of Chandelles. So Turton came to us, which brought our numbers up to forty one. He had done a bit more flying than we had, most of it on Harvards, but *no IF* and had *no time in the Link Trainer at all*, so he was banished to the Link for the first two weeks to learn the rudiments of flying in cloud while the rest of us became acquainted with the Harvard.

That evening we lay on our bunks studying the pilot's notes for the Harvard and speculating about how we would get on with it.

'You know Doc' said Cliff Lock 'This is like EFTS all over again.'

'This aircraft is nothing like a Tiger, we shall have to learn everything all over again and remember to put the wheels up and down all the time as well.'

'Still, it flies the same way.'

'I dare say it does, but it won't feel the same, and what about the runways?'

'Well what about the runways?'

'Well there are no blades of grass to tell you when you are at thirty feet and if the wind isn't blowing straight along them, which it probably won't be most of the time, we shall have to do "out of wind landings" all the time as well as everything else.'

As it happened the weather came to our aid here. The runways were totally covered with ice. You could land sideways and still skid to the end in a straight line, although our instructors discouraged this.

'I shouldn't worry Cliff, no one fails to solo on a Harvard.'

At least we hadn't heard of anyone who had.

'Well I hope you're right Doc.'

Before flying the Harvard we had practically to sign our birthright away. A printed sheet called:

'RAF Pilot's log book endorsations' we pasted into our log books and we had to sign this in three places to say that:

We had read and understood:

Station flying orders.

The file of information for pilots.

Notices for pilots.

These were all long lists of forbidden and mandatory things. Also that we had been instructed in and fully understood:

The operation of the hydraulic gear
   (wheels and flaps).

Gasoline and brake systems
   (go and stop).

Were familiar with the cockpit drill
   (what all the levers and switches did).

Emergency exit.

Fire extinguishing gear
   (In case we thought we could put it out instead of hitting the silk).

Knew the safe endurance with full tanks.

And finally:

Had noted and knew where the authorised low flying area and forced landing areas were.

This was then countersigned by the instructor after we had carried out a blindfolded preliminary 'tarmac check' and vital actions in a satisfactory manner. (You had to be careful here not to actually unlock the undercarriage or you failed the test on the spot.)

This took all the morning. These instructors were really nervous guys. Life might be tough. Each instructor had two pupils. I had Harvey and so did Clough. We spun a coin for first flight and I won.

Outside on the airfield it was about −20°C. The aircraft were all lined up in the open in front of the hangars with a lot of freezing erks standing by. They were well rugged up but they still looked frozen. We climbed in and, with their help, fastened the straps then set about starting. Starting an aero engine is usually complicated. Aeroplanes are seldom stolen because the incredible routine needed to get them going is too much for the average thief. Starting the engine had to be done by the pupil. The Harvard could not be flown solo from the rear seat, where the instructor sat, so the engine starting controls were all in the front. The first improvement we noticed from the Tiger was that instead of the Gosport tubes we had proper earphones in our helmets and microphones to talk into, which improved communication no end. However if the connecting jack on the wire became partly unplugged during flight the first the pupil knew of this was when the poor instructor, unable any longer to talk to his pupil, undid the locking spring on his control column and taking it out of its socket leaned forward and used it to hit him on the head. The more intelligent pupil at this point tumbled to what was wrong and hastily pushed the jack back in.

The Harvard had an electric starter, but to save the battery there was a hand-starting crank too. It helped to keep the erks warm, although they could have told us a better way, and didn't look upon hand starting with too much relish. The engine a 550 horse power Pratt and Whitney Wasp, four times the power of the Tiger's Gipsy engine, was started by the inertia of a flywheel. This was set in motion either by the electric motor or by the aforementioned erk standing on the wing and cranking the handle which fitted into the port side of the cockpit. If the batteries were a bit low the motor took so much current that there was not enough left to make the plugs spark which was why the erk had to wind the handle. However it was usual to assist the erk by giving the motor a little blip to start the flywheel because, starting from scratch, hand starting was rather slow. It would probably take the erk two or three minutes hard winding before the flywheel was going fast enough to turn the engine over, and if it was engaged too soon the engine failed to start, the flywheel stopped and the whole business had to be done again. The usual practice therefore was to let the erk get the flywheel up to its maximum speed, judged by the whining noise it made, any noise made by the erk was ignored, then, just before the erk reached the point of total collapse engage the flywheel with the engine and hope it started. If not, get a new erk and start again. An erk's life was hard. However if all want well, as the engine turned over it made urgent sucking noises, and just when you thought it would stop one of the cylinders fired, an immense cloud of smoke emerged from the exhaust pipe and engulfed the cockpit and after one or two strangled coughs, interspersed with gouts of flame from the exhaust, it burst into life. During this time the pilot was pumping frantically on the hand fuel pump with his left hand. With the other hand, as he dare not stop pumping, he hastily reached across to move the throttle handle slightly to 'catch the engine' as it fired, then hurriedly switch his right hand back to the priming pump on the dash-board if it seemed likely that the engine might falter and stop. After a bit of juggling with these three controls it either gasped into silence again or, more usually, settled down to a steady throaty roar at about 1000 revs to warm up. The pilot, suspicious of its intentions, continued to work the hand pump until he was quite sure that this monster had settled down, then he slowly relaxed and proceeded with the rest of the pre-flight business. He tested the rudder, ailerons and elevator, tested the operation of the flaps — but not of course the undercarriage, unless he was dreaming, as occasionally happened — checked the oil pressure and temperature, fuel gauges, battery charging meter, and then, with the engine warmed checked the magnetos, maximum revolutions and propeller pitch controls. Then, all being well, he waved the chocks away and set off for the downwind end of the runway.

Vital actions TMPFF. In the Harvard the significance of these letters came home to the pilot. Now, completely ready, he turned toward the runway at the end of the taxi strip and waited for the green light. The runway van in Canada had no need of the machine gun which the scorpion at Sealand sported, it was simply a heated caravan with a look-out dome on top.

'Now take off is exactly the same as you did in the Tiger', so spoke Flight Lieutenant Harvey, 'Only you will find that it takes a bit longer because the Harvard is heavier. I'll do the first one — you follow me through on the controls.' Getting a green Aldis from the van he turned on to the runway. There were two parallel runways in each of three directions forming a large double triangle. With anything up to three or four dozen aircraft flying at the same time they were needed.

Now you line yourself up with the runway then run forward a bit to make sure that the tail wheel is straight and won't cause you to swing. Now open the throttle smoothly to full throttle and rest your hand behind it to stop it vibrating back.

As he did so the Harvard began to move forward. I had the feeling that I should feel much the same if I had been trying to fly a steam roller so solid was the Harvard. However it gained speed rapidly, the tail came up and it was soon bounding along at a frightening speed. It lifted off quite easily and began to climb steeply into the Canadian sky.

'Right — undercarriage up.'

This also could only be operated from the front cockpit. I pulled up the handle of the lever to unlock it and moved it backwards. The wheels came up and thudded into their housed positions.

'Check the undercarriage lights.'

'Yes Sir — both locked up.'

'Good, now we'll climb up at 110 knots. Close the hood — its chilly back here and pull back the throttle a little and the pitch lever to give 1850 revs. We don't want to deafen everybody on the ground.'

In fine pitch at full power the Harvard's propeller made more noise than the engine due to the blade tips becoming supersonic. Increasing the pitch slowed it down and the noise diminished considerably.

'We'll climb up a bit and you can see how she handles — Right you've got her — keep her at 110 knots and climb to 3000 feet.'

For an hour and ten minutes we did climbs, gliding turns, steep turns, stalls, spins and several landings and take offs. Canada as far as the eye could see was flat. A few bits indeed looked flatter than the rest and were frozen lakes. The whole vista was white, a few smudges here and there were villages. The only clearly visible feature apart from the town of Kingston itself and Lake Ontario was the railway which looked black. From end to end the country was blanketed with snow — map reading was not going to be so easy. The sun shone and the sky was blue and outside the cockpit, pleasantly warmed by the sun and the cockpit heater, the temperature was about −30°C. For nine days, in which we flew for about nine hours, our flying time interspersed with ground subjects, we did mainly circuits and bumps. Because we had to fly dual at this stage the instructors did twice as many hours as we did, nerve racking vigils which left them weak. Then again came the first solo. Not quite the ordeal it had been in the Tiger but the first solo on a new type would ever be a flight to remember. We did not really think we should fail and none of us did.

For two months we did all the things we had done in the Tiger. The Harvard was faster and when it stalled it fell quicker and faster. When it spun in gyrated more viciously. When it bounced it bounced harder and when it scared you it scared you worse than the Tiger, but it was a fine aircraft and we loved it. It was much easier to do aerobatics in the Harvard. Loops, rolls, the famous chandelles, the roll off the top — 'the Immelmann turn' — another from the First

World War, we did all these, not to use in combat, and no one was ever failed for doing them badly, but to become familiar with the aircraft and the way to fly it. Aerobatics were forbidden in all but a few operational aircraft, although sometimes done nevertheless, but steep turns and steep dives and good landings were what we needed to be good at.

The retractable undercarriage had 'arrived' only about three years before, at the beginning of the war. A few aircraft like the Swordfish and the Lysander still had fixed undercarriages. Even the proper pilots, like our instructors, had usually learned to fly when all the undercarriages were fixed, and people used to forget. It was not uncommon to see pilots blithley coming in to land with the wheels up. A red Very light from the runway van jerked most of them out of this forgetfulness. To discourage it a loud horn had been put in the cockpit which blew a deafening blast in the pilot's ear if he closed the throttle while coming in to land with the wheels up. However since he also had to close the throttle to spin or glide, a button was provided to stop the horn. Many a pilot coming in to land with his wheels up automatically pushed the button to stop the horn which was 'making such a noise he couldn't think' then happily landed, wheels up, wondering who the red Very lights were being fired at. The RAF had invented a mythical character called Pilot Officer Prune who awarded 'Putty medals' called 'The Most Highly Derogatory Order of the Irremovable Finger' to pilots who did this, and other careless things, which became known as 'finger trouble'. The average pilot never had girls very far from his mind, even when he was flying, but had to be shown that there was a time and place for everything, and everything in its place, and that included the wheels when you were proposing to land, and the MHDOIF.

When we were not flying or engaged in other professional duties we could discover Canada. At night as we lay in our bunks we watched the Northern lights. Wonderful curtains of crimson, green, gold and blue chased each other across the sky or gave it an eerie light behind the clouds. Off duty we went into Kingston. We put on our balaclava helmets, greatcoats, woolly scarves and over-shoes and queued up for the bus while beards of ice from our frozen breath formed on our chins. In Canada however we soon found people don't queue. They just stand in a clump round the bus stop. When the bus came they surged forward in a mob, pressing against the side of the bus which slid bodily sideways across the icy road until it met the snow bank on the other side. When it had absorbed the mob it moved off. No vehicles used chains on their wheels in Canada and with the banks of snow on each side of the road the bus had to stay on it. So long as nobody used their brakes the traffic seemed to miss each other most of the time without too much difficulty, and travelled at normal speeds. Vehicles were never parked with the brakes on as they froze and wouldn't come off.

Once in Kingston, as soon as we left the warmth of the bus, we dived into a cafe. The cafes were cozy places with little alcoves and what did we eat in Canada in January with the temperature −20°C *ice cream*! Lovely peach melbas with nuts and maple syrup and coffee with lumps of cream in it. After that a visit to the movie house then back to camp. It was too cold to walk about and look at the sights such as they were, in any case they were covered in snow and ice.

The weather, too, disrupted the social life of Simmers. Accustomed to open air romance he soon realised that in this country he was quite likely to lose vital parts to frost bite if he wasn't careful. Besides it seemed to him unlikely that he would find any young cuties sufficiently hardy or starved of affection to risk frost-bite themselves, especially to their more intimate parts. He wrestled with this problem for a long time, then hit upon a solution. He persuaded one of his lady friends to invite him to her home. All went well for the first couple of visits, while he was still in the preliminary stages so to speak, but after arousing the young ladies interest he found himself snookered.

'There wer'nt no where to go' he told us 'I couldn't tak 'er to t'bedroom, well could I? we couldn't go outside. The kitchen wer'nt no good people kept comin' in.'

'An eskimo would build an igloo.'

'Maybe 'e would — I don't know 'ow to build an igloo, in any case when things get properly underway there's no time to stop and build igloos.' We could see his point.

'So what did you do?'

'Well I found a sort of seat under the stairs. It wer'nt much better than the kitchen but people only passed through the 'all they didn't stay there. Still we couldn't get down to anythin' really serious.'

And that was it, the romance never really blossomed. He tried the same ploy once or twice more, but never with any success, and the back row of the cinema was about the best solution he could find. Poor Simmers. He glowered darkly in his frustration. 'Bleedin' weather. When does it warm up in this part of the world?'

Our pay, even with flying pay, didn't really allow us to splash out very much. It paid for cigarettes and ice cream. The bars in Kingston were a disappointment. They were not cozy like the cafes, but resembled more a railway waiting room. The beer was, to our way of thinking, not up to much and we couldn't afford the whisky. So we led good abstemious lives, which considering one thing and another may well have been a good thing.

At the end of two months we had the CFI test then, judged reasonably competent in the Harvard, started on the second half of the course which was operational flying training. It began with some intensive IF, English weather was well known to our instructors, and formation flying. Then we went to the satellite aerodrome at Gananoque, where the Link Trainers came from, to do some concentrated night flying, more formation flying and an introduction to the use of radio. Up till then we had never used radio. It was like a new toy and we played with it while we flew, learning the jargon — Roger — Wilco — and so forth and being vaguely surprised when anyone answered our calls. Aboard ship we knew we would never use it as there was always radio silence at sea.

The night flying was romantically primitive. The flare path was made up of genuine 'Goose neck flares.' These were rather like teapots with wicks stuck in the spouts and burned kerosine oil with a large smokey flame, which flickered in the wind, and that was all there was. Probably they had been left over from World War I. In the Tigers one solo flight at night had been our lot. At Gananoque we spent hours doing night circuits and bumps and night cross country trips too. Sometimes it was so cold, about −30°C, that the flares would not burn; then we retired gratefully to the mess to while away the evening.

By day we had now graduated to gunnery and bombing. We were introduced to the gunnery gradually. First we attacked a target on the ground using a camera gun. When we had shown that we could hold the target in the sights as we dived on it we were allowed to use bullets. From that we graduated to attacking a drogue towed for our benefit by a Lysander. This was quite exciting — for the tug too. The tug flew up and down over a specified strip of land where the local civilians had been warned off. We had to locate the drogue then make diving attacks from astern. When the camera showed that we had learnt to distinguish the drogue from the tug they gave us bullets. The tug pilots were understandably wary of us because wherever the bullets went it was not into the drogue. I think they used the same drogue for the entire war. The pilots of 41 pilots course, between them, during the whole time we were at Kingston managed to put two holes in the drogue. We managed to miss the tug too. They did use a very long tow rope.

One morning Clough strolled out to his aircraft fuming silently about an imagined wrong. During an earlier flight he had climbed in after another pilot had been flying and the engine was running. As he strapped himself in the erk obliged by holding his oxygen mask out of the way. Unfortunately the tube was out in the slipstream where the idling propeller was sending back a freezing gale which shot straight up the tube and into Clough's face. Remembering the trick he had played on his instructor at Sealand he was convinced that the erk was doing it deliberately because he didn't like him, and resolved to get his revenge. As he climbed in for the second time that morning the engine was stopped, but he made sure his oxygen mask was not in the way as he did up his parachute. When he reached for the seat straps he could not get them because the erk was holding them out of reach. He had turned away to speak to someone and did not notice that Clough was ready to put them on.

'Straps man' bellowed Clough, whereupon the poor frozen erk nearly jumped out of his skin and dropped the straps.

'Clumsy idiot.'

Convinced that the erk had been deliberately teasing him he decided to vent his anger on this 'fool erk' who needed, he thought, to be taught a lesson. To begin with he let the erk wind the flywheel without any help from the motor. To make sure that he got the message he let him go on longer than usual. When the flywheel was screaming round at full speed he engaged the engine then opened the throttle as it fired. It leaped into life and blew the erk clean off the wing into the snow.

'Serves you right' he muttered. The erk, livid with justifiable rage, picked himself up.

'You stupid bugger' he yelled 'Don't you know how to start it yet?' But Clough couldn't hear him. He waved the chocks away and departed blissfully on his flight his good humour restored.

As well as two runways there was also, in front of the control tower, a taxi strip, and between that and the hangars a concrete apron. Coming in to land one day along this runway, soon after the landing direction had been changed because of a shift in the wind direction, I noticed one of the Lysanders taxying towards me. Obviously he had landed on the other runway before the runway change and was about to turn off on to the apron. I continued my approach. He was being a bit slow about it but suddenly speeded up and turned off out of the way. I landed and went back to the crew room.

'CO wants to see you.'

'Me, why?'

'I don't know — but you've got to report to the control tower right away.' I went, puzzled about what it could be.

'Hadley, why did you land on the taxi strip?'

My heart sank. So that was it. No wonder the Lysander had hopped quickly out of the way when he saw a mad pupil pilot about to land on him.

'I mistook it for the runway Sir.'

'Didn't you see the Lysander?'

'Yes Sir, but he moved out of the way.'

'Are you surprised? Jolly good job he did or there'd be a heap of wreckage there now.'

'I'm sorry Sir.'

'You'd better be chum. Just pull your finger out.'

'Yes Sir.' I withdrew chastened.

Then there was bombing. We only used eleven and a half pound practice bombs but they were about the size of Indian clubs. We did glide bombing and dive bombing, the main difference being the height we started and the angle at which we came down. Occasionally a bomb, not properly hooked on to its rack, fell off before it should have and one or two fell in the outskirts of Kingston but nobody was hurt although they did complain a bit.

At the end of our time at Kingston we should get our 'wings', the 'flying badge' as the navy called it. Then we should be split up; some going to train as fighter pilots and some for TBR — The Torpedo Bomber Reconnaissance aircraft — with one or two for seaplanes.

'What are you going to apply for Doc?' It was Rowe-Evans speaking.

'I don't know yet Rowe — fighters I think. The thought of flying a Spitfire appeals to me.'

'I'm going for TBR. Fighters are defensive, I want to be part of the strike force.' He had something there of course. 'I'm a Stringbag man myself' said Rowe.

'Well it may be something better by the time we leave here.' I said. 'I hear that the Barracudas are coming into service.'

'That would make a difference. What do you think it would be like flying straight and level at 100 feet straight at a battleship shooting at you with everything it had?'

'Dicey I should think but it wouldn't be for long, and if your fish hit — well it seems to me that would really even things up. Still it would be fun to fly a Spitfire.'

'Yes, but they might not give you one, it might be a Wildcat.'

'Well perhaps I'll join you in the TBR. Of course whatever we ask for they'll probably give us the opposite anyway, that's the way the official mind works. What about you Pat?'

'I'm going for TBR I'd like to have some company when I'm flying. An observer to do the navigating seems a good idea, and a gunner to look out at the back and tell me if anything is coming makes for a quiet life I'd say, then I can concentrate on what I'm good at.'

'What's that Pat?' I dodged the pillow that flew towards me. So It was decided.

One day Roberts set off on a cross country exercise. Feeling somewhat bored he swooped down to ground level well out of sight of anywhere and skimmed across the surface of a frozen lake at nought feet. The surface was as smooth as a billiard table and gleaming, dazzling white. As he roared across, not quite able to judge the height, he suddenly noticed a loss of power. He hurriedly climbed up and came home. As he flew round the circuit we noticed that the aircraft was making a funny noise. His landing was all right then he taxied round to the hangar and stopped. It was only then that both he and we perceived what was wrong. As the propeller stopped turning we saw that three inches at the tip of each blade had been bent back at right angles. He made the journey to the control tower.

'Explain.'

'Well, Sir. I was doing a practice forced landing Sir, and came too low.'

'For a practice forced landing you are supposed to break off at 200 feet.'

'Yes Sir I misjudged the height.'

'By 200 feet?'

'The sun was on the snow Sir.' The CO looked at Robert's log book.

'Roberts'

'Yes Sir'

'You were not supposed to be doing forced landings, you were on a cross-country at 2000 feet.'

'I thought the engine was overheating Sir, I just came down to see what the ground was like in case I had to land, in case it stopped Sir.'

'And after what you did it might have. You have damaged the propeller and may have shock-loaded the engine.'

'Yes Sir.'

'You will be grounded pending a Court Martial for unauthorised low flying.'

'Yes Sir.' At the Court Martial he was found guilty and sentenced to fourteen days in the Toronto Glass House.

In due course he returned. He looked thinner and a little subdued. He joined up with 43 pilots course and eventually got his wings but not a commission.

As our final month at Kingston drew to an end the coming of spring was heralded by the ice on the runways melting. The result of this was a spate of ground loops as pilots accustomed to landing at all angles and skidding playfully about suddenly found wheels gripping the runway. We just had time to learn to land properly again before the final CFI test and the award of our 'wings.' We assumed that there might be a passing out parade for this with our wings pinned on to us by the CO. However we simply drew them from the clothing store and stitched them on ourselves. No doubt the RAF thought that this honour should be left to the Navy to bestow. The Navy however viewed wings askance. It would have preferred that its flyers, like its submariners wore no distinguishing marks at all and for many years the observers wore no wings. The pilots wings however had been awarded by the Royal Air Force. Not wishing that its pilots should wear RAF wings it conceded that Naval pilots could wear wings, so long as they were unobtrusive and worn on the left sleeve and the letters RAF replaced by an anchor as was appropriate to a sailor. The left sleeve was not seen by the person taking the salute at a march past. Actually this arrangement was very much to our liking and gave us a touch of glamour denied other mortals. It must have irked their Lordships somewhat that even the King proudly wore his wings on the sleeve of his Admiral's uniform.

And so our time at Kingston came to an end. We still hadn't learned how to fight but pilots we were, trained and qualified and entitled to full flying pay of six shillings a day. We were sent off on two weeks leave to recover, then assembled again at Monkton to await passage home. We had liked the Canadians and they liked us. Cliff and I spent a happy two weeks at the home of Mr and Mrs Marco Smith of Stoney Brook, Long Island, U.S.A. The Americans liked us too.

Chapter 8
Back to England

At Monkton we waited to be shipped home. With our newly won wings we were able to regale the incoming courses on their way to Kingston with highly coloured tales of derring do. We were also able to sell them items of kit which we would no longer need ourselves when we were commissioned. This was doubtless illegal but we needed the money as we had returned from leave broke and they needed to replace items of kit they had lost. Simmers even managed to sell a pair of skates although it was April and all the ice had gone. Still, as he said, there was an ice rink in Kingston. I had an old uniform cap which had gravitated to the bottom of my kit bag. It had been compressed by the clobber on top of it. When I pulled it out and separated it from the boots it looked more like a meat loaf that had been dropped than a hat.

'You can't sell that Doc.'

'I might.'

'Who ever would want that?'

'Perhaps I can straighten it out.'

More in hope than expectation I tossed it into a basin of water to see what would happen. It slowly opened out, like a Japanese bamboo flower, and resumed its proper shape. I dried it, brushed it and sold it for two dollars to a fellow who had lost his cap overboard on the way over.

'Doc you're ruthless.'

'Rubbish, he needed a hat, would have cost him more in the slops.'

I was able to sell my field training boots in Monkton for four dollars.

There was nothing to entertain us in Monkton so we were delighted when we had to board the train again for Halifax. Of Halifax we again saw nothing as we immediately boarded the SS *Louis Pasteur*. Not surprisingly with a name like that she was French. She had not been modified to the extent that the *Andes* had and we were scattered about the ship in random groups not in cabins of course but in holds, corridors or small open spaces called flats. As we came on board we were each handed a long soft package tied with rope like a vast continental sausage. These we recognised as hammocks but being airmen rather than seamen we had not been issued with them when we joined. No instructions accompanied this hand-out. We carried them to our allotted corners then looked at them with interest.

'How do you think they work Doc?'

'I've no idea we shall have to experiment.'

'Fear not beloved, deliverance is at hand.'

'You know how they work Pete?'

'No brethren, I shall consult the good book.'

'What's *that* going to tell us?'

'Quiet Doc, oh ye of little faith.'

With that Pete dived into his kit bag and came up with a book.

'Chapter one verse two on page one of your Seamanship Manual.

"To sling a hammock up, and secure the lanyards.

The bight of the lanyard is placed over the hammock hook and the end rove through the ring, the hammock is then triced up to the height required, and the end secured with a double or single sheet bend."'

'Well I must say I'm surprised at their Lordships. To put "How to sling a hammock" on page one of the Manual of Seamanship either shows greater perspicacity than I give them credit for, or it could explain the skill of the average sailor in getting his head down at every possible opportunity.'

'I daresay the average seaman never reads beyond page one of the Manual and may even have difficulty getting to the bottom of the page.'

'Does it give any instructions about the technical part?'

'What technical part?'

'Well after all that stuff about the lanyard being rove through the ring and triced up, which sounds as if it might be painful, it finishes up with technical talk about a single or double sheet bend.'

'Ah, I see what you mean' he flipped the pages, 'Well if you turn to chapter three verse five on page 64 you will find instructions, and a carefully labelled illustration, on how to make a sheet bend (or swab hitch).'

'What's a swab?'

'The good book doesn't say.'

'Perhaps we can manage without a swab.'

'I hope so.'

'And where are the hammock hooks?'

'Well, this not being a ship-of-the-line, there aren't any, so I suppose we use anything which looks strong enough.' And this we did. As, however, the hammocks were all of regulation naval size intended for hammock hooks set at regulation intervals apart, by the time we had 'triced them up' to water pipes, lamp brackets, scuttle clamps and various other protruberances some of the hammocks were more like boards and others had a deep 'U' shape, neither version being particularly comfortable.

We practised getting in, and, immediately afterwards following a barely perceptible pause, getting out. In time we learned how to stay in long enough to study the dynamics of the hammock sufficiently to risk going to sleep.

The *Louis Pasteur* was a fast ship. So fast in fact that her Captain thought that it would be better not to waste time zig-zagging at sea when the time saved could be spent more safely in port. So he set her bows towards the English Channel opened the taps and made a bee line for England at 32 knots.

Thirty six hours out he thought he smelled a submarine so he turned sharp right and headed South. Two days later we were somewhere off the coast of Florida. When he thought he had shaken the submarine he turned sharp left, whacked up the boilers to even greater fury and made 33 knots all the way to Southampton. We were put ashore into buses and taken to HMS *Daedalus* at Lee a year after we had left there almost to the day. We had been whittled down to thirty five of us, who had been at Sealand, and about the same number who had done their elementary training at Elmdon plus about a dozen survivors from Pensacola still in America. Driving into the airfield at Lee we glimpsed, for the first time, the Barracuda. There was a squadron of them and they looked very menacing as they crouched round the perimeter at their dispersal points arranged to minimise damage if the airfield was attacked. We watched one coming in to land. It was using a lot of power as it hung on its propeller with its wheels and its flaps dangling beneath it like some massive locust.

However, now, we only had thoughts of leave. We drew travel warrants, a list of officer's clothing required and a cheque for £145 to spend at a naval outfitters. Thus equipped I went 'ashore' and then boarded the Gosport ferry to carry me to the 'hard' at Portsmouth there to visit Gieves, naval outfitters par excellence since before the days of Nelson. In fact the Lord Admiral himself bought his uniform there. I was speedily fitted out with two of most things and four or five of such things as shirts and socks, measured for the uniform then, that done, I crossed the road to the harbour station and took the train home. During the war tailors worked like galley slaves and a week later I got the uniform by post, got married, had a honeymoon and a month later arrived at the RAF Station at Errol on the shore of the River Tay near Dundee to be groomed for Barracudas. With a bride of only a month I had no wish to live apart. Enquiries in Errol elicited the information that the district nurse was going on holiday. I rented her cottage and Patsie and I set up home.

Of the seventy odd pilots who went on leave from Lee, four went off to fly seaplanes, thirty to fighters which left forty-six of us. Eight of us including Cliff and myself were to train on Barracudas — the rest would fly Swordfish. But first we had to spend a month at Errol 'converting' by flying the Master. The Miles Master was the English equivalent of the Harvard, and some RAF pilots trained on it. It was designed to look and behave like a fighter, and it did. Without the engine it flew like a brick. It spewed oil out of all the gaps in the cowling. It made us realise that once we left behind the well behaved Harvard life was not all beer and skittles.

'What puzzles me' said Pat 'is why we have to fly it anyway. It's nothing like a Stringbag.'

'No, but it may be something like a Barracuda.'

'But I'm not flying a Barracuda.'

'No, but you might one day. You won't fly Stringbags for ever.'

'I'll do my best.'

'Well anyway the Navy thinks you should have a more liberal education.'

'I don't think they *think* at all.' He was probably right there.

For three weeks we flew the Masters round the place doing the usual things after which we were ready to move on. The Operational Training Unit was at Crail in Fife where we should learn to drop torpedos. As they were not quite ready for us the chaps at Errol arranged a treat. They had a Hurricane which they said we could fly. Now the blinding truth which strikes the pilot at this point is that in a single seater your first flight is also your first solo. The pilot's notes become, so to speak, the key which opens the lock. All you know about the aeroplane is what the little book says and of course any pearls that pilots who have flown it toss in your direction. We had reached the stage in our training where we realised that if you can fly at all you can fly any aircraft there is, although it may not be quite the piece of cake you expect. When it came to my turn I knew enough of the pilot's notes to get off the ground. I hoped that my guardian angel was sufficiently clewed-up to cope with things from then on. After all you do expect an angel to know a few basic facts on aerodynamics.

I strapped myself in and started the engine. The Merlin engine heard from the ground was one of the sweetest sounding engines.

Heard from inside the cockpit I wondered if it was all right. The noise resembled a concrete mixer which had been filled with old nuts and bolts. However it seemed to be going all right and all the dials had correct readings. I looked over toward the fitter to see if he was making frantic signals for me to stop but he appeared unconcerned. Either the engine was all right or he was just waiting to collect on his bet with the rigger that the engine would fall out just as I got the wheels up. I decided to call his bluff, waved the chocks away and taxied round and took off. Suddenly I was going twice as fast as I'd ever been in my life before. I could actually see the ground moving underneath me. It was like the power of a galloping horse. The Hurricane *really* flew. It whipped round the sky doing steep turns as if gravity didn't exist. I flew round in a dream. For an hour and twenty minutes I enjoyed the sheer bliss of flying the finest aeroplane ever built. As I joined the circuit I felt I was loitering until I noticed I was still doing 250 knots. After making an extra circuit I managed to rein it back to 130 knots so that I could put down the wheels — then brought it down to land. It landed like a piece of thistle down. I could not resist the temptation to make another circuit. So this was what I'd passed up for Barracudas.

We also had a go in a Swordfish. There were no dual Swordfish either but we were happy to try anything. It was like the Tiger Moth in a magnificent way but seemed unwilling to land at all; however I managed to coax it down at what seemed to be walking pace.

One Saturday evening Patsie and I went down to the village for a drink. As we neared the village hall there was something strange going on.

'Look at that building.'

'Yes, it seems to be pulsating.'

'There's a throbbing sound isn't there?'

'Yes.'

'You know I think it's actually jumping up and down.'

'Let's have a look inside.'

As we approached, the noise and the vibration increased. We opened the door and a blast-wave engulfed us.

'My God what is it?'

'Look!'

Inside the hall was a cloud of dust about eight feet high. Discernible in the middle of this cloud, and gyrating, there was a mob. It resembled, vaguely, a rugger scrum. It was jerking and heaving rhythmically to a band which was invisible on the far side of the hall. From time to time a body flew out and hit the wall. Helped up by spectators the casualty was dusted off and returned to the fray.

It was, I believe a mixture of Scottish and Russian dancing. There was at Errol, in addition to ourselves, a party of Russians. They had come over to collect Albermarles. The Armstrong Whitworth Albermarle was a medium day bomber, designed to replace the Blenheim. Before it ever got into service it was out-classed by the American Boston and Mitchell bombers which were very much better, and it never had a chance. Left with a heap of brand new junk, so to speak, the government set about trying to get rid of some of them, some were used to tow gliders.

'What can we do with all these Albermarles George?'

'I don't know Sir, use them for training perhaps?'

'Not enough of them for that.'

'Can't we convert them into transports?'

'No, don't carry enough.'

'Communications?'

'No, too expensive and slow.'

'I know, why don't we sell them to the Russians?'

'What a good idea George, do you think they'll have them?'

'Well they're always asking for aeroplanes.'

'But Albermarles?'

'Well we can try Sir.'

'Oh all right, well see what you can do.'

Now the Russians, who are nobody's fools, were not of course taken in by this ploy. However they said that if, as it seemed, the British Government didn't want these valuable aircraft they would be prepared to take them off their hands if a satisfactory price could be arranged and what sort of figure had the British Government in mind? On hearing the price suggested they pointed out that Russia was in a desperate fight for survival, vast territories had been over-run, their resources had been almost exhausted by the war but nevertheless they did need these most useful aircraft but could afford only about a quarter of the price asked. Naturally said the British they sympathised deeply with the plight of their Russian allies but could not think of letting them go at such a figure and if the Russians did not want them they could easily sell them elsewhere. The Russians then said that if that was so then that might be the best solution which was a pity as they really did need them. The British Government then, feeling that it might lose the sale, said that if the Russians really wanted them so much they would, in the circumstances, be prepared to accept a much lower figure, and eventually a bargain was struck. It was only necessary for the Russians to ship the required number of roubles, preferably in gold bars, over to us and they could have the Albermarles. The Russians then agreed that though this would undoubtedly be a satisfactory arrangement they had not, they said, been taught to do business in that way. However if the British Government would allow the Russians to come over and learn to fly them then they could, in due course, fly them to Russia and the roubles would be dispatched forthwith. Not having much choice, and not wanting the Albermarles anyway, the British Government agreed. So that was how the Russians came to be in Errol. Eventually the Albermarles became a gift I believe.

The Russian pilots being young high spirited chaps, they naturally spent the evenings down at the pub like everyone else. It did not take them long to make friends and that was how they came to be invited to the 'ceilidh'. We left them to it. Back at the airfield the Russians contented themselves doing seemingly endless circuits and landings which all appeared to be perfect. They were still at it when we left Errol, but doubtless flew to Russia eventually. Flying at Errol was the last time we were instructed by the Royal Air Force. The Navy now welcomed us back. We had in fact spent a couple of weeks at the Royal Naval College at Greenwich mainly learning how to enjoy a Naval Ward Room and exhibit the proper Officer-Like-Qualities required of us. The course included a little Naval History during which we learned, among other things, the interesting fact that the Royal Naval Volunteer Reserve was actually somewhat older than the Royal Navy itself. Old sea dogs like Drake, Raleigh, Hawkins and Frobisher were really reservists, being country gentlemen who only put to sea as privateers or adventurers except in time of war when they took command of the ships of the fleet. The full time professional Navy only appeared shortly before the great Nelson himself.

One other thing happened at Errol. We acquired George Monilaws. George had been on the course ahead of ours but had been ill. He was probably the best pilot I ever met. He treated the Barracuda like a fighter. He had flown it a few times before he joined us and before we flew it. He did all the things which were not allowed like 'steep turns straight off the deck' and aerobatics but his general flying was so good he was always rated above average and the instructors smiled indulgently at his indiscretions. George was a born pilot. He was also a wag. 'My dear, my interest in you is purely sexual' was his reply to a Wren officer who queried his motives for asking her out, during a ward room party one evening.

Chapter 9
R.N.A.S. Crail

The Lapwing, or Peewit, during its courtship display, demonstrates the most perfectly executed aerobatics. It half-loops, rolls, does stall turns and figure eights with natural ease and beauty. Its most spectacular feat is a vertical dive to within a foot of the Earth's surface where it pulls out and skims the ground at grass top height, zig-zagging furiously, before zooming up to join its mate.

We did not appreciate this when we joined the Royal Naval Air Station at Crail in Fife. The Admiralty, in its wisdom, had christened the place HMS *Jackdaw* despite the fact that although jackdaws were a little scarce, as were trees, plenty of lapwings lived there. At all events their presence was appropriate. The standard method of attack by torpedo bomber at that time could have been modelled on the flight of the lapwing.

It was here too that we encountered the mighty Barracuda. The Barracuda was like no other aeroplane ever built. Designed to take over from the Swordfish and Albacore it was the latest, most up to date, most powerful strike aircraft in the Royal Navy. The wings were thick and bristling with radar aerials, boundary layer fences, grab handles, flaps, the pitot head and bomb racks. The undercarriage looked massive as indeed it needed to be for the crunching deck landings it would sustain. It had the most powerful Rolls-Royce Merlin engine ever built, boosted to about twice its intended power by a giant supercharger. However, owing to some misguided influence on the part of the 'Lords who rule the water' it had been designed not so much as a torpedo bomber but as an Observer's aeroplane. The wings had been set high on the fuselage and large bay windows made of perspex built into the sides of the Observer to 'spot the fall of shot' which at the Battle of Jutland 27 years earlier would have made the day for Beatty and Jellicoe. This explained the excessively long legs of the 'Barra' and its peculiar high tail, which two features both ruined its performance and gave it some of the odd quirks for which it became noted, eccentricities which made it lethal to those not familiar with its habits. An American pilot when shown the Barracuda walked slowly all round it in awe.

'Gee, I guess that's the finest flying machine I ever did see,' he said 'but it'll never replace the airplane.'

Patsie and I moved into rooms in Crail opposite to 'The East Neuk' where we 'Barra' pilots often gathered in the evening to quaff a little ale and talk about our remarkable aeroplane. There were no dual control Barracudas so a study of the pilot's notes and a few words from our instructors, plus a useless hop as back seat passengers was all we got by way of introduction to it. Now our instructors, excellent chaps though they were, were also new to the 'Barra'. They had been flying Swordfish and Albacores, both biplanes, and they were apt to fly the 'Barra' with the same careless abandon, sometimes with fatal consequences. This had given it a bad name. Several had recently come from a Swordfish squadron which had distinguished itself by attacking the Bismark. Not so well known was the fact that shortly before that they had swooped out of low cloud in their Stringbags one foul foggy day and dropped eleven torpedos on HMS *Sheffield* by mistake. The Captain of *Sheffield*, sharp as a tack, had observed this blunder without too much surprise and combed the torpedo tracks as they sped towards him. Happily the torpedos were faulty and those close enough to hit failed to explode. The pilots, suitably 'combed' themselves by their own skipper when they returned to their Carrier hastily re-loaded with new torpedos for the successful attack later which had brought them such fame.

'Well chaps you will find the 'Barra' quite easy to fly. We have mostly Mark IIs but there are a few Mark Is. They have the Merlin 30 which is not so powerful as the Merlin 32 in the IIs so we don't use them to carry fish as with too great a load they show a marked reluctance to fly at all.'

Now there are one or two things the little book doesn't tell you. When you take off don't be in too much of a hurry to get the wheels up. Although with the wheels down it is barely capable of flight try to get up to about twenty feet or so before you retract them because as the wheels go into their housing in the wings they upset the airflow to such an extent that you will drop several feet. Another thing to remember is the radiator shutter. On the ground you must have it wide open or she'll boil before you get to the take off point, but if you don't at least half shut it before you take off it causes so much drag you will never reach flying speed but go through the boundary fence at the end of the runway. Just beyond the airfield boundary fence is a minefield.

When you come in to land bring it in at 65 knots. You will need quite a bit of engine because with everything down the drag is enormous. Any questions?

'Do we need flap for take off Sir?'

No, not when you're light but with a fish on put on 15°; oh and don't forget if the flaps get stuck in the dive brake position it puts the stalling speed up about 20 knots so I should come in at about 100 knots for safety. Any more — right, go and do an hour's local flying to get used to it then come back and do a couple of landings.

Not surprisingly starting the engine proved to be a bit of a pantomime. The Hurricane had a Merlin engine of course so that the priming and throttle settings were much the same, but whereas the Hurricane had an electric starter like a car — just press the button and it went — the Barracuda had a Coffman starter. Doubtless named after its inventor rather than because of the noise it made, it was a sort of adaptation of the shot gun. A magazine held five large blank cartridges. Pressing the starter button fired a cartridge which drove a spiral shaft through a cog wheel to spin the engine. This was accompanied by a sharp report and a puff of black smoke. The propeller spun, the engine — if correctly primed — fired and a ten foot flame shot out of each set of exhaust pipes past the pilot's ears. He then had to tickle the primer and throttle until the engine condescended to go. However, the magazine of the starter was worked by a long wire, rather like the brakes on a bicycle, and as the wire became stretched with use the magazine often failed to line up properly. When the starter button was pressed the starter merely emitted an asthmatic wheeze and the propeller did not move at all. The starter was of course out of reach of the fitter on the ground — the Navy didn't have erks, only fitters and riggers, which is what the erks really were — so when this happened he had to get a pair of steps or an old oil drum to stand on so that he could prod the thing with a screwdriver to make it work. This meant that the parking area was always littered with pairs of steps and old oil drums which were blown about by the powerful slip stream in an indiscriminate and hazardous sort of way.

We spent the next two weeks getting to know our new mount. Take off was unique. As the Barra clawed its way unwillingly into the air under the fantastic power of its overblown engine going flat out, it gave an unnerving lurch to the left and right as first one wheel clicked up then the other. Vastly relieved of this burden of drag it started slowly to climb. The pilot then shut the canopy to reduce drag a little more, urging it on with care and prayer until what was casually called 'a safe height' was reached. Once actually flying it shrugged off its initial lethargy and behaved in a manner more befitting the Navy's number one hunter/killer. Its predecessor on the production line had been the Fairy Fulmar, which although slow was a highly manoeuvrable fighter, and the 'Barra' displayed the same agility.

In the beginning, many years ago, the torpedo had been invented to fire from ships or submarines. Then, inevitably as soon as aircraft had been invented and as soon as they were able to lift a bit more than just the crew someone had had the bright idea:

'Why don't we drop torpedos from aeroplanes?'

'Well why not?'

And they did, and they found that if it was dropped from too high it just went down and stuck in the sea bottom. And if it was dropped too low or too fast it bounced out of the water like a flat stone skimmed across a pond and the torpedo's engine, without the resistance of the water to work against, raced itself to destruction. They persevered until they got it right and the old aeroplanes used to bumble along just above the waves and lob the fish in about a mile or so from their targets. This was fine until the war started then it was noticed that even a mile away the hooligans on the other side started to shoot at them so that many of them never actually got close enough to drop the fish. To counter this unsportsmanlike activity a new type of torpedo attack was developed, and this was what we now began to learn.

> Now chaps this is how we play it; we fly to the target in a loose vic formation at 10,000 feet. I will manoeuvre to bring us a mile or two ahead of the ship. Then I will signal line astern by pointing aft with my thumbs. Number two you will drop back to about 300 yards behind me and number three you go about 600 yards astern. When I judge that we have reached the right place I will dive. Watch me closely and as soon as you see me go, slam on the dive brakes and come vertically down, balls out, keeping station on me so that we come down together. Putting on the brakes makes it very tail heavy so you must trim forward. You will also need a fair bit of left rudder trim. Diving like this with the brakes on it won't exceed 260 knots and you can come straight down from as high as you like. At about 1000 feet start to level out and finish your dive at 200 feet. As soon as you are level take the brakes off and *remember, trim back* or you will

nose into the sea. Watch the rudder trim too, you don't want to skid or the fish goes in squiff and breaks up. By now you will be doing about 200 knots and should be about a mile from the target. If I get it right we should be running in simultaneously at angles of 30°, 60° and 90° on the bow. Get it level, check the speed and height then drop the fish. After that fly like a demon and get the hell out of it, weaving as you go. In this way we give them three targets to make up their minds about instead of one, or six if another flight comes in from the other side as well, and the faster we are moving the more difficult we are to hit.

'When do we put on the torpedo settings?'

Ah — I was just coming to that. As soon as you have identified the ship set on its maximum known speed — it will most likely be going flat out if it hasn't been surprised. If it has you have to judge from the look of the wake and bow wave. On the way down set on the angle you will be running in on. It may not be exactly 30°, 60° or 90°. Then at the last minute if you see a kick in the wake as the rudder goes over the ship has altered course, set the avoiding action lever either towards or away then aim for the centre of the ship. Right have you got all that — good — well lets go and have a bash at it. Of course we shan't carry fish to start with.

Cliff and I walked out with our instructor Lt O'Shea to the aircraft. He was a flamboyant youth with a bull terrier called Rastus. The dog's favourite toy was a dustbin lid which it seized in its teeth by the handle then ran off. Unable to see where it was going of course it soon crashed into something or somebody at full speed which stunned it a little. We always felt that it may not have been quite right in the head but O'Shea seemed fond of it.

We took off, formed up then climbed slowly to 10,000 feet. Steaming up and down the Forth was a little paddle steamer the PS *Glenavon*. O'Shea took us to a point a little ahead of it then waved us back to start the attack. We took up our extended line astern positions and waited. The *Glenavon* we knew did about 9 knots which I set on the torpedo control. Being in the middle I should be running in at 60° or thereabouts on her starboard bow when we got down so I set that too — I could adjust it later if I needed to. Then O'Shea put his nose down.

'Right, this is it, nose over — dive brakes on and *dive* — trim, trim — that's better.' I hurtled straight down. From 10,000 feet to sea level is just under two miles. At four miles a minute this was going to take about 20 to 25 seconds. As we screeched down I watched the

Glenavon. She was holding her course and speed. I gave the angle a nudge to 70°.

I must start to pull out at 1,000 feet — the altimeter lags in a dive so by the time I get to 1500 feet, on the clock, it should be about right — we've misjudged the angle more than I thought, I shall be running in at 90° not 70° — nudge the lever again — boy look at that altimeter unwinding — right 1500 feet back on the stick — the 'G' squashes you down — level at 200 feet — dive brakes off — *trim back* or you'll be in the drink — rudder, rudder quick, she's skidding, trim the rudder — wings level — what's the range? — probably about 1500 yards — did she avoid? — I don't think she did — range OK — height OK — speed OK — wings level right press the tit — now get out — avoiding action, boy this is fun — O'Shea's waggling his wings — reform. So that's what it's all about — I could get to like this.

Mounted in the wing was a camera. When the torpedo release button was pressed the camera took a photo of the target. When we returned to the aerodrome the photograph was checked to see whether we had hit or missed. The camera held enough film for five pictures but as we only needed one we had to press the button twice before the attack and twice afterwards to get the target on the middle shot in case the ends of the film got fogged or damaged. It was one more thing to remember.

We practised these attacks diligently two or three times a day, sometimes with dummy torpedos, in addition to low flying over the sea to get used to doing it until our instructors thought we should try with a 'Runner'. The runner was a torpedo with a practice head. It was set to run underneath the target and at the end of its run it came to the surface and gave off smoke so that it could be picked up. At £2000 a time the Navy liked to get its torpedos back. With a runner you could see where it went although we still took photos. We also went low flying over the sea at night. Skimming along the moon's reflection at 50 feet. On starlit nights we relied on the radio altimeter which was so sensitive that it oscillated gently up and down over the wave crests. One day we would be doing this in ernest.

Our targets varied. Sometimes we had old paddlesteamers like the *Glenavon* or the *Whippingham*, which had come all the way from the Isle of Wight for our pleasure or a cruiser or destroyer. One day HMS *Nelson* steamed out of the Forth on some battleship business. It was a chance too good to miss. Lt/Cdr Thorpe briefed us:

Today we shall attack *Nelson*. We have nine serviceable 'Barras'. I shall lead. Hadley you will be my number two, Lock number three. Lt Connolly will take Scorgie and Barr and Lt O'Shea, Monilaws and Black. We'll do a stream take off and form up over the Isle of May in three vics of three and climb to 10,000 feet. *Nelson*, four escorting destroyers and a cruiser will be steaming North East. I shall try to get ahead of them unobserved. When I give the signal my flight — red flight — will attack out of the sun to starboard. Blue flight, Connolly will come in from port. O'Shea — yellow — will follow me in from starboard but one minute behind. This will give us time to drop and get out of the way before you come down O'Shea. We shall all carry runners. Radio silence of course. Don't forget to click the camera twice before the attack. Remember a battlewagon is *much bigger* than the targets you are used to. At 1000 yards it looks enormous. Don't drop the fish too far away and remember to make the switches to arm it before you press the tit to release it. Any questions?

'What speed do you think she will be doing Sir?'

'Flat out she probably can't make more than 18 or 19 knots — about 10 I should think. Any more questions — right good luck chaps.'

I wandered out with Barr. 'Glad you're flying these instead of Stringbags now?'

'No I'm not. The Stringbag is a gentleman's aeroplane, these, well they're bloody dangerous.'

'I wouldn't say that. You're in and out much quicker. After all who wants to fly at a battleship at 90 knots when you could be doing 200.'

'Yes but all that winding trimmers and flaps. In a Stringbag there's nothing to do. You just aim the fish and drop.' We reached the aircraft.

'Well, see you later.'

We climbed in and started up. As each pilot got ready he raised his arm to signal the leader. As soon as we had all indicated our readiness we moved off. We taxied round and queued at the downwind end of the runway. Thorpe got a green and we followed each other round on to alternate sides of the runway and opened up. As each pilot took off he jinked to starboard to get his slipstream off the runway, away from the aircraft behind him. We flew round in a climbing turn towards May Island and formed up. We could see the fleet off to port. Thorpe took us Eastwards out to sea as we climbed, then led us round in a wide circle well ahead of the fleet. They were wallowing slowly along, the cruiser in the lead followed by *Nelson* and two destroyers either side. We should have to approach over the destroyers or between them to get in to attack *Nelson*. Over the top looked too dangerous so it would have to be between.

There was a layer of cloud, about 6/10, between us and the fleet. Thorpe brought us right round so that we could approach the ships from the North. About five miles off we caught a glimpse through a hole in the cloud. Thorpe gave the signal to form line astern. We took up our stations and headed for the position on the starboard side. He would be the one to come in on the 90° bearing if the destroyers were not too much in the way, myself at 60° and Cliff at 30°. I set 60° on the dial, 10 knots on the ship's speed setting, armed the torpedo, set the release switch and waited. After a few moments I saw his nose go down.

'Right — stick forward — brakes — throttle back — dive' and down I went. The cloud was a thinnish layer at about 5000 feet. Going flat out I plunged through it. When I emerged there was the fleet. Thorpe had judged its position pretty accurately before he dived. I could see that I should finish my pull out just astern of the leading screen destroyer.

1500 feet — stick back — level at 200 feet — full throttle — brakes off — trim back — trim rudder right — speed 220, it'll fall off a bit more yet — my God it's enormous — wings level — she's turning away! — move avoid lever — 170 knots, 90 feet, wings level — range 1500 yards, I think, should be OK — drop fish — steep turn to starboard and stay low — *watch out for the destroyer* — the battlewagon couldn't shoot at me though with that so close — home James — I think we must have scored a few hits — we'll know when we get back.

We gathered in the crew room. Thorpe didn't look too pleased.

'Well chaps, out of nine aircraft we got one hit — on the stern, it's not good enough. Most of you dropped too far away. I warned you about its size.' Barr spoke up.

'The destroyers were in the way.'

'Of course they were, that's what they're there for, you have to get round them somehow. Oh well better luck next time.'

A few days later Thorpe was again bending our ears when:

'Lootennant Commander Sir there's a telephone call for you.' Thorpe went to the phone — we could hear him.

'Le'tennant Commander Thorpe here — did what! anybody hurt? Oh well that's something, what's the damage? — none! — well that's bloody lucky — all right I'll send someone down for the bits.' He returned.

'Right, who dropped his fish over Crail?'

Osborn put his hand up. 'I think it was me.'

'You prune — you might have killed somebody — how did you do that?'

'I made the torpedo switches when I took off so I shouldn't forget them in the heat of the moment when we got to the target and then forgot they were on when I clicked the camera.'

'Oh — know where it went?'

'No Sir, I thought I was over the sea.'

'Maybe you were, but they travel in flight after you drop them. You hit the police station.' We all dissolved in laughter.

'The bobby's a bit annoyed. Lucky he wasn't killed.' We laughed again.

'It's not funny.' Then Thorpe too burst out laughing. 'Just get your finger out young Osborn.'

'Yes Sir.'

'I expect Commander Flying will bawl you out for this.' He did.

To help us in our work the Navy had invented the Torpedo Attack Teacher or TAT. They had installed a Link Trainer in a round building which had the walls painted in a seascape. Some of it was with a calm sea, a blue sky and a horizon and some rough and foggy. It was illuminated to simulate various times of day. Fitted under the Link and connected to it by a computer was a projector which threw on to the seascape the white silhouette of a ship. As you flew towards the ship it got bigger at a rate linked to the speed of approach. The shape of the silhouette varied according to the bearing of the aircraft from it. Changes of speed of the ship and avoiding action could also be simulated. The movements of the silhouette gave a very realistic illusion as the pilot flying his Link, without the hood of course, made his attack. He approached — dived — made his torpedo settings, he had to identify the ship first of course before he could set the speed, then at the last minute decide if it was turning towards him or away. When he had everything right he pressed the button. The computer did its sums, everything stopped and a light appeared below the ship where the torpedo had hit or in the sea ahead or astern if he had missed. We cheerfully sank the *Bismark* the *Tirpitz* and a number of Japanese aircraft carriers several times a week.

This was much more popular than IF on the ordinary Link. It had all the thrills of a giant funfair toy. Another, possibly insignificant, fact was that whereas the ordinary Link had always been operated by a slightly bored Flight Sergeant, the Navy had the genius to put an attractive Wren officer, Third Officer Collie Morford in charge of the TAT, a point noticed at once by one lad who lost no time in attempting to try and coax her into accompanying him to the local hostelry.

This shows the clean athletic lines of the original Barracuda II *(Charles E Brown)*

The De Havilland Tiger Moth 82A. There was no self starter or brakes. We had to learn to fly the hard way and in the cold in November. *(F.A.A. Museum)*

The North American Harvard II. These aircraft are flying over the International Bridge near Kingston, Ontario. The Harvard was a lovely aircraft and I spent many happy hours in it. *(F.A.A. Museum)*

'A brick with wings and a permanent oil leak' was the Miles Master I. *(F.A.A. Museum)*

Your first flight in a single seater, such as a Hurricane, was also your first solo on type — a sobering thought. *(F.A.A. Museum)*

The Barracuda II. This shows the Youngman flaps in the dive brake position. The Barracuda did not have to be 'peeled off' to start a dive, it had a special valve in the Merlin 32 carburettor, which meant that the 'Barra' could be simply 'pushed over' into it's dive without the motor cutting out. *(Charles E. Brown)*

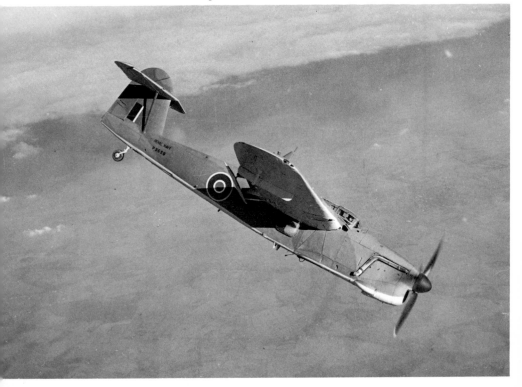

Fairey Barracuda II in operational trim complete with radar aeriels, boundary layer fences, stub exhaust pipes and a flying tail on the Fish — this came off when it hit the water. It also has a crew and a few dents. *(F.A.A. Museum)*

Practice attack on paddle boat — probably P.S. *Glenavon* — 1315 hours 4 November 1943. This photograph was automatically recorded by the wing camera on the aircraft behind me being flown by Cliff Lock as he dropped his fish. The fish appears to be running, off Crail (May Island in the background). *(Author's Collection)*

My first deck landing — 16 December 1943, HMS *Ravager*, batsman Lt Cunningham, Barracuda No P9887. *(Author's Collection)*

Deck landing number 8 in Barracuda BV 680 — 17 December 1943, exactly 40 years since Wright's first flight. HMS *Ravager*, batsman Lt Cunningham. This completed my flying training. What a sight it looks with everything hanging down. *(Author's collection)*

Barracuda going round again following 'cock up' on approach — probably too high, too fast and too far to starboard. Off Arran in the Clyde. *(F.A.A. Museum)*

My personal aircraft for two whole days, here lurking in the jungle of Ceylon. I learned a lot from my little Stinson Reliant. *(F.A.A. Museum)*

One circuit and a slow roll was all I had time for in the Fairey Fulmar in 15 minutes but it was fun. *(F.A.A. Museum)*

HMS *Queen* ploughing through the Oggin. Any similarity between her and *Ravager* is purely coincidental. *(F.A.A. Museum)*

The Wildcat taking a wave off, this might have been Harry Beeston declining my advances but actually it is not. *(F.A.A. Museum)*

Grumman Avenger leaving the booster — note wire strop, which attached the aircraft to catapult, falling away. *(F.A.A. Museum)*

'She's a bit of all right eh.'

'It's no good old boy she's married.'

'Well 'er 'usbands not 'ere is 'e.'

'No, but he's a two and a half Squadron Commander and much better looking than you. You've had it chum.'

One day Southern and Barr went off with Lt Camidge on a normal routine practice attack. Three quarters of an hour later only Southern and Barr came back.

'What happened?'

'Don't know really. We dived down together in the usual way. At the bottom we pulled out and Camidge went straight in. We flew round to see if he had got out but there was nothing to see.'

'Poor old Camidge.'

'Perhaps he forgot to trim back when he took the brakes off.'

'He might have, but I think he'd have had time when he felt it getting nose heavy unless he was going very fast, then it may have been too quick for him to stop it.'

'There's something else.'

'What's that Cliff?'

'Well the other day I was *practising* avoiding action. I was just flying along skidding from side to side, you know to put the enemy gunners off because they can't tell which way you are going when you're skidding, it upsets their aim, when suddenly the tail shot up in the air and I came straight down like a bullet. I was at 5000 feet and I'd lost 4000 by the time I'd pulled out. I don't know what happened.'

'Camidge might have been skidding if he hadn't wound on the rudder trim, when his foot came off the rudder after the dive.'

'Yes, just flying it like he used to fly the Stringbag.'

'If he'd done what I did he'd have had it.'

'Just a great splash and he wasn't there any more, I couldn't believe it.' Said Barr.

I was due to fly myself so I decided to try Cliff's experiment. I climbed to 5000 feet then flew straight and level at cruising speed pushing the rudder pedals alternately so that the 'Barra' was skidding violently from side to side. After four or five oscillations, which were increasing in size, the tail suddenly shot up, the Aldis lamp leaped off the floor, the seat rose up and my head hit the roof and we plunged straight down. Although I was expecting it to happen I still lost 1000 feet before I regained control. I felt sure this was what happened to Camidge. I believe that skidding the 'Barra' threw the highly placed elevators out of the slipstream on one side. At the end of a dive when pressure on the port rudder pedal was released the tail swung violently to port, the slipstream hit the underneath of the starboard elevator and threw it up. The propeller revolved clockwise, when viewed from behind, and would throw upgoing air on to the elevator, because with the tail mounted so high on the rudder post the starboard elevator only would be in the slipstream.

We had all lost friends in the war but no one on 41 pilots course had been killed. We all knew it could happen though, especially when we started flying to the limit in operational aircraft. But if somebody bought it you tried not to let it worry you.

'It shakes you doesn't it.'

'Could happen to anyone. As Cliff says he was probably skidding. We've done all our training in 'Barras', we shouldn't make that mistake. He's not the first to treat the 'Barra' like a Stringbag and get the chop. It's a tricky aircraft. It's bad luck on Camidge, but that's the way it is. A front line pilot must accept these things. What we have to think of is the future.'

'So that's it — when you take evasive action in a 'Barra' *don't skid*.'

There were other minor hazards too not all connected with flight. Coming home from night flying one evening on Patsie's bike I was stopped by the policeman in Crail.

'Where d'y think you're going?'

'Home Officer.'

'You've no got a light.'

'It must have gone out.' He shone a torch on the empty light bracket.

'No front light.' He shone his torch on the back bracket.

'No rear light. I shall have to report this Sir.'

'Oh really.'

'Name and address please.'

A week later I got a summons. I was charged:

1 That I did ride a bicycle without a front light, for which if convicted, the penalty was a fine of up to £5 or three months in jail or both.

2 That I did ride a bicycle without a rear light, for which if convicted the penalty was a fine of up to £100 or three months in jail or both.

Did I wish to plead guilty or not guilty? If I pleaded guilty I could do so by post.

I thought that it might be unwise to fight the law on what seemed to be an open and shut case and posted off my guilty plea. Two weeks later I had another letter. I had been tried in my absence and found guilty of both offences. I had been fined two shillings and sixpence on the first charge and five shillings on the second. Would I send a postal order for seven and sixpence by return — or else. I did and that would have been the end of it except that I mentioned it to the landlord of our digs who was the driver of the local bus. He was most indignant and berated the policeman, who was a friend of his, (they used to go poaching together) for daring to apprehend a tenant of his for such a minor offence. The Bobby was very sorry and said that if only he'd known he would never have thought of doing such a dreadful thing. However, perhaps he was still smarting a little from the torpedo landing in the police station yard.

Sometimes instead of drinking in the East Neuk we went into St Andrews where we drank in the Cross Keys. Here one evening Patsie, Cliff and I were sinking a few with some Norwegian soldiers.

'Skol'

'Skol'

'What does Skol mean?' we asked.

'Well it's really Dien Skol, Mien Skol, Al a Flicker Skol — at least that's what it sounded like — which means your school, my school, all the little girl's schools — Skol.' He drank his drink. Slowly his eyes glazed. He was leaning against the wall and his feet began to slip along the floor. He slid gracefully down the wall until he was sitting on the floor legs outstretched — 'Skol.'

There was always a good chance that if we survived after being shot down, or the engine packed up for some reason we might be taken prisoner. We were, therefore, given lectures on how to escape. The intelligence officer taught us how to write letters in code and showed us the escape equipment like buttons which concealed compasses and showed us how to conceal hacksaw blades in our clothes and other useful dodges.

'It is the duty of every captured officer to try to escape' he said. 'Many have succeeded so do not give your parole that you will not try to escape except perhaps for short periods for some essential reason. Even if you escape but don't get away it helps because it means the Germans have to keep a lot of troops looking for you and trying to recapture you.'

'When is the best time to try?'

'Straight away after capture if you get the chance. When they have only just caught you they won't really be expecting you to escape. You will take them off guard, also they won't have had a good look at you or got a photo.'

'Aren't we likely to get shot doing that?'

'That's something you have to take into account. If the risk is too great don't try it, bide your time.'

'What do the Geneva Conventions say about escaping?'

Quite a lot. If you are not in uniform you may be shot as a spy, on the other hand they are not supposed to shoot you out of hand. Still I wouldn't rely too much on the Geneva Conventions.

Now to give you an idea of what it would be like we have laid on an exercise. You will be taken in a truck and dumped some miles away. You will be wearing uniform but you can leave your caps behind and disguise your uniforms any way you can think of. You must make your way back into camp without being caught. You are not allowed to speak English. If you come across any military vehicles which have not been immobilised as they should have been you are at liberty to steal them but not civilian vehicles. Lastly the Army and the Home Guard will be out looking for you. There is a prisoner of war camp about five miles away and the POWs often work on the farms so watch out, they may mistake you for real POWs and you know what the Home Guard are like.

'Do we have maps?'

'Yes, take the maps you would normally be carrying but it is assumed that you would be lost so we shan't tell you where you are to be dropped.'

We discussed the forthcoming exercise. 'Doc, can you lend me a sweater or something? I've got nothing to disguise my uniform.'

'Yes Bristow, here, you can borrow this.' I fished out my old jersey which I wore under my flying suit.

'Won't you need it? what are you going to do?'

'I shall turn my uniform jacket inside out and wear that.'

'Won't it look rather funny?'

'Yes it will, but people might think it was an old coat of some sort that I had found and was using to work in.'

Hubbard and I had been paired off. He had an enormous Colt .45 pistol which he had got from somewhere.

'You're not planning to use that I hope.'

'It's not loaded.'

'I dare say not but the Home Guard won't know that.'

'I'll be careful. I'll keep it in my pocket and only bring it out if it is essential.'

'Nobody said anything about being armed.'

I still felt a bit worried.

We all climbed into the back of a truck and the back was closed with a canvas cover so we couldn't see where we were going. After about twenty minutes they started to drop us off two at a time. When

Hubbard and I got out we guessed we must be about fifteen miles from Crail, but we had no idea where.

'Well what do we do now?'

'I suppose try to get to St Andrews then we might be able to pinch a truck. We don't want to walk all the way back to Crail.'

'Yes, but which way do we go.'

'I suggest hitch hiking.'

'We're not allowed to speak English.'

'We could simply say St Andrews — I mean if we were in Germany we could say Berlin without being able to speak German. We needn't say anything else.'

The first thing to come along was a lorry carrying potatoes. We had by now disguised ourselves and looked incredibly scruffy. We waved our thumbs at the driver and he stopped.

'St Andrews?'

'Aye, hop in.'

We did. The driver eyed us curiously but he didn't say much. Perhaps he would drive straight to the police station. The lorry was noisy, talking was difficult, he had to shout. Luckily he didn't say much. We just grunted replies. It wasn't long before we got to St Andrews and to our relief he put us down without any fuss.

'Well that's a good start. Now all we have to do is find a truck and drive it back.'

It never crossed our minds that there would be any difficulty about this. We assumed that St Andrews would be littered with unattended army lorries. So we set off confidently looking like a couple of tramps. Hubbard had merely pulled his pusser's jersey over his uniform. It bulged in all the wrong places but at least it didn't look like uniform. He thought he looked like a fisherman.

'A fisherman! I suppose you hooked that jersey out of the water.'

'Well I look better than you do.'

He had something there, I didn't look like anything for which there was a reasonable explanation. We wandered round the place getting more and more despondent. There were no trucks in sight. We had almost decided to try to pass ourselves off as normal passengers and go by bus, we had no intention of walking 14 miles, when we saw a 15 cwt truck standing outside a cafe.

'There's our transport, there's no one in it.'

'If we can get it going. I can't see anyone anywhere near it either, there won't be any keys in it.'

'They must be in the cafe. Perhaps, if we can start it, we can get away before they notice.'

'How?'

'I've heard if you pull the wires out of the ignition switch it will start.'

We strolled over to it.

'Look' said Hubbard 'They've left the keys in — quick jump in.'

He turned the key and pressed the starter. It started first time and we drove off.

'We did it!'

As we did so I saw four or five soldiers come tumbling out of the cafe and start to run after us.

'We are being chased.'

'They can't catch us by running.'

At the end of the street we turned into a dead end.

'Hell's bells we can't get out this way, we'll have to go back.'

'They must have known it was a dead end, that's why they are running after us.'

We turned and went back the way we had come. The soldiers watched us and stood in a line across the road, Hubbard stopped. A furious Sergeant came over:

'What the hell do you think you're doing?'

Hubbard produced his pocket howitzer and pointed it at the Sergeant.

'You're dead.' he said. The Sergeant looked a little taken aback.

'What is this?'

'We're on an escape exercise. We're going back to Crail. We have permission to steal any military vehicle we find so we stole yours.'

'There's one thing puzzles me.' said the Sergeant.

'How on earth did you get it started?'

'Just pressed the starter.'

'But it never starts when we do that. We have to fiddle with the choke for hours. That truck is the most obstinate truck in the whole army.'

'You havn't got the touch mate.'

'And how are we supposed to get the truck back, I'll probably be put on a charge for failing to immobilise it. If you take it I'll be in the guard house for a year at least, that is if they don't shoot me.'

The poor man looked really worried. We took pity on him.

'Come with us, we don't want to keep the truck. When we get to Crail you can have it back, no one will know.'

The Sergeant brightened at once.

'In fact you can drive. I'll sit in the back with my pistol pointed at you and you can take us through the gate.' Said Hubbard.

'Right come on chaps, pile in.'

So off we went. The sentry on the gate let us through without a glance and we returned the truck to its rightful owners and that was that. Somehow I don't think it would have worked in Germany.

While this was going on Patsie had been shopping in St Andrews and of course knew nothing about it. Sitting in the bus on the way home she suddenly saw my jersey on Bristow. She didn't know Bristow who was also sitting in the bus looking decidedly sheepish. She stared at him, deeply wondering whether there was some gruesome secret to explain why this unkempt youth should be wearing my jersey. He began to look more and more uncomfortable and consumed with embarrassment, blushed a little. He handed the fare to the bus conductor without saying a word then shrank into his seat as the bus conductor eyed him. At Crail he got off and made off towards the camp, on foot.

Connolly had teamed up with O'Shea. After being put down they tramped aimlessly along the road for a bit then rounding a corner came across an RAF petrol lorry parked outside a farm. This was unusual to say the least and not a little suspicious. They looked about but there was no one in sight or inside the cab and again the keys were in it. They jumped in and drove it back to Crail. Thinking that perhaps they would be recognised at the gate they left the petrol lorry outside the police station at Crail then made their way back to camp by a detour round the guard room and went undetected. They told the policeman where they had found the lorry later so that when the driver noticed that it had gone he would be able to retrieve it safely.

Later that evening my landlord knocked on our door.

'I've heard all about the goings on today.'

'Oh have you!'

'Yes — my friend the policeman.'

'Ah I see.'

'The driver of that petrol bowser was worried sick.'

'Serve him right, he shouldn't have left the keys in.'

'Y' see he was na supposed to be there at a'.'

'No?'

'No, y' see he's got a little affair going wi' the farmer's wife. He'd just popped in for a quick one and when he came out his bowser's gone.' he chuckled 'Man was he worried? He didna' care aboot the tanker he was just feared in case somebody found out aboot the farmer's wee wife.'

Now the Swordfish pilots also trained at Crail alongside the Barracuda pilots. Their course was two months as against three for the 'Barra' pilots as the Stringbag was considered easier to fly. They made the same type of attack as the 'Barras' but being somewhat slower, they attacked at 90 knots instead of about 150 to 200 knots. They had to drop the fish from 50 feet instead of about 100 to 150 feet. One morning when a flight of Stringbags returned, the news came across that Adrian Rowe-Evans had gone in. Apparently he had pulled out of his dive a bit late and hit the sea. We were all briefly shocked by this news but the two pilots who returned thought he was OK as they had seen him get out of the aircraft. However a chap might be lost even if he had got into the dinghy. We waited anxiously for further news.

During the afternoon, round about tea time, a truck turned up carrying a grinning Rowe. It was, he said, a misjudgement on his part which had landed him in the oggin. He had, however, climbed into the dinghy and waited hopefully to be rescued. The word had gone out though, and very soon the Anstruther lifeboat came and picked him up. As he seemed a bit damp and chilled they had warmed him up with a goodly dose of the best lifeboat rum. By the time he got back to Crail he was very well oiled. Naturally we all congratulated him further in the ward room that evening.

Now your Fleet Air Arm pilot was a specialist. He had been selected and trained principally to do one thing. In our case this was to deliver a torpedo at an enemy with a reasonable chance that it might hit. However, there were other tasks which from time to time we were expected to carry out with the same degree of skill and competence such as dive bombing, drinking, gangway watch in harbour, making whoopee, spotting the fall of shot (not that again) also airfield defence against the enemy or, if they were not around, the Army or Home Guard — a much more serious business.

So one evening we were equipped with rifles, a handful of blank cartridges and boots and gaiters just like a school officers training corps on field day, and scattered round the airfield at the aircraft dispersal points to defend them against invasion. Several hours we waited in pitch darkness while the Army and the local Home Guard slithered towards us on their stomachs with their faces covered in shoe polish. At last, sensing that the moment for attack had come the captain of the invading army fired a Very pistol to signal to his troops that it was time to break cover and advance. We didn't know what the significance of this signal might be but George, who was guarding one of the 'Barras', thought it seemed such a good idea that he climbed into the cockpit, picked up the Very pistol kept there and fired one himself. What the effect on the troops might be we had no idea.

Doubtless the wheels in their brains whirred a little as they pondered the meaning of this signal and their Captain gnashed his teeth in frustration. The idea caught on at once, and others climbed into the aircraft and fired various coloured Very lights to brighten up the proceedings. It was soon like Guy Fawkes night. The attack collapsed in disarray. Wolf, a white Alsatian which lived in camp rushed over and bit Connolly on the bottom then charged into the perimeter mine field and blew itself up in a tremendous explosion. This brought the invasion to an end and we all retired to the ward room to drink gin.

Soon after this our course came to an end. We had notched up about fifty hours in the Barracuda and made about eighty or ninety practice torpedo attacks. There was just one small detail of our training to complete — Deck Landing

Chapter 10
Deck Landing

'Nobody but a nut would ever try'

In order to learn this crazy art we came to the Royal Naval Air Station at East Haven. A stone frigate — a nissen hut frigate would be more accurate — not far fron Dundee, HMS *Peewit* she was. HMS Seagull would have been more like it, because as everyone knows, the seagull is probably the best deck lander there is. In fact a seagull can not only land on the deck but on almost any part of the ship at all. So too can the Fleet Air Arm, and not infrequently did, although without the skill and finesse displayed by the seagull and rather more expensively. Like any other 'ship' we had a Captain and Commander and a complete crew, but the man who ruled with a rod of iron was Commander Flying or 'Wings' a dedicated, fanatical specialist in the wizardry of deck landing.

The first pilots who had tried, many years before of course, all made their own judgement of speed and attitude on approach to the deck to 'land on'. But after a time it was found that an experienced man standing on the flight deck could judge the approach of the aircraft — 'duck everybody he's going to prang' — and feel the movement of the ship better than the pilot who, sitting behind a large engine, couldn't see much anyway and the DLCO or Deck Landing Control Officer, better known as the batsman, was born. Initially he gave his signals, holding flags or bats in his outstretched hands, *advising* the pilot whether he was too high or too low, too fast or too slow or whether he was so much off line that he would miss the ship altogether. When the aircraft arrived over the ship at such a speed and in such a position that the pilot could land he was given a signal to 'cut' the motor. The aircraft then fell to the deck, the hook caught a wire and the flight deck party rushed out from hiding and grabbed the aircraft in the traditional manner evolved by Squadron Commander Dunning, the first pilot ever to deck land at sea. If the pilot made a mess of it or the ship suddenly plunged into the waves, and it wasn't too late to change his mind, the batsman waved one of the bats round his head. When he did this the pilot opened up to full throttle and the aeroplane staggered up and away in a nail biting period of suspense. If it *was* too late the plane came down anyway, the flight deck party crouched down in the walkways, behind gun emplacements or anything else handy and all waited for the crunch, then rushed out to gather up the wreckage, and console the pilot.

Such was the success of this arrangement that the Navy went a stage further and put the batsman *in charge* of the landing. This meant that so long as the pilot did exactly as the batsman told him he would land on the carrier and if he crashed it would be the batsman's fault not his. This was of course a great comfort to the pilot and made training much easier because all you had to do was to convince the pilot of the skill and omnipotence of the batsman and any idiot could do a deck landing. The Americans however retained the advisory system; moreover the signals they used were exactly opposite to ours, which didn't matter unless you tried to land on one of their carriers.

To indoctrinate us in the *method* the aerodrome had been marked out like an aircraft carrier's deck. All landings were controlled by a batsman standing beside the runway end and we spent nearly all of most days doing Aerodrome Dummy Deck Landings or ADDLs for short. When not doing these we went for periods of slow flying practice. Now the stalling speed of a 'Barra' with its wheels, flaps, hook, grab-handles and everything else down was 60 knots. The recommended approach speed for landing was given in the little book as 75 knots and it was recommended also that for deck landing we should 'approach with ample engine power at 5 knots less than for a normal landing'. So much for the little book. We had been approaching at 65 knots ever since we started flying them.

'However' said our instructors 'you will never get on the deck at *that* speed, you must come in at 61 or 62 knots.'

Now at this point I must say that I found flying at 61 knots or even 62 knots decidedly dicey, so I continued to approach at 65 knots.

'Hadley you're coming in too fast.'

'Yes Sir'

'61 knots Hadley'

'Yes Sir.'

So I went off to practise slow flying. The 'Barra' didn't seem to like slow flying very much although it was quite good at it. It became sluggish and I had the feeling that it might be just about to lose control of itself and bite me. One day, after a spell of this sort of humming-bird stuff, I thought that I would see just how slowly she would fly. So I put the wheels and flaps down at several thousand feet, put the throttle at the usual 'approach to land position' then deliberately stalled. She stalled at 55 knots, I just kicked the rudder to pick up the dropped wing, opened the throttle a bit and she came out. I tried again with a bit more engine and the same thing happened. Then I tried again on about half throttle, or a bit more, and she didn't stall until the speed had dropped to 45 knots! I could scarcely believe it. Of course the 'Barra' was mushing down, but when I kicked the rudder and opened the throttle a bit more she didn't come out as she had before. She couldn't really fly at that speed I suppose and she just flicked into a spin. I'd lost quite a lot of height by this time and was only at about 1500 feet and there was a 600 foot hill underneath covered with trees. However I had no choice but to do a proper spin recovery, so I closed the throttle, put on full opposite rudder, and pushed the stick forward. She came out of the spin straight away but I could see that I was going to hit the trees during the pull out. I suppose your mind works faster on these occasions because it came to me in a flash that if I pulled the Barra into a steep turn I should lengthen my path to the ground. I did this and it worked and I was back in control doing a steep turn with the wing tip skimming the tops of the trees.

This little episode increased my respect for the 'Barra' a good deal. I was not only surprised to find that with enough power it was controllable down to about 45 knots, but the speed and ease with which it recovered from the spin I found most encouraging. I felt that we should get on well together.

After I landed I related my experiences to the others but I think they may have thought I was shooting a line. Simmers especially was unimpressed, he had his nose deep in a book. He had not been able to organise a girl friend here yet but had somehow come by an unexpurgated copy of 'Lady Chatterley's Lover' which had been printed in Sweden and imported illegally, so he settled down with that to pass the time until his next flight was due.

Deck landing is a highly specialised art. The aircraft had to be brought down exactly on to a rectangle on the carrier's deck somewhat smaller than a tennis court and moving away at 30 knots. It was also pitching and rolling, sometimes quite a lot. But the main snag was that because of the way that the aircraft was built, with a large engine in front, the flight deck, in fact most of the ship, disappeared from the pilot's view under the aircraft's nose at the very moment that he arrived. The only way to land was to approach in a low curve. That way you could just manage to keep the batsman in view along the edge of the cowling until he gave you the cut, after which you just sat and waited. Our instructors gave us the gen.

The carrier circuit is at 300 feet. Get your wheels, flaps and hook down and the hood open and bung the prop into fine pitch, then come round in a steady curve with plenty of power — hanging on the prop. Watch the batsman and do exactly what he tells you. You will get fairly gentle corrections to your attitude to begin with to get you on the right line but as you get closer to the ship you must act more quickly as there is less time for the aircraft to respond. The batsman will bring you gently down to finish your turn just before you reach the round-down — that's the end of the flight deck. When you get the cut chop the throttle shut and the aircraft will sink on to the deck. If you get a wave off open the throttle wide, only pull the wheels up as soon as it's safe to do so and fly off. Don't pull the flaps up until you get a bit of height and speed. For practice on the aerodrome you don't put the hook down of course — just touch down and go round again.

So off we went — round and round like clockwork mice doing a landing every four minutes or so. Mostly the batsman held his bats steadily outstretched as we came round, indicating that we were coming in at the right speed on the right line. As we got nearer he lowered his bats to bring us down — then the cut, usually a bit higher than we would normally do it, and we thumped down. Both bats down — come down. Both bats up — flatten out a bit or go up. One up and one down — get the wing up on the up side. One bat held behind the back — too fast, slow down and get the tail down (I always seemed to get more than my share of these), both arms circling — too slow, bats crossed — cut! and these were orders to be obeyed, and pretty sharp too, not polite requests. The fierceness of the signals increased the closer we came to the landing. If correction in the space available was impossible the batsman waved us off vigorously then it was push the throttle wide, but not too fast in case the engine cut out, and hope.

Sometimes the Commander Flying — Commander R.N. Everett RN — the great *wings* himself — came out to bat us in. He radiated fierceness and batted with a fanatical zeal which was unmatched. I'm sure he could have batted a Lancaster bomber in to a landing on a matchbox. He could hypnotise us from at least half a mile away. He had his own special groove in the sky and you were in it — or else. He became so enthusiastic as the aircraft roared towards him that he danced out on to the runway, willing the aircraft to the very spot he had chosen, so that he had to duck under the wing as the aircraft hit the ground. He surely got us down all right but it was more shattering than the usual ADDL as he always disappeared under the nose much sooner than the other batsman used to, so that our period of guesswork was longer. He was the Navy's top batsman and he knew it. I think even the birds obeyed him.

Round and round we went, day after day, hundreds of ADDLs we did until we got it right. At night the batsman held two lamps and had another strapped to his chest, all connected to a car battery at his feet which prevented him running very far. Night deck landing was a prospect too dicey to contemplate but we had to train for it and a number of pilots actually did it at sea.

During this time we had one day off when, for a treat, we went to RNAS Arbroath for a go in the decompression chamber. This was a diabolical device rather like an old boiler with port-holes cut in it. As we sat inside watched through the port-holes by a Machiavellian doctor the air was sucked out until the pressure was the same as it would have been at 25,000 feet and we had to use oxygen to breathe. Our oxygen was then cut off to show us what would happen if we forgot to put it on when we were flying. When this happened to me I was asked to do mental arithmetic, which I got wrong, then set to writing my name which I did a number of times — each time more badly — before passing out.

Radnor and Southern were talked into playing draughts. Then they cut off Southern's oxygen. The game proceeded normally for a short time then Southern began to lose. Believing himself to be a better player than Radnor he became more and more angry. He then accused Radnor of cheating, picked up the board and threw it at him, then he passed out. He could remember nothing about the game when he recovered and vehemently denied that he could ever have behaved like that. However after watching another pilot in a hypoxic state trying to put marbles into a jar with rather less skill than the average drunk, then putting his shoes in his pockets and asking us where they were after he came round he conceded that perhaps it would be wise to use oxygen for high flying after all. Then back to deck landing.

At the end of three weeks we were just good enough to try the real thing in good weather on a calm day. We packed our gear and set off across Scotland by train to join HMS *Ravager* lying off Greenock on the Clyde.

December was cold and wintery. HMS *Ravager* swung restlessly round her anchor as we went out in a tender to join her. The sea was grey and choppy and a thirty knot breeze whipped the tops off the little waves in the Clyde. We climbed the accommodation ladder, saluted the quarter deck, and went aboard our first real ship.

Ravager was an Escort Carrier. She had been built in America by Henry Kaiser to a design which was really a single screw merchant ship modified by the addition of a flight deck. The funnel had been squashed and now emerged as two tubes, one either side of the flight deck. The bridge was the now standard 'island' on the starboard side. She was 14,000 tons, 400 feet long and 98 feet wide, and that ain't much to land a six ton aeroplane on at 61 knots, especially as you only have the stern half of the flight deck to land on anyway. The other half is used for parking the aeroplanes on after they have landed and there is a triple wire barrier to catch anyone who fails to hook an arrester wire after landing.

We arrived on board about tea time so we didn't fly that day. *Ravager*'s batsman Lt Cunningham gathered us together and told us of the plans for the morrow.

You will each have to complete eight deck landings. We usually have two of you going round at once then one can land and take off again while the other is in circuit. Now come in on a nice curve at 61-62 knots. After you land let the aircraft run back a bit then brake so that the wire can be unhooked, there are eight wires, you will then be pushed back to the take off position for another run. When you take off I shall give you the signal to go, probably just as the bow is going down. This allows you to accelerate rapidly. By the time you reach the end the bow will be coming up and help to throw you into the air. Now, if you make a hash of the approach I shall probably wave you off before you realise it is hopeless. You get three goes the first time round. If you get three wave offs fly over to Machrihanish and land there.

'What happens then Sir?'

'You go back to East Haven for more training.'

'Do we need flaps for take off Sir?'

'With 30 knots over the deck, and light, you could take off without, but you'd probably be better off with 15°'

'What if the deck is obstructed by the other aircraft as we come in?'

'Continue to approach — it will probably be clear by the time you arrive, if not I shall give you a wave off, then hang about until we clear it.'

Next day it was still cold and grey and windy. *Ravager* got up her anchor and we set off down the Clyde. Her top speed was 18 knots and if there was no wind this was barely enough for flying, but there was seldon a day in the North Atlantic or North Sea when the wind was less than 10 knots and that was what Henry Kaiser counted on when he built the Escort Carriers. They couldn't keep up with the fleet which steamed at 25 knots, unless it was held up by the more elderly battleships, but for convoy escort they were fine. Browse and Cliff were the first to go.

'So this is it then.' Cliff said. 'For what we are about to do may the Lord make us truly thankful. That sea looks mighty cold.'

'Don't worry, there's a Motor Torpedo Boat following behind to pick you up if you fall in.' I said.

'I'll throw you a life belt' said Southern.

'With the skill at your command I'd rather you didn't, you'd probably hit me on the head and kill me just before the MTB arrived to pull me out.'

'I doubt it, but it might damage the life belt.'

Cliff and Browse picked up their helmets and went up on to the flight deck. The rest of us crowded into the walkways to watch. Two Barracudas were parked one either side of the after end of the flight deck. They had chocks both in front of and behind each wheel to stop them rolling about and a member of the flight deck party lying on his stomach on either side holding them in place. Other members of the flight deck party were untying the ropes attached to the wing tip grab handles as Cliff and Browse climbed into the cockpits. They settled themselves in and as the DLCO signalled to them, by twirling his right arm round, started the engines. The ship started to swing round into wind and the flight deck was cleared of tractors and other odds and ends ready for flying. There was now a cold 30 knot gale whistling over the deck and the ship was pitching gently as she headed into it. After running up his engine Cliff gave the thumbs up, followed shortly by Browse. On the island they hoisted the aeroplane flag and 'wings' gave the signal to commence flying. Lieutenant Cunningham, the DLCO, held up his clenched fists to remind the two pilots to put the brakes on then waved the chocks away. The handlers picked them up then scuttled to the walkways fighting the gale as they went. Cunningham beckoned Browse forwards then guided him to the centre of the deck, held up his fists again then gave him the signal to lower his flaps. Satisfied that all was well he raised his arm to Wings on the island. A green light told him to go ahead. Raising a green flag above his head he circled it round while Browse opened the throttle until the engine was going full bore and creating a deafening cacophony, preventing any speech being heard. He held the flag steady as he looked down the flight deck towards the bow. It was pitching about four feet. He waited until it came up. At the top of the pitch he brought the green flag rapidly down. Browse let go the brakes and the 'Barra' began to move slowly up hill along the deck.

With a 30 knot wind against it its acceleration looked all too slow. As the deck came level then started tilting down it gathered speed. As he passed the island the deck started up again. Browse roared on over the end and disappeared. He didn't appear to be going all that quick and we waited for the splash. He had dropped a little bit as his wheels left the deck but mostly his apparent sink was due to the bow coming up and hiding him from our view. As the bow went down again we saw him climbing gingerly as he jinked to starboard. He got his wheels up then started on his way round the circuit. Cliff meanwhile had been moving up for take off and followed him off.

As Browse flew round, the supports under the arrester wires came up to lift them clear of the deck and Cunningham moved on to the batsman's platform on the port side almost at the stern end of the flight deck. It was about six feet square and jutted out over the walk-way and sea at the edge of the flight deck. It had a screen partly to keep the wind off the batsman but also to make him more easily seen by the approaching pilot. Just below it was a net to catch him if one of the aircraft came too close and he had to jump for it. Lying in the net was a rubber dinghy in case he jumped clean over the net by mistake to land in the sea 40 feet below. He had on a yellow waistcoat and in each hand a brilliant fluorescent yellow bat like a large ping-pong bat. As Browse, going downwind, came level with the ship he banked round to start his approach. Cunningham held out his bats and watched him come round. Browse was a good pilot and came steadily on holding a good line. As he got nearer Cunningham lowered his bats a little and the engine note changed slightly as Browse eased the throttle slightly back. Cunningham continued to give him lower signals as he came in. Just as he reached the round down Cunningham held one bat behind his back briefly, indicating 'too fast'. The nose went up a fraction as he came over the deck with a roar. 'Cut.' Cunningham crossed the bats, Browse chopped the throttle shut. The 'Barra' dropped like a stone about two feet and landed heavily with a crump which echoed across the hangar deck below, and could be heard even in the cabins below that. The hook caught the second wire which pulled out with a rattling scream as the arrester mechanism took up the strain. The 'Barra' jerked to a halt. As it started to run back the aircraft handlers rushed out and seized it by the grab handles, tail and undercarriage. Two of them unhooked the wire and clicked the hook back into the fuselage. Then they pushed him back the few yards to the end of the flight deck. He gave a thumbs up and Cunningham waved him off again as Cliff began his approach. Cliff had followed round too closely behind Browse so that by the time Cunningham was ready to receive him he was too close to get 'in the groove' and Cunningham waved him off. He opened up and flew over the deck and followed Browse round again, this time making a wider circuit. Browse came round and made another good landing then Cliff was on the approach. Going wide had thrown him off a bit so that when he started his approach he had fallen too far astern. He dragged it in from a long way back but because he was coming straight in he couldn't see Cunningham properly and drifted off to starboard to get a better view. Cunningham didn't want him there of course and started to give him frantic left bank signals to bring him back. He banked left to get back into the groove and of course promptly lost the batsman under the nose. By the time he had got back on to the port side again and aligned himself on the proper approach he was too high and Cunningham was urgently trying to bring him down. He closed the throttle a bit to lose height, sank viciously and opened it again as he crossed the round down a bit too high and fast. It wasn't brilliant but Cunningham decided it would do and gave him the cut. He floated over four wires and caught the fifth still flying. This pulled him out of the sky with a sickening jerk. The flight deck party did their stuff and he was soon off on his next circuit.

Southern and I watched all this with growing apprehension.

'I reckon this is the diciest thing we've done yet.'

'You're telling me.'

'It shouldn't be allowed.'

'Anyone in his right mind would know it was impossible.'

'Hadley' Cunningham called to me during a brief lull in the flying. 'When the next aircraft lands change places with the pilot, keep the engine running.'

'Aye aye Sir.' Cliff was just coming in for his fourth. As he hit the deck and caught a wire I climbed up and went over to him. When the flight deck party had pushed him back he put the brakes on as they put the chocks under the wheels then he undid his straps and climbed down.

'What's it like?'

'Out of this world Doc — good luck.'

I climbed in and did up the straps, adjusted the seat and checked the gauges. It looked OK. I looked over to Cunningham and gave him the thumbs up. He glanced at the island, got a green and raised his flag. The flight deck party scampered away and I started to open the throttle, holding the 'Barra' on the brakes. As I sat there with the Barra throbbing under full power it was an odd sensation to feel the ship heaving under me. My eyes rivetted on Cunningham I waited.

He paused a moment or two then dropped the flag. I released the brakes and the 'Barra' surged forward. I was conscious of the deck moving slowly past. We passed the island then ambled gently over the bow with the grey sea a mere 40 feet below. It was like a slow motion film only it was real and I was in it. I did not feel any sink as she went over the round down; by the time we got there we were flying.

'Hope the motor keeps going, can't really manage without it just now, good old Royce. Jink to starboard, wheels up, then turn to port on to the downwind leg. Start the turn in when abreast of the ship, remember she's going away at what amounts to 30 knots.' And there she was like a shoe box floating in the sea — it's impossible. 14,000 tons with a Captain and a crew of about 200, 50 of them gathered round the flight deck their eyes glued on me. The whole ship's company poised and thinking of one thing — me. Will he make it? — will be prang? Well this is where we find out.

Hood open — wheels down — flaps down — hook — fine pitch — seat up — slacken throttle nut a trifle to make it easier to control — tighten straps, Hell they're as tight as they can go already, here we go. The batsman must be there somewhere — where the Hell is he — where's his screen — ah I've got him now — Lord he looks small — I can hardly see what he's signalling. Ah — arms outstretched — so far so good, keep going like this and I should be OK — a piece of cake. He does look small though still I suppose from half a mile away anyone would look small. Those two bats and his yellow waistcoat just make a little line of three blobs. He's leaning over to port now — wants me to tighten the turn a bit. One bat behind his back — too fast. Hell I'm only doing 62 knots what does he expect. Getting closer now — signals coming faster. Down — down, bank to port. I'll lose him under the nose in a minute — there, he's gone oh Hell! turn a fraction to starboard now I see him again. Down — down — still too fast I'll never make it. There it goes round and round — the wave off. Full throttle and hold on tight.

Six feet off the deck she stops sinking and roars slowly up the deck overtaking the ship at only 30 knots. I could see the exasperation on Cunningham's face as he swept under the wing, and all along the walk-ways and all over the island faces — the goofers — all waiting to see if I should make it. I could see them all as I held the 'Barra' off the deck by the skin of its teeth. Once over the round down I lifted the wheels and set off for the next try.

This wasn't quite like the first solo it was more like a fight, a trial of strength, who would have the upper hand me or the 'Barra'. Well it was going to be me. I'd lick this pesky 'Barra' into shape. Down with the wheels and flaps and trim it back to 60 knots this time, and power, power until it hung on the prop and I dragged it round. I'd got it where I wanted it now, and there was Cunningham waiting like a wicket keeper as the fast bowler ran up to bowl.

Down, down — that's it — down, down — cut. Crump — we hit the deck a mightly blow and bounced up. I was hurled forward against the straps as the hook caught and pulled me out of the air as the wire screeched out, and we hit the deck a second mighty blow, but we were down and apparently still in one piece. Right, let it run back a bit — brake — hook up, then, back to the stern as the flight deck party took over. So that's what it's like. It's incredible that the aircraft stands it — it must be as tough as old boots. Six tons and it lands like a suet pudding being dropped. I took off again under the fascinated stares of the goofers — all 98 of them including the Medical Officer and the man in the asbestos suit waiting to haul me out if the cab pranged and caught fire, the flight deck engineer juggling with the arrester wire controls and the crash barriers, the fire party, the tractor driver and the fork lift driver waiting to shift the bits. The Captain and the Navigating Officer wondering whether I should get down before they had to change course to avoid running aground on the Isle of Arran and Wings perched on his seat on the island lording it over the flight deck and yelling through his bull-horn from time to time to liven things up, and Cunningham, standing on his little platform, one eye on the aircraft coming in and the other on the wind speed and direction indicator at his feet as he kept a check on what the ship was doing, as well as watching the flight deck.

Three more landings and that was my lot for the day. I was half way through the task and I hadn't bent the aircraft yet. The other four pilots had a go in the afternoon then the Captain turned round and we steamed back to Arran and anchored off Lamlash for the night. We who had flown in the morning joined the goofers in the afternoon. It was just as exciting to watch as to do. The next day was 17th December 1943. The same day that exactly 40 years before the Wright Brothers had made their first 12-second hop, but no one on board remembered. Wilbur was dead, not killed in an aeroplane as many people supposed but, from typhoid fever in 1912. But Orville was alive still. What did he think in 1943. 'Land a plane on a ship, you must be mad' is that what he thought? But perhaps not, after all people thought *he* was mad to fly at all. I think he would have enjoyed watching us. That day I completed my eight landings and so did Cliff and Browse but the weather began to blow and flying was stopped. We came back and anchored off Lamlash again. This was the end of our course. We were now officially 'on leave' and Christmas was coming, yet here we were stuck in the Clyde at anchor. A tender came over in the evening. Cliff and I approached Cunningham.

'Would it be all right if we went ashore in the tender? We might be able to get a boat across to the mainland in the morning. If we stay on board until *Ravager* goes back to Greenock we might be here for days.'

'Yes, I don't see why not, you've done your landings.' So off we went.

We hadn't of course given the matter very much thought. At 9.30 that evening we arrived in Lamlash to look for a bed. A small village on a Scottish island in wartime on a cold December night during the blackout is scarcely the place. The pubs had shut half an hour before — those were abstemious days in Scotland. The prospect, to say the least, was bleak. We began to wish we had stayed in the warm conviviality of *Ravager*'s wardroom when we found ourselves outside the policeman's house. We knocked.

'Could you tell us where we might find a bed for the night please?'

'Ach wheel ye'll no find one at this time.'

'Oh.'

'And how long wud ye be wanting it?'

'Only for tonight. We're hoping to cross to the mainland in the morning.'

'Aye, wheel we have a spare bed, I think my wee wifey will put ye up if ye don't mind sharing.'

'No we don't mind, thank you very much.'

It was freezing in the policeman's spare bedroom and not much warmer in the policeman's spare bed. Cliff and I endured the night and early next morning went down to the harbour to find the drifter which had brought us ashore and was going to Ardrossen on the mainland with mail. We climbed aboard and set off. I had never felt sick in a large boat nor even in an aeroplane no matter what manoeuvres I had been doing but the motion of that drifter was unsettling. The voyage was chilly as well but after about an hour we arrived in Ardrossen. We disembarked bleary and cold and set off along the quay. A voice hailed us 'Hi!' We looked about. We could see the head and shoulders of a young Naval officer sticking up above the edge of the quay. We walked over and found him standing on the cabin top of the MTB which had been following us about for the past few days.

'Come and have a drink.'

Was he mad?

'It's eight thirty in the morning.'

'So it is but never mind that, Christmas is coming. Have you had breakfast?'

'No.'

'Neither have I. Come aboard.'

We were cold and hungry and I at least feeling a bit queasy. We climbed down to the MTB.

'This is the wardroom.'

It was a box about six feet square.

'Gin?'

'For breakfast?'

'Why not?'

'Yes why not, just the thing, we have something to celebrate today anyway.'

'Cheers, what's that?'

'Cheers, we've just finished our training.'

'Well good for you — have another. I've been watching you, waiting to pull you out of the oggin when you fell in.'

'Well I must say we were very glad to see you there. How many of us have you fished out?'

'None so far, very boring, still I haven't been on this job very long.'

'Well better luck in the future. Why aren't you out there now?'

'My oppo is doing it today while we re-victual. Have another gin.'

Breakfast lasted about an hour as we helped him consume most of a bottle of gin.

'Where's the rest of the crew?'

'Buying supplies I hope. They went off early with most of the petty cash.'

'Well they won't be able to get any more gin until the pubs open.'

'No, I was hoping they might come back with some food as well, I'm starving. Have another drink.'

'No more thanks we have a train to catch.'

We staggered up on to the quay and waved goodbye. We hadn't been drunk before breakfast before.

'Thanks chum you've saved our lives even if you didn't have to rescue us to do it.'

We lurched drunkenly along to the station and caught the next train to Glasgow. There we parted.

'Bye Cliff.'

'Cheerio Doc — see you soon I hope.'

'Yes — bye.'

I went on leave and Christmas with Patsie to await my appointment to a squadron.

Part II

The Squadron Pilot

Chapter 11
822 Squadron

This was it. This was what it had all been for. To be a front line pilot.

Christmas Day had gone by and so had the New Year. I was on indefinite leave waiting for an appointment. I might have to wait weeks, or even months, but this was unlikely. Each day that passed a chap wondered if he might have been forgotten. It had been known to happen, some mix-up in the filing system no doubt. Once a man was mis-filed he might be lost for years and only found by accident, if at all.

My speculation was abruptly brought to an end by the arrival of a buff envelope from the Admiralty at Queen Anne's Mansions.

To acting Sub-Lieutenant (A) D.L. Hadley RNVR
'I am commanded by the Lords Commissioners of the Admiralty to inform you that you are appointed as pilot to 822 Squadron.

I am further commanded to order you to proceed forthwith to the Royal Air Force Station at Tain (Railway warrant enclosed). Acknowledge to the Commanding Officer Royal Air Force Station Tain.'

This, from the Secretary to the Admiralty. It was flattering to see my name and rank officially in print for the first time, but why were they always in such a hurry? Forthwith indeed! Nelson was always in a hurry and left their Lordships gasping and floundering in his wake; doubtless the habit stuck. So forthwith it would have to be. Where was Tain anyway? I exchanged the warrant for a ticket to Tain. At least the railway knew where it was, the ticket said via Inverness. Until that moment I hadn't realised that there was anything beyond Inverness except a few sheep and John O'Groats — and there wasn't very much there as far as I knew. If you went any further you fell off. The Admiralty had banished as much of its Fleet Air Arm as it could to the wilds of Scotland. This kept it out of their hair and it didn't matter too much what they got up to there because there was hardly anybody to notice.

I packed my gear, said goodbye to Patsie, and puffed my way up to the frozen North. The weather in January '44 was particularly cold and it got colder with every mile further North we went. The train was packed. All the seats occupied, so were the corridors, with people wedged into corners and sitting on cases or each other. People's breath steamed and the whole train seemed to be damp, steamy and full of smoke. Everybody had luggage, the army more than most. The army always went everywhere fully equipped. Part of their esprit no doubt, ready for instant battle. So that in addition to kit bags they also had enormous back-packs full of blankets, ground sheets, mess tins, spades, spare boots and so forth. They also had belts full of ammunition, rifles and tin hats, as well as gas masks like the rest of us, so that they took up a lot more room. Happily being now an officer and a gentleman I travelled first class, and so was crammed into a first class compartment with seven or eight other first class officers all exercising their privileges. After a night and a day of intermittent travel with snatched meals at station buffets, if the train deigned to stop when they were open for long enough to drink a scalding cup of tea, we arrived in Edinburgh. Here I had to break the hundred yards world record carrying a case and a kit bag to catch the connection to Inverness, which the guard signalled out as soon as he reckoned the passengers had a sporting chance of catching it on the run. At Inverness I boarded the local train. Years in the highlands had given it character. It chugged happily along not missing a single station or wayside halt and frequently stopping in between as well for some reason that seemed adequate to the driver, until at last we arrived at Tain. In order to give no help to the enemy, the station names, if there were any at all, were written in very small writing and put where they were difficult to see, so that every time we arrived at a station the station master or a porter had to bawl it out, and as few people could make out what was said all the passengers crowded to the window to peer out and bawl enquiries as well. Once it was established where we were, then the appropriate passengers disembarked. At Tain there was no competition and I was the only passenger to get off. It was freezing. The wind howled unhindered from Siberia, bringing snow. It was late at night.

The platform was deserted. I felt like a character in a ghost story. The guard blew his whistle and waved his flag and the train, which was probably the only link with the outside world, departed. Lurking in the station was a grizzled highlander who I supposed was the station master and doubtless also the porter and the signalman. I approached him with some misgiving. He might also be the local ghost for all I knew and not really there at all.

'Excuse me but do you know if there is any transport to the RAF station at Tain?'

He shook his head.

'Noo — probably did na ken ye were coming.'

Then he brightened a little.

'But I could give them a ring for ye.'

'Thank you, that would be kind.'

I waited in the dark, cold, evening. After half an hour a truck arrived.

'Sub — Lootenant Hadley?'

'Yes'

'Didn't know you were coming Sir, is this your gear?'

'Yes — well they should have had a signal.'

'I expect the signal will come tomorrow — we're a *long way* from the Admiralty here.'

I climbed in beside the driver and we set off.

'What's this place like?'

'Pretty bleak Sir, but the grub's all right. We share it with the RAF of course — Typhoon Squadron.'

'Are you from 822 Squadron?'

'Yes Sir, I'm a fitter.'

'Who's the CO?'

'Lootenant Commander Woods Sir. An observer.'

He said it as if he didn't really hold with observers commanding squadrons. Being a fitter he may have felt that an observer would be less sympathetic to a man of his trade than a pilot would — unjustly of course.

'Really.' I had never heard of an observer in command of a squadron before either. In the RAF the fact that the pilot was always the captain of the aircraft meant that the squadron commander must be a pilot too, whereas in the Navy the captain of the aircraft was always the senior officer on board regardless of whether he knew anything about flying. However the situation was usually resolved amicably, because if the pilot said 'Bale out' the observer was never likely to argue. So there was no reason why an observer should not command a squadron. Everyone knew where they stood, or jumped, as the case might be.

In due course we arrived.

'Where do you want to go Sir?'

'I've no idea.'

'I'll drop you off at the steward's hut. The leading steward will know where to take you.'

'Thank you.' I got out unloaded my gear and knocked on the hut door. After a long time and a lot of knocking the door opened and a head appeared wreathed in smoke. The door opened a bit more and the head's owner came out along with more smoke, coughing. I could see that the dim interior was full of smoke.

'What on earth's going on in there?'

'Stove's smoking Sir, lucky you knocked or we'd all be dead.' Leading Steward Hutchins plunged back inside and roused his mates to open a window then returned.

'Have you just arrived Sir?'

'Yes' I said 'Can you find me a cabin?'

'Yes Sir. It's very late. The mess will be closed but I'll put you in one of the empty ones and we can find the proper one in the morning.'

'Thanks' He did and I retired, cold and hungry, for the rest of the night.

In the morning as soon as I had had breakfast I made my way to the Squadron office and knocked on the door.

'Lieutenant-Commander Woods?'

'Yes — come in, have you just arrived?'

'Yes Sir, I came last night.'

'Had breakfast?'

'Yes Sir.'

'Good — come and meet the rest of us. Would you be Hadley?'

'Yes Sir.'

'Yes, they said you were coming, this your first squadron?'

'Yes Sir.'

'Tom, here's a new pilot for you' he addressed a cheerful dark haired pilot from New Zealand. 'Lieutenant Bassett, Senior Pilot, this is Sub-Lieutenant Hadley. What's your christian name?'

'Dunstan, but I used to be a medical student, everyone calls me Doc.'

'Hello Doc' Bassett extended his hand 'been flying 'Barras' long? Meet Killer Crane he's another pilot.'

'Yes Sir — we were the first course to train on them at Crail, hello Killer.'

'Ah well you should understand them a bit. Most of us learned on Stringbags, 'Barras' *are different*.'
He introduced me to the other members of the squadron.

'Right, now this morning you can fly with Reggie Soden, his pilot's got a cold. Reggie!'

Reggie came over. He was a very experienced chap. He had been on the Taranto raid as a gunner then trained to become an observer. Observers, as they grew more experienced, tended to be wary of new pilots and I could see that he viewed me with the deepest suspicion. However, he wasn't to know that I had never flown with a crew before, never even carried a passenger in fact, and I wasn't about to tell him. He didn't say much as we went out to the aircraft and took off on a practice bombing run. I dropped the four 11½ lb practice bombs and came back and landed.

'Nice landing Doc.'

'Thanks' After that we were good friends. We didn't fly together except once more as he had a regular pilot but he respected my ability.

822 Squadron had nine aircraft when I joined it, and twelve crews. I was the most junior spare pilot which meant that I had no aircraft of my own but had to fly other peoples. This irked them a bit as they were always afraid I might break it or upset the trim in some way. My next observer was Sub-Lieutenant Burbidge, known as 'Hiram' as he had spent some time with the Americans. He always flew with a vast array of equipment including a compass he had acquired from somewhere which was about the size of a football. He carried this and his Bigsworth chart table, a computer and a number of other items in a large green kitbag which he loaded into the 'observation lounge' of the 'Barra'. He was a good observer but I only flew with him four times before one of the more senior pilots grabbed him to replace his own observer who had been sent elsewhere. I flew with one or two others then eventually settled with Sub-Lieutenant Trevor Heaney with Leading Airman Feltoe as my gunner. We stayed together until May when I at last got my own aircraft, and a different crew, as the squadron was increased to 12 aircraft.

Formation flying was one thing we had to practice, because on a strike we always approached the target in formation before attacking. Heaney and Feltoe were new to a front line squadron, as I was, and I wondered how much they really knew about flying. They could probably recognise a good landing, but they wouldn't have had much experience of torpedo attacks, if any, and would never have done a deck landing. I plugged in the microphone jack.

'Can you hear me Heaney?'

'Yes skipper.' I felt a glow of pride, skipper I was.

'You Feltoe?'

'Yes skippper.'

'Good, I'm going to start up — you both OK?'

'Yes' I went through the routine and the 'Barra' burst into life. I coaxed it until it was running smoothly with its usual growling rumble then waited for it to warm up. It was a bitterly cold day but with the radiator shutter closed it didn't take too long. I ran it up, all was well. I waved away the chocks and we taxied out. I followed Killer Crane and Tom Bassett. At the downwind end of the runway we halted and did our vital actions. I called the crew.

'Stand by for take off.' Bassett got a green from the Scorpion and taxied round on to the runway. Crane and I followed. We would take off in succession — as we should on a carrier — a stream take off. I watched the other two surge ahead then opened my throttle to follow close behind. Slow at first the powerful thrust of the propeller soon had us gathering speed. The tail came up, we bounced a couple of times and we were off. I waited a moment or two then pulled up the wheels.

'Good take off Doc, wheels locked up.' I had forgotten I had a crew.

'Thanks'. Bassett was climbing fast and turning to port. Crane and I turned inside him to join up as soon as possible. By the time we had reached 1000 feet Crane was tucked into his position just behind the starboard wing tip and I was to port. There was cloud at 4000 feet but there were a few holes in it. Bassett headed for a hole and climbed through then levelled out and flew close over the cloud. As we skimmed low over its velvety top we could suddenly see how fast we were travelling. It was like flying about six feet above ground at 150 knots. With the next aircraft almost close enough to touch, it suddenly looked very dangerous and a little shudder went through the formation as Crane and I edged a little further away.

'My God Doc aren't we too close?' Recovering from the initial fright I began to move in close again.

'No Heaney, it's just that when you are close to the cloud you get this sensation of speed.'

'This is not just a sensation Doc. It's what we're actually doing.'

'Yeah — makes you think doesn't it.'

After a while we climbed up higher and left the cloud behind. Once again we appeared to be stationary in the sky as we tightened up the formation. Bassett turned his head to look at me then waved his hand over his head. This was the signal to go into echelon starboard. I pulled up the nose slightly and slid across the top of my two companions to settle down on the starboard side of Crane.

'Why over the top Doc?'

'It's the rules old boy. Above when you move to starboard, below when you go to port. Saves a nasty mess in mid-air if two aircraft change places at the same time.'

'Ah, I see.' Echelon was a harder formation to hold than the V or Vic we started with, as Crane who was formating on the leader could not keep as steady as he was. We circled round a couple of times, once with me on the inside and then on the outside, then Bassett signalled line astern and we both dropped back. Crane was just under Bassett's tail and I under Crane's. This was a much easier formation to hold and I had a chance to look round a bit. I could see the Dornoch Firth below and in the distance Wick. After a while Bassett waggled his wings and we resumed the Vic to fly back to the airfield. As we reached the circuit I was waved back to echelon starboard again. This was a preliminary to landing. We flew along the upwind leg of the circuit then Bassett 'peeled' in a steep turn and flew crosswind to begin his approach. Crane flew on for about half a minute and then did the same, followed by me half a minute later. Deck landings were made at about half minute intervals which was just enough time to land, fold the wings and taxi forward of the barrier before the next aircraft landed on. Peeling off had a joyous feel about it and I pulled the Barra over into a really steep turn to follow the other two round. Then, it was — open canopy — wheels down — check green lights — flaps down — propeller to fine pitch — trim — seat up to top of travel and then settle into the groove for landing.

Bump — bump — keep straight.

'Good landing Doc.'

'Thanks.' We taxied round, parked the aircraft and went to lunch. After lunch we gathered in the briefing room before going on the ALT. As we went in the sky was overcast, there were large thunderheads and lightening was flashing on the horizon. It didn't look very hopeful. The briefing officer called us to order.

'Now your target this afternoon is 'Manxman'. She is a fast minelayer. She can do over forty knots if she wants to so you will have to judge her speed carefully. It will be good practice for what you are working up for.'

'What's that Sir?'

'I can't tell you that yet, but you must get all the practice you can on fast ships, and don't talk about it.' A ripple of excitement ran through the room. 'Now Manxman is out in the Moray Firth somewhere. You will be given her position when you take off. You will form up at 10,000 feet and steer to intercept her. Recognition signal today is TF or two reds followed by a green Very light. That's all I have to say, any questions — right, met man give us the weather.'

An owlish little man stepped forward.

'Well the weather looks OK. There's a front approaching but it won't be here before tonight. There's a little scattered cloud, wind 210, 20 knots.'

We looked at him in stunned silence.

'Have you been outside recently?' the met man laughed.

'No, I don't need to. In any case I've been too busy since breakfast reading the teleprinter and making a weather chart for you lot.'

We rose to our feet and closed round him. He began to look a little worried. We picked him up.

'Hi what are you doing?' We carried him outside. The lightening was flashing, the thunder crashing and the rain coming down like stair-rods. He stared open mouthed.

'Care to revise your forecast?' He hurried inside. We returned to the mess to spend the afternoon in simple pursuits.

Next morning we again assembled for our ALT on *Manxman*. The weather was perfect and we lined up for a stream take off. Heaney, Feltoe and I were number three of the nine aircraft taking off. All seemed well as we roared along the runway. 'Have you done an ALT before?'

'No — have you?'

'My dear chap — ' then I realised he was joking.

'What I don't know about ALTs isn't worth knowing.'

We flew on in silence. Another New Zealand pilot, Bill Ringer and I were formating on Killer Crane who was in the lead. The other nine aircraft were grouped about us. Killer had the CO with him. After about half an hour *Manxman* came into view and we shifted into the extended line astern formation used for the attack. I kept my eyes glued on Killer. His nose went down.

'Right — hold on to your hats.'

I slammed on the dive brakes and began to plummet down. We went straight down and I pulled out at 150 feet. I had already set the switches and we went streaking towards *Manxman* at about 200 knots, I took aim, pressed the tit and pulled round into a steep turn just above the waves, zig-zagged about for a minute or two then assuming I was probably out of range, if they had been shooting at me, climbed up to reform at 2000 feet.

'Good Lord, is it always like that Doc?'

'Yes, usually, sometimes you have to dive through cloud and that makes it a bit more tricky. How did you like it?'

'I reckon I could get used to it — exciting isn't it?'

'How about you Feltoe?'

'I can take it if you can skipper.' We flew back to Tain.

In the evenings we relaxed in the mess. Drinking, smoking, playing liars dice, singing and sometimes having crazy games. Burbidge had a trick which I had seen neither before nor ever since.

'I shall now do the double chair somersault trick.' he said. Turning the occupants out of two wooden club chairs he arranged one chair in the centre of the room facing him. The other chair he set on its back a few feet beyond the first with the legs pointing away. Going back to the end of the room he turned to face the first chair.

'And now, before your very eyes, Hiram the death defying Human Cannon Ball, will fly.'

So saying he handed his beer to a WAAF officer to hold for him and started to run. Just before he reached the first chair he took off and dived head first into it. The chair flipped on to its back. Hiram somersaulted as he flew over it then hit the second chair with his backside in the seated position on the seat in order that his speed would turn it up to its normal position on its feet and he would finish the trick sitting comfortably in the chair holding out his hand for his beer. Unfortunately the club chairs at Tain were not the solid naval arm chairs he had used to perfect the trick and the second chair could not stand the strain. As Hiram the Human Cannon Ball hit it at full speed it disintegrated into a cloud of flying sticks and cushions leaving the surprised Hiram sitting on the floor amid the wreckage. The officers mess erupted with mirth. Even those who had seen the trick before had never seen such a devastating demonstration.

'Attaboy Hiram!'

'Good show — have a drink.'

He picked himself up.

'I should have known better than to use RAF chairs.'

At the beginning of February we moved to Crail for a spell, to improve our skill at torpedo dropping. After a couple of days we started using runners. We felt sure we were working up for something big, and the runners seemed to confirm it. When not flying we spent the time on ship recognition and discussing tactics amongst ourselves according to which ship we might be attacking. HMS *Implacable*, a 28,000 ton fleet carrier was waiting to take on aircraft and we felt sure it must be us. In the evenings we played liars dice or cardinal puff and sang bawdy songs while we waited for the signal.

Then the signal came, we were to move. We were to fly to Burscough and be prepared to go aboard. Next morning we loaded the squadron stores into trucks and assembled in the crew room.

'Let's hope no one goes unserviceable.' said Killer.

'Shouldn't do, we've got all the ground crews on the top line. When they pull their fingers out they're good.'

Heaney, Feltoe and I went out to our aircraft.

'Well this is it then.'

'Yes nice to be doing the real thing at last.'

The CO called his squadron on the radio

'Hello 822 this is the CO. We'll do a stream take off then form up and make a pass over the runway before we set course for Burscough. Once airborne we'll keep radio silence, don't want to attract any stray fighters. Right follow me out.'

We began to move off, sorted ourselves into the correct order for take off and taxied round to the end of the runway. The nine 'Barras' looked very businesslike as they trundled along. Crews still about the place stopped what they were doing to watch us go by. Killer stopped at the Scorpion and waited for the squadron to catch up. Getting a green he taxied to the right hand side of the runway and started his take off run. The air of Crail was filled with the roar and the ground vibrated as nine Merlins opened up in quick succession. The last aircraft had already turned on to the runway before Killer took off.

As I roared down the runway I began to feel that something was wrong. We were not gaining speed as fast as we should. The 'Barra' felt sluggish. I glanced at the dials. We were getting full boost, the revs were all right but something was holding us back. With most of the squadron, seven aircraft, behind me this was no time for dawdling about. Suddenly I remembered — the radiator shutter! I hastily reached down and wound it shut. The 'Barra' immediately gained speed and I felt the wheels leave the ground. I swallowed hard. A little bit later and I wouldn't have made it.

'What happened then Doc?'

'I forgot to close the radiator shutter, sorry.'

'Never mind we made it but I thought for a time we weren't going to.'

'Me too mate. I won't do it again.'

Observers and gunners were a long suffering bunch.

We climbed to 5000 feet and headed for Liverpool. We flew in a loose formation because the weather was foul, and in due course came to Burscough. Like any Fleet Air Arm squadron trying to impress we roared round the circuit at 300 feet and landed, then taxied round to line up outside the control tower. We booked into the mess. It would only be a matter of hours before we were ordered to fly on board HMS *Implacable* cruising round in the Clyde or the Irish Sea, just waiting for us. While out there in the Denmark Straight or the Atlantic was our target, oblivious to the highly tuned torpedo squadron waiting to pounce.

It was the end of February. Leap year day and March 1, my birthday, I spent doing an intensive instrument flying course on Oxfords, while the rest of the squadron pilots, who had already done it, lounged about. The evenings I spent with Patsie in digs in a house in Ormskirk belonging to Mrs Kegan. Why this instrument course was thrust upon me at the last minute I never found out and I never flew Oxfords again.

822 Squadron January 1944

Pilots

Crane, Vernon (Killer, Senior Pilot)
Whatmore, John (Dizzy)
Moore, Derek
Heliwell, Dick
Essencourt, Tom (Fingers)
Grimsdale, Harry (Grimmers)
Carruthers, Jock
Pratt, Norman
Culbertson, Johnny
Wilson, (Busy)
Williams, Dave
Ringer, Bill
Hadley, Dunstan (Doc)
Bassett, Tom (Left as I joined ex-senior pilot)

Observers

Woods, Gerry (Boss, C.O.)
Harsant, Freddy (Senior O)
Burbidge, Jim (Hiram)
Pearce, Eric (Poorly)
Lawton, Jerry (Dormouse)
Ryan, Peter (Bambi)
Knell, Bobby
Robertson, Jamie (Robbie)
Soden, Reggie
Issacs, Joe
Heaney, Trevor
Stevens, (Steve)
Laurence, Alfie
Solly, Harry
Overed (Springs, may have been 823 Squadron)

Telegraphist Air Gunners

Boddy, Bailey, Wotton, Dimmock, Feltoe, Challinor, Smart, Skeldon, Kerr, Stevens, ? White, ? Long.

Chapter 12
A Pier Head Jump

The 'defence of India' and a little smuggling.

As we waited, curiosity about the future mounted. The *Tirpitz*, doubtless, was lurking in some Norwegian Fiord. Each day at Burscough I looked forward eagerly to the day when we should take off to fly on board HMS *Implacable*. It was at this point that something entirely inexplicable happened. The Admiralty suddenly blew a fuse and we took what was known in naval circles as a 'Pier head jump'. The whole thing was suddenly 'scrubbed'. The aircraft were flown to Speke and loaded on to a carrier for transport and we, and the officers and ratings of three other squadrons of Barracudas and two squadrons of fighters, were hustled willy-nilly into the Royal Mail Steamer *Strathnaver* — an ex-cruising liner — and bundled off to the East. On the day we sailed I believe no one, from the First Lord himself downwards, had the slightest idea where exactly we were going, or why, and probably didn't care. Three weeks later we arrived at Port Said. By then the Master Ludo Players in Queen Anne's Mansions must have thrown the dice a few times and decided where about on the board they should move us to. At Port Said we were hastily unloaded and packed into a coal burning British India boat SS *Aronda* for onward transmission. We believed we were bound for Madras. In fact the Admiralty had somehow located a remote and barely inhabited part of India, called Ulunderpet, where it hoped it would lose a goodish portion of its troublesome Fleet Air Arm, with any luck, until the war was over.

The *Strathnaver* had been airconditioned in parts but not so the *Aronda* and we stewed in some discomfort through the Red Sea. For no obvious reason we swung round the anchor in Aden for a week getting hotter and hotter, then sailed South East through the Indian Ocean with the temperature rising all the way, the unfortunate fitters and riggers in the squadron travelling steerage of course. We officers were packed into cabins, much in the manner of fish into a hay box, to cook. As the final stroke of genius the Admiralty had permitted aboard this vessel *two* ladies. One was the wife of some colonial servant, she was joining her husband in India, the other was her daughter.

Now it is true to say that attractive though these two ladies were, and despite the fact that they were heavily outnumbered, or possibly just because of it, they were left largely to their own devices. However, one or two souls sniffed the air with hope rising in their breasts and one of these was my observer Trevor Heaney. It didn't take him long to be in there pitching. However, he was not alone. A number of eager rivals appeared but they were slow off the mark. Quite early on our second day on board he was busy trying to interest the daughter in the seagulls and kites, which flocked round the ship for scraps, when real competition loomed up in the shape of Kit Farmiloe who was in 827 Squadron. Now Kit was the genuine Brylcreem Boy. Always impeccably dressed and groomed — he usually wore whites with his wings pinned on while most of us wore khaki without the trimmings. His hair was carefully brushed, his nails clean and polished and a faint aura from some expensive after-shave lotion pervaded the air about him as he smoothly moved into action.

'Look' Trevor was saying 'See that one, that's a kite, he grabs the food with his feet, see, not his beak like a seagull does. Look there's another'. The girl had spied Kit approaching and answered in an absent sort of way.

'How interesting'. Kit opened fire.

'Hello.'

'Hello' she said. 'Have you come to watch the birds too?'

'No' said Kit 'I came to see what you were doing. Are you interested in birds?'

'Oh yes, I'm a dancer you see' she gushed 'and birds are so graceful — like dancers themselves. Are you interested in dancing?'

'But of course,' he chuckled. The girl blushed prettily. 'However I'm sure we can pass the time in a game of shuffleboard.'

Trevor, completely thrown by this suave and skilful ploy could only gasp agreement.

'Yes, what a good idea.'

'Oh I'd love to,' said the girl 'you can be my partner.' She turned to Trevor 'and you can play with my mother'. Now the Mother, although old enough to be his Mother too, was none the less a pretty hot number herself so Trevor was not unduly put out by this suggestion.

The four of them glided off to find an unoccupied shuffleboard court. This wasn't too hard as because of the heat there was not much enthusiasm for games among the rest of us despite the unrelenting efforts of our CO. We preferred to laze in deck chairs or in our cabins and in any case would rather watch these two ladies displaying their charms at shuffleboard than play ourselves. The game gathered quite an audience though, which soon began to take sides with ribald comments.

'Oh well played Sir.'

'Good shot Madam.'

'Knock him out, knock him out.'

'Oh well done.' The time passed pleasantly enough in the contemplation of what might have been. At meal times the two ladies naturally sat at the Captain's table. This was regarded as distinctly unfair by both Kit and Trevor who reckoned that the daughter at least was much too young for the senior officers at the Captain's table. However, there was little they could do about it so they had to content themselves with the time between meals when the two appeared on deck in revealing tropical clothing. Their cabin, of course, was well tucked away among those of the ship's officers and quite inaccessible to Sub-Lieutenants on passage so they did their best to locate dark corners of the boat deck to pursue their nefarious plans. The flirtation continued throughout the voyage. Kit always cool crisp and very urbane sometimes had the daughter's favour. At other times it seemed that the diffident charm of Trevor was what tickled her fancy most. We watched the play with idle interest. Nothing it seemed would come of it, and nothing did.

Eventually we docked in Madras. The girl and her Mother were met by high born civilians wearing solar topees who drove away with them, in style, in horse drawn carriages. The aircraft were unloaded on to the quay, and, there being no other way to move them, and to the amazement of the inhabitants of Madras, taxied, wings folded, through the streets to a metal landing strip which had been laid on the beach at a place called St Thomas's Mount. Their passage through the streets caused no little excitement and the powerful slipstreams blew all manner of things in all directions. Barrows, baskets of fruit, paper and clouds of dust took off and scattered. One lady standing idly by to watch us pass was instantly disrobed by the blast from the propellers and when last seen was completely nude but making very good time up an alley in pursuit of her sari. At St Thomas's Mount the aircraft, which of course hadn't flown for months, were carefully inspected. Then my crew and I took off to fly to our new home, the Royal Air Force station at Ulunderpet, 120 miles South West of Madras in the middle of nowhere.

Now the Royal Air Force station at Ulunderpet was quite new. The airfield had been built on the top of a low hill. Why this had been done was a mystery. It had two dusty runways made from metal plates linked together and set approximately at right angles across the hill so that the airfield resembled a large hot cross bun. Standing at one end of the runway the other end was out of sight. The control tower had been put near the intersection at the top of the hill so that the controller at least could see both ends at once. This was very necessary as the local inhabitants were somewhat vague about aeroplanes and were apt to wander across the runways when the notion took them.

The Americans had supplied runways but a local contractor had been engaged to provide living quarters and baths. The living quarters were palm leaf huts. They had been built in a circle like a tribal village. They kept out the sun very well, and the rain fairly well, but of course had no doors or windows so that the wildlife moved freely in and out, and much of it came in to live with us. The flying things came in and out as they pleased. In the roof lived a number of lizards of assorted sizes which ran about or fell off and from time to time discharged what appeared to be sulphuric acid. Chipmunks also visited us. They nibbled the backs off our books and ate the fly buttons off our trousers. Large centipedes lurked in our clothes and snakes of an irritable nature and with deadly poisonous fangs, cobras, kraits and such like, roamed about in search of their prey, of which there seemed to be plenty in our huts. They were inclined to curl up for a sleep if they came, in their travels, to a quiet comfy place such as our beds.

All this awaited us as Heaney, Feltoe and I purred across the plains of Southern India wondering what the place looked like. We spotted the runways after about an hour in the air, the 'Barras' were even slower in the torrid heat of India than they were in Britain. As we gazed down I noticed something odd.

'You know there's something funny down there, there seem to be lumps on the runways, mounds of earth or something. You don't think that perhaps they haven't finished building them yet?'
Trevor got out his binoculars and had a look.

'They're cows, blackish sort of cows, I think they must be water buffalo.'

'Let's go down and have a look.' Sure enough water buffalo they were.

'I'd better buzz them'. We roared down the runway about twenty feet up. Some of the beasts got up and ambled away. After two more passes the runway was clear, we came in and landed. The water buffalo of course were sacred and cared nothing for aircraft. In fact they didn't care about anything at all. Being sacred they could sit where they liked. If they sat in the road you had to drive round them. They could eat and drink whatever they fancied wherever they found it, or whoever it belonged to, and go wherever they liked. They were very holy. To the Hindu all life is sacred and the buffalo more sacred than anything else. The only exception to this rule seemed to be tax collectors, who were fairly regularly knifed, but this animosity to tax collectors is not unique to Hindus.

For three months of the year the climate at Ulunderpet was terrible and for the rest of the year worse. We were lucky to have arrived during the terrible months. It was fiendishly hot, dry and dusty. As we climbed out of the aircraft the sun hit us like a club. We made for the huts where cool water was kept in earthenware 'chatties' hanging in the windows. The moist surface of these chatties also appealed to the frogs and during the night they sat on the outside to cool their feet, and croaked.

The contractor had also been commissioned to supply baths and this he had done.

'What's that thing over there Doc?'

Near the middle of the compound was a cement trough about six feet long, three wide and two high.

'It looks like a horse trough.'

'Do you think when the contractor was told that six squadrons were coming he thought they meant cavalry?'

George Monilaws strolled up; he had arrived earlier with 817.

'That, is a bath.'

'A bath!'

'Yes. You will see there is a plug hole in the bottom.'

We looked. 'But there is no water'.

'Ah well no doubt they would carry that up in chatties — as much as you want'.

Trevor had been studying the gutter leading away from the plughole.

'That drain is going up hill'.

'Yes, most of them do that. Bathing obviously is not practised much here; with the stream close by, I don't suppose they feel the need'.

'Perhaps that is why it is out in the open so that the locals can gather round and see what goes on'.

'Yes, I don't think that bath is very practical. It is obvious to me that plumbing, and even the basic principles of water finding its own level is not a subject that is in the builder's apprentice's curriculum. I expect he wondered what on earth he was making.'

The cookhouse was equally primitive but here the contractor was on safer ground. Cooking was universal and Manoel, the Goanese cook, felt quite at home in the basic kitchen provided. He produced curries of incredible heat with a delayed action so that half way through the meals we turned gratefully to flagons of excellent limeade he also made from fresh limes to douse the fire in our throats. There was also gin, made locally, what out of we had no idea, but it tasted quite good.

Trevor and I shared one of the huts with about eight others. There were five double cabins under one roof with communal livestock. We slept inside mosquito nets of course with revolvers under our pillows in case of snakes or robbers. The robbers it was said would slit your throat as soon as look at you, if you woke up while they were on the job. The sanitary arrangements were thunder boxes.

During the heat of the day, the sun beating on the aircraft made them almost incandescent. We passed the hot time in intellectual pursuits, like sleep or cards, flying in the early mornings. It was 30 miles to the coast so that an ALT took about two hours but we practised them assiduously. No doubt the Admiralty had it's reasons for basing its latest strike aircraft so far from the sea but we felt that perhaps their Lordships were still trying to think of some way to keep us out of mischief. They dealt us a pretty crippling blow quite early on by sending a signal to the spare parts store at Coimbatore:

'Owing to the fact that the propellers of Barracudas have been found to strike the deck during deck landing three inches will be sawn off the tips of each blade.' The zealous stores officer set about his task at once so that all the seventeen spare aircraft he had in store should be instantly ready for operations if required. No sooner had he finished than another signal came singing through the air:

'Re the last signal, for Barracudas read Seafires.'

The poor old 'Barra' could barely manage with what it already had, with its propeller blades shortened by three inches it just looked funny. Fly! it could not.

One day as Trevor and I were peacefully melting in our cabin during the siesta, bathed in sweat and swatting flies to pass the time there was suddenly a loud bang and a revolver bullet whizzed through the hut. It hit the chattie hanging in the window on its way through causing an instant deluge.

'God! what's going on?' We rushed outside. Another shot went off as people ducked on all sides. On the far side of the compound near the kitchen was a mob of people capering about. All seemed to be armed and firing with wild abandon at something. 'It's a cobra!' It slithered rapidly over the ground and disappeared into a hut. As the posse converged on the hut the occupants emerged with the speed of light and were almost shot by mistake. At last the snake was baled up inside, but what to do now? The cook came to the rescue. Cobras didn't cut much ice with Manoel. Seizing a forked stick he marched into the attack. He was a big man with feet like a couple of york hams. As he advanced the ground shook. He disappeared into the hut and shortly emerged triumphant and smiling with the cobra dangling over his stick.

Somewhere between Liverpool and Ulunderpet we had acquired a Captain. He must have put up a magnificent, unfathomable black at some time to have landed in command at a dust heap like Ulunderpet. Possibly his crime was learning to fly, as he sported wings, and from time to time climbed into a Hellcat to pulverise the local airspace. By taking to the air he was of course doomed never to rise higher than Rear Admiral. After all any naval officer, especially a senior naval officer, who was sufficiently feather-brained to fool about with aeroplanes would, in the eyes of their Lordships, be hardly likely to be any good with a fleet of ships. However, as the Captain of a warship has his own private motor boat, so the Captain of six squadrons of aircraft should have his own private aeroplane, or so he reasoned. So, using the four gold rings, with the executive curls, on his sleeves he leaned on a quivering supply officer.

'I need an aeroplane.'

'I'm not sure whether there is any establishment for such a requirement I ...'

'I think that little Stinson Reliant over there is just what I need.'

'Well Sir, that one actually belongs to ...'

'We must have a communications aircraft. Every Royal Air Force Station has a communications flight and we need one too.'

'Yes Sir, but I'm not sure whether King's Regulations and Admiralty Instructions cover this ...'

'Arrange for a pilot to fly that one over to Ulunderpet tomorrow. One of my pilots will fly your pilot back.'

'Well Sir it may have to be another one, that one belongs to ...'

'Another one will be fine — first thing in the morning then.'

'Aye aye Sir.' The supply officer crumbled. Our Captain then looked for a pilot. I was still a spare pilot, not yet having my own aircraft. He called me over.

'I'm getting a communications aircraft, a Stinson Reliant, can you fly one?'

'I'm sure I could Sir.' I had no doubt I could fly anything at all given the chance.

'You haven't flown one before?'

'No Sir, but once I know the taps it will be a piece of cake.'

'Good then you can be my communications pilot.'

'I don't want to leave the squadron Sir.'

'Oh no you won't have to, we can't afford that, but from time to time there will be errands to do such as fetching stores or taking me to staff meetings and so forth.'

'I'd be happy to do that Sir.' I could scarcely believe my ears — my own private aircraft. The world had suddenly become my oyster. I hoped that the Captain would have plenty of staff meetings in places like Bangalore or Ceylon or perhaps a Hill station like Ootacamund.

'Good, well that's settled then. A station pilot will bring it from Coimbatore tomorrow. You will fly him back and he can show you the controls on the way then come back here and report to me.'

'Aye aye Sir.'

Next morning the Stinson Reliant duly arrived, as promised, soon after breakfast and I went off in it with the pilot one Lieutenant Langdon. There was very little going on in Ulunderpet so an observer came too. The Stinson was a four or five seater. To Harry Solly lunch in Coimbatore seemed a good idea. Solly was a clever young chap but when he wasn't actually navigating an aircraft he usually got his head down for a nap, or even while he was flying if there wasn't much to do. He could do a very good imitation of Nellie Wallace singing 'My old man said follow the van'. He eventually became my regular observer.

We flew to Coimbatore without incident, then had a good lunch after which I pottered round to the Met office to get the weather forecast. The Met officer handed me a piece of paper.

'Here you are.' I studied it.

'This is yesterday's forecast your clot.'

'Oh is it — oh well it's the same today.'

'Oh, thank you.' I needn't have bothered.

I returned. The weather had been the same for weeks — still you never knew it might change one day. One liked to know these things. I collected my observer and went via the control tower to the plane. Lunch was beginning to wear off as I started up and taxied out. On the way down to the take off point it seemed to me that I kept having to correct the plane from being blown to one side.

'There's a cross wind on the runway' I said. 'That lunatic in the Met office doesn't know his arse from his elbow.' I turned into wind and began the take off run. The aircraft kept swinging off course and I had to use the brakes to keep it straight.

'There's a hell of a cross wind' I said, 'I'll have that man's balls.' With a final lurch I took off. The aircraft slewed violently to one side and I had to bank steeply to keep straight and begin to climb, still skidding violently to starboard. It was now apparent that the wind was not to blame.

'There's something mighty wrong with this heap' I said. 'I'll have to get a bit of height if I can then try to get it down again.'
Solly moistened lips as I gradually edged upwards.

'Have a look and see if anything has jammed the rudder cables in the tail' I called to my anxious passenger. He looked hopefully about.

'Can't see anything — what's wrong?'

'Don't know — it just isn't responding properly to the controls'. I looked about vaguely at the dials and switches in the cockpit hoping for some inspiration but they only told me what I knew already — that I was skidding violently to starboard and the engine seemed to be OK. In fact it was doing its stuff manfully. I decided that when I got to 1000 feet the best thing would be to fly round and make the best approach I could and land on one wheel and hold it as long as I could before the wing touched or the other wheel came down on to the ground. Then suddenly I spotted a strip of red metal on the cockpit floor. I hadn't noticed it before. It ran to the rudder pedals. I gazed at it stupefied thinking that it was part of the operating linkage then I realised, *it was the rudder locking clip*. I bent down and unclipped it. The aircraft immediately began to fly normally.

'Some stupid erk must have done that while we were at lunch.' I said. 'Well it's OK now.' We flew back to Ulunderpet.

Soon after we landed a Barracuda taxied out to take off on what was generously called a test flight. What the pilot was testing was not defined but the aircraft had just been serviced and he was probably simply proving that it would in fact still fly and that nothing vital had been left off or a screwdriver still lurked somewhere near the compass. He roared down the runway in the usual lethargic fashion of the Barracuda and as he lifted off, his undercarriage began to retract. He had pulled it up too soon. All was well until the wheels reached the wings then the 'Barra' sank majestically to the ground. Going flat out the propeller was the first part to touch. It shattered and a cloud of dust rose into the air. Next the radiator was torn from beneath the engine and a cloud of boiling steam and glycol coolant merged with the dust. The aircraft ground to a halt about fifty yards further on and began to droop and fizz. As the dust cleared the pilot emerged grubby, but otherwise intact, from the wreckage, mouthing threats about his blameless rigger.

'I think it's a write off' he observed.

'Yeah — you'd better start filling in your A 25'.

This was an accurate assessment as the aircraft appeared to have been reduced almost to its component parts and most of them bent. It had split in two at the cockpit and the pilot simply had to walk away. The bits were gathered up and stacked at the edge of the airfield and gradually became incorporated into the architecture of the nearby village. They fitted a new propeller to one of the stored Barracudas at Coimbatore and 822 was re-equipped.

After that little bit of excitement I set off in the Stinson again to fly to Madras for some spares which I had to deliver to the stores in Coimbatore. This would mean spending the night there so Solly decided he would risk it again and come with me as did another observer, Alfie Lawrence. Madras was only one hour's flying time away but in the opposite direction to Coimbatore, so after picking up the spares we took off from St Thomas's Mount again for the trip back to Coimbatore. It was getting late by this time, and I knew we should arrive almost in darkness. There was no flare path at Coimbatore.

A mountainous spine runs up India in these parts. It gets up to 8000 feet round Coimbatore but there is a pass at Salem between peaks of 4000 feet or more and the railway runs through here and then to Erode 30 miles further on. Trusting my instinct rather than two observers' dubious navigation I flew south-west from Madras until I hit this railway then followed it to the pass. There was a huge line of thunder-heads ranged along these mountains and going up to about 30,000 feet with the mountains well buried in the cloud base which was down to about 2500 feet above the ground. We could not go over the top so we had to go underneath. As we approached the pass the cloud seemed to be coming down and the mountains closing in either side until we were flying in a tunnel with cloud on top and rock either side. I realised then that the cloud was not coming down, the aircraft was being sucked up. We were in imminent danger of being ingested into the cavernous black maw of this gigantic thunderstorm above us. If we were, we should most likely be spat out as fragments at about 35,000 feet and scattered over all India, so violent is the weather inside such a storm. I hurriedly pushed the nose down and dived. The cruising speed of the Stinson Reliant was about 120 kts. By the time we stopped gaining height we were diving at 155 kts. For the next thirty miles we dived at 155 kts. and lost no height at all, barely keeping pace with that fearful updraught trying to gobble us up. At last the suction eased and in due course we arrived at Coimbatore just before dark. In fact the extra speed had helped us to arrive with only moments to spare and I put the plane down as the last glimmer of twilight faded.

'What would you have done if we had arrived in the dark?' I asked the Duty Officer.

'Don't know really, put a lorry with its lights on at the end of the runway I expect.' I expected so too and was glad it hadn't been required. It was 19 June; I had been married on this day just one year before so we celebrated our double deliverance from aerial disaster that day in suitable fashion that evening, then in the morning set off back to Ulunderpet. We had with us another passenger, Lieutenant Charters. I don't remember why he chose to risk his life with us but doubtless he had some pressing business in Ulunderpet. I returned to squadron duties.

While at Ulunderpet we went dive-bombing and once we even did some night flying. This was quite exciting as there were no flare path lights or glide path indicator; in fact no lights at all. All we had was the landing light in the port wing of the aircraft, and the moon. The moon enabled us to glimpse the stunted trees just off the end of the runway as we came in to land and I suppose the beam from the landing light must have done some good. We had never used it before, landing lights were never used in Britain as they attracted the enemy, but doubtless it helped to illuminate the ground for the last few yards of the approach and would have shown up a buffalo, probably not in time to avoid it though. However after the first experience we didn't go night flying again so I suppose it must have dawned on the CO that he might be pushing his luck to persist. I dare say Killer, and the CO's own pilot Dizzy Whatmore would have pointed out that brilliant though the pilots of 822 were you had to be able to see where the ground was to land on it and miss the trees.

After we had languished in Ulunderpet for about two months the master ludo players must have thrown a six or something because orders came for us to move to Ceylon. There did not seem to be any particular reason for this as the enemy was still a thousand miles away and no aircraft carriers anywhere near us but anything would be better than Ulunderpet. There were rumours of course of action in the Pacific. Moving to Ceylon might be the prelude to something.

'Sub-Lieutenant Hadley!'

'Yes Sir.'

'The Barracuda squadrons will be moving to Ceylon. We will be based in Katukurunda. You will take the Stinson with my gear.' Thus spoke our captain.

'Aye aye Sir.' I had been planning to do that with my own gear rather than send it by transport when it might get lost and which would mean that in any case I would be without it for a week or so. However I guessed that there would be room for the Captain's gear and my own. When I got back to the squadron office the CO called me over.

'Ah Doc, the Captain tells me you will be taking the Stinson to Ceylon.'

'Yes Sir.'

'You will be able to take my gear.'

'Yes Sir.' By now I was doing some rapid mental arithmetic on the capacity of the Stinson.

'There is something else', the CO went on

'I've got the Captain's gear as well Sir.' I said hoping to stop the flow.

'It's only a small thing.'

'And my own stuff Sir.'

'Yes, well this is most important.' He showed me two enormous stone flagons of gin. 'We have to take this.' It was true the need was urgent. We had learnt from a brief visit to Ceylon already, to do a dummy torpedo attack, that the only available liquor there was, apart from some terrible beer and arack — a native drink made from the tops of palm trees — nothing to drink but South African cherry brandy or Australian creme de menthe. Known respectively as port and starboard lights we drank this stuff in numerous thimble fulls but it was not exactly thirst quenching or suitable for a pre-dinner drink. The gin was obviously a dire necessity.

'They are pretty big Sir.' — Each one held about five gallons —

'I shall be overloaded with these.'

'Oh I don't think so, one will fit on the radio bracket' — there was no radio in the Stinson — 'the other can go on the front seat beside you.' That was the trouble with 'lookers' they never really understood a pilot's problems or the mechanics of flight.

'It's smuggling isn't it?'

'Ah well, it will be all right if you fly straight to Katukurunda, just like from one ship to another, besides there's no customs officer there.'

'I might have to land at Puttulam to refuel, or Columbo and there are customs officers there.'

'Well as long as you don't prang they won't be likely to bother you. Anyway we can't leave the gin behind.'

There was no doubt about that, the gin had to go no matter what. I carefully loaded the little Stinson and took off. The luggage covered the entire floor of the cabin to a depth of about three feet. Two of the seats had to be removed to make room for it. With the smuggled gin strapped to the seat beside me the take off run seemed very long. Towards the end of the runway and going smartly downhill I heaved it into the air and set course South. In view of the overloading, the gin and the customs, I decided that a non-stop journey would be best, if possible. I decided to take a straight line across the sea, rather than follow the coast and the intervening islands which we were supposed to do, thereby saving a good few miles. Hell, I thought, if a naval pilot can't fly over the sea who can? I began to work out the fuel consumption as we flew along, rather a chancy thing to do really.

After an hour and three quarters we had reached the coast. The Stinson had two 30 gallon tanks. I had used 15 gallons in the first hour and I decided I would have to switch to the second tank in about 10 minutes. However it would be unwise to do this over the sea in case for some reason the fuel flow ceased, so I changed tanks early while still over land and reckoned I still had 15 minutes in hand if I needed it later. I crossed the coast and droned on towards Katukurunda. The coast receded until it was about 20 miles away on my port beam. By the time I rejoined it near Columbo, which was the last chance to refuel, I reckoned I had about 30 minutes fuel left. Katukurunda was 40 miles further on. I decided I was OK. After 20 minutes I still hadn't found it. Katukurunda, I knew, was just a strip carved out of the coast jungle, there was nowhere else to land — the jungle was solid down to the waters edge. I might just manage a crash landing on a bit of beach but there were a good many fallen coconut trees to impede progress. I was wondering what to do when the airstrip came in sight. I sighed with relief, made a hurried circuit and landed on the last few drops of fuel. One tank dry and about half a pint in the other the fitter said later. The gin was safely brought to Ceylon. It was hurriedly removed to the Ward room bar — still in bond so to speak — where 'The immortal memory' was duly toasted.

From Katukurunda we flew more training flights with, from time to time, trips across the island to Trincomalee, on the other side, to attack various practice targets. In the evenings we ate curries and drank port and starboard lights again when the gin ran out and waited for something to happen.

The Captain lost his Stinson without ever flying in it as the Admiral decided that being now so close to Columbo he wouldn't need it, whereas of course the Admiral might, so I had to fly it to Columbo to hand over to a grinning officer on the Admiral's staff. I learned a lot from that little Stinson, and kept my guardian angel pretty busy I think. Still, probably quite a good idea to keep him alert.

Chapter 13
In the Garden of Eden

At Katukurunda the living quarters were palm leaf huts much like those at Ulunderpet, and in the windows hung earthenware chatties for the same reason. At night the frogs at Katukurunda, no different from those at Ulunderpet, congregated on them and croaked for the same reasons. They also had the advantage of static water tanks built outside the huts, in case of fire, which they shared with a number of turtles which had come to live in them. The tanks, being sunk in the ground, were a minor hazard for officers returning from the mess in the evening. And the wildlife moved in and out in an identical way as chipmunks, lizards, bees and mosquitos and snakes made free with us or our possessions, eating anything edible like toothpaste and many things not normally considered to be.

One evening I was sitting in my cabin writing a letter. I carelessly moved my left arm without looking what I was doing. As I put my elbow on the table it was instantly seized by something with a million teeth. I went cold with fright. I had put my elbow on the bristles of my hairbrush. The wildlife really had us twitched.

The plumbing at Katukurunda, however, was better. Vast water tanks had been set up on poles and from these, pipes led to open air showers which delivered a chilly deluge when a chain was pulled. As the temperature was usually verging on the maximum shade temperature ever recorded in meteorological history this was all right. It rained too. Every day from midday to about 1245 the heavens opened and rain fell. Fell, perhaps, is the wrong word. It was more like being under a rainwater butt as it split. You were soaked to the skin in one second. This did not matter too much either, unless you had a packet of cigarettes in your pocket, because when the sun came out again it only needed about 15 seconds to dry off. Sun dried cigarettes though, which had a drooping, wrinkled look, never smoked very well. The other thing which fell noticeably in Katukurunda was night, which came down with a thud about seven o'clock each evening usually just as a chap was walking over to the ward room. At the same instant about 50 million fireflies lit up and the same number of cicadas came on the air.

There was also at Katukurunda a sort of palm leaf village hall where the occasional ENSA show appeared, or an old film was shown. The roof of this place leaked too of course. An attempt had been made to waterproof it with pitch or tar but the sun melted it and some of it had dripped through on to the seats. One day as I sat in my cabin Harry Solley came in. He held up a pair of trousers.

'Look at these Doc.' I looked.

'They are full of holes.' They were too. The seat was like a colander — just as if someone had blasted them from 20 yards with a shot gun.

'What can I do with these?'

'I don't know, have you tried catching fish with them?'

'The dhobi did it.'

'Did you wear them to the last ENSA show?'

'Yes, I think so.'

'Ah well that explains it.'

'How?'

'Well as I expect you noticed when you took them off the seat was covered with small spots of tar.'

'Yes.'

'Well the dhobi just hit them on the stones until he got all the marks out. As you see they are beautifully clean.'

'But I can't wear them like this.'

'No, I should give them to the dhobi.'

'He doesn't wear trousers.'

'No, that's a point, well that's the best I can suggest.'

Harry Solley drifted mournfully away.

We started flying from Katukurunda as soon as the fitters, riggers and the rest of the squadron with the stores arrived. To begin with this was mostly dive-bombing. There was nothing to torpedo anywhere near Ceylon but the East Indies were in the hands, temporarily, of the Japanese and there were targets there suitable for dive-bombers. The Barracuda was a good dive-bomber. In the past the odd one had shed its wings on the way down, which was a little worrying for us crews, but once we had changed all the wing locking pins for new ones we could come down like the clappers. There were some old, time-expired, bombs in the stores so they gave us these to practice with. Some went off and some didn't but we soon got quite good at it. We came straight down from 10,000 feet much like we did with the torpedos, only we dropped the bombs off at 2000 feet on the way down then pulled out so as not to be included in the fireworks.

After a time, however, we went back to dropping torpedos. HMS *Victorious* when she had finished bashing the Germans in Norway, had followed us out East. Now, we thought, at last we might get aboard, although for what purpose we had no idea. When it came to dropping torpedos we had to fly across the Island to Trincomalee where the Naval Air Station at China Bay had the torpedos. As we were getting ready to go I heard Harry, who had become my regular observer now, give a yell.

'Look at that.' A centipede about six inches long with long legs fell out of his shirt sleeve just as he was putting it on.

'Did it bite you?'

'No, but it was going to.'

'Thought better of it I expect.'

'Where did it go?' It had fallen amongst his flying kit but was nowhere to be seen.

'Ran off I expect.' He carefully shook out his gear then we went over to the aircraft.

As we taxied out I followed Bill Ringer and Killer Crane. We took off and flew Eastwards in a loose formation.

'You know I don't much like the look of that jungle, Harry.'

'No, nor do I.'

'It looks like solid trees in all directions as far as you can see. They are so close there is no room between them. It looks more like the ocean. It's supposed to be the original Garden of Eden you know.'

'Is that so, well in that case I'm not surprised Adam and Eve quit. What happens if we have to make a forced landing?'

'I don't know, there doesn't seem to *be* anywhere to land. It's not even flat and the rocks sticking out of the top are no good either.'

'I suppose we should have to bale out but those trees are 200 feet high. If you land on them it's still a long way to the ground.'

'Well lets hope the motor keeps going, it sounds all right.' I checked the dials and the fuel they seemed OK.

'Did you notice the aeroplane bouncing about as we taxied down to the runway?'

'No, was it?'

'Yes, going up and down like a pogo stick.'

'Probably taxied over a bit of rough ground.'

'Yes perhaps so.' We continued the flight in silence. We landed at China Bay. It had been quite cool flying across the Island at 7000 feet but as soon as we landed the sun hit us again. As we took off our helmets I heard Harry shout again.

'Aaaaargh!'

'What is it?'

'Look — inside my helmet.' It was the centipede. Squashed between his head and the helmet it had been unable to move. Now it gathered itself and rushed out as Harry dropped his helmet like a hot potato. It made off across the scorching ground at full speed.

While we had lunch the aircraft were loaded with runners. A little way out to sea HMS *Cumberland* with her escort was steaming up the coast, just right for a little target practice. The aircraft were almost incandescent when we got back to them so we climbed in gingerly uttering yelps as bare flesh accidentally touched bare metal, then started up and set out for the runway end. The runway at China Bay was almost two miles long. Now this was not for our benefit. The Barracuda only needed eight or nine hundred yards, even in the tropics, downwind, and with a fish on; this enormous runway was for the Americans. They kept a squadron of Super Fortresses at China Bay and *they* needed the runway. The Boeing B 29 Super Fortress was a real giant of an aeroplane. In addition to a couple of pilots and the usual gaggle of navigators, bomb aimers and radio operators it also carried a bus load of cooks, medics, stewards and so forth who did duty on the machine-guns or perhaps they were gunners who passed the time in other pursuits when not actually gunning. At all events it carried as many bombs at one time as our entire squadron and when fully equipped had enough ammunition and fuel and food for a day or two, which it could stay up for, and it even had dried blood plasma which could be reconstituted for any one who might need it on the trip if they happened to get short of blood for some reason.

By the time we reached the end of this runway the wind had changed and was now blowing at 10 knots the way we wanted to go. To taxi the two miles to the other end when several of the aircraft were already boiling was out of the question, so we hurriedly lined up on the runway and opened up as soon as we could. Even downwind with a runner the 'Barra' should be off inside two miles.

It was at this point that I began to have trouble. I had noticed the unusual bounciness of the aircraft and hanging the fish on the bottom had made it worse. In fact it was so bad on the way round to the runway that I had had to stop once to let the bouncing settle down. However, I figured that once in the air it would be OK and I could sort it out when I got back. I opened the throttle and set off down the runway. All went well, the tail came up and with the wind behind we gathered speed fast. Then just before I was ready to lift off we hit a small bump in the runway. The 'Barra' leaped into the air but not having flying speed came down again. Now normally it would have stayed on the ground to gather a bit more speed — but not today. It bounced straight up again slightly higher than before, tried to fly, stalled and came down again. And so it went on. I and my anxious crew roared down the runway in giant kangaroo hops, never quite getting enough speed to fly. At this point I would have cut short the take off, but with seven aircraft behind me I could not, so I continued to make giant hops down the runway, hoping that on one of them we would fly, until I realised that I wasn't getting anywhere and that even a two mile runway ends eventually. There was only one thing to do. I pulled the emergency boost knob and determined that on the next bounce, come what may, I would hold it in the air. We zoomed up on the next bounce but even with the added boost started to come down. As I held on grimly,the end of the runway flashed beneath us. Luckily the ground fell away a few feet beyond the runway end and sloped down to the shore of a lagoon about four miles long beyond the runway. The 'Barra' continued to sink, then, just a little above the water, decided to fly.

Immensely relieved I held it there waiting for it to pick up speed. Harry had been silent up to now, his mouth a little dry. He had stoically borne the insane lunges the 'Barra' was making well aware that, whatever the trouble was, I was doing my best to get airborne, but as we surged across the lagoon at four feet his curiosity broke through. He pressed the microphone switch.

'What goes Doc?'

Now if I could have answered I would. Unfortunately I was still deep in strife. In my right hand I held the stick not daring to let go so close to the water. My left hand held the throttle lever. In the flurry of take off I had forgotten to tighten the friction nut. If I let go and the lever came back, even a quarter of an inch, we would lose enough power to drop us in the lagoon. There was another problem too. I had forgotten to lower the seat before we took off. As the 'Barra' had been designed to be flown by a gorilla whose hands reached to its knees, even if I had let go of the throttle I could not reach the undercarriage lever to pull the wheels up, which in any case I could not do until the 'Barra' had gained a few more feet or, again, it would sink down into the lagoon as the wheels clicked into the wings upsetting the airflow over them and thereby the lift. Now although the lagoon was four miles long, even at only 90 knots, which was all the 'Barra' was doing, it would still get to the end in a little over two minutes and at the end was a stand of palm trees about 60 feet tall, and all this of course depending on whether the engine could stand the boost over-ride for long enough to get us out of trouble, five minutes being the limit Rolls-Royce recommended.

Very gingerly I eased the stick back a fraction and the 'Barra' very slowly began to climb. When we got to about twelve feet I put my knees against the stick then leaned over and hurriedly tightened the throttle friction nut with my right hand. So far so good. Then holding the stick in my left hand I lowered the seat with my right. I was now about half way across the lagoon and up to about 15 feet. Changing hands again I could now reach the undercarriage lever and I pulled up the wheels. The effect was immediate and after its initial lurch the 'Barra' started to climb. I cleared the palm trees by a shade leaving their fronds lashing in my slip stream then started to chase the squadron which was now well away. Returning the boost over-ride knob to its normal setting I switched on the microphone.

'Sorry fellas — I don't know what's got into it. When we get back I'll put it U/S. There seems to be something wrong with the undercarriage.'

'I thought we'd had it there for a bit.'

'Yeah it was quite dicey for a time.'

Killer had seen our take off and watched with curiosity as we skimmed the lagoon leaving a ruffled wake in the water behind us so low were we. He was relieved to see us climb away at last and come up to join. Bill and I were flying at numbers two and three to Killer again, and Bill gave the thumbs up as we joined. As we got to 10,000 feet it got quite chilly. We always wore long trousers and long-sleeved shirts in case of fire but they were only cotton drill and after a time we either shivered or turned on the cockpit heater, so we were very glad to see *Cumberland* below at last. We split up into our attacking formation then came streaking down. We had forgotten what a big ship looked like and not wanting to drop too far away came too close as we levelled out. Most of us just about got it right but one pilot misjudged it badly and pulled out much too near. He didn't have time to level out properly before he dropped. His torpedo hit the water and shot out again like a flying fish. It soared high in the air and flew right over the fo'castle of *Cumberland* causing the ratings working there to fall flat on their faces, then plunged into the sea on the other side never to be seen again. This impressive little trick was not appreciated by the Captain of *Cumberland* and the pilot got a rocket when we got back.

'Hell.' he said. 'I don't know what they're fussin' about — it was only a practice head on that torpedo.'

When we landed back at Katukurunda the 'Barra' was still bouncing like a tennis ball. I turned it over to the riggers who promised to investigate. The fitters were feeling quite pleased with themselves as they had just found the cause of a curious squeaking which had been coming from the propeller of one of the other 'Barras'. When they dismantled it they found that inside the spinner a chipmunk had built its nest and objected when the engine was started. They soon sorted out our problem. It seemed that the oleo legs of the undercarriage had been blown up with air but somebody had forgotten to put in the 'oleo' to damp out the oscillations.

There is a little play called 'Love in a Mist'. This takes place on Dartmoor in the winter in a fog and is full of references to how cold it is, and what a freezing draught there is, and will somebody shut the door. The actors put on scarves and overcoats to keep warm. The cast consists of only three men and three women and the scene is one room inside a country pub so it was an ideal play for a travelling company like ENSA. It is of course a comedy but in the tropical heat and humidity of Katukurunda it was a wow. As we watched them striving with their lines while dripping with perspiration until their overcoats were sopping we gave them louder applause than they had ever had. After claiming to have 'sunk' the *Cumberland* we felt we deserved no less than this farce to round off a good day.

One of the curiosities of Trincomalee was an Italian warship. The *Eritrea* had been the flagship of Italy's fleet in the Red Sea. More like a yacht with a couple of pop-guns she had a very good table and wine store well stocked, and had been much liked by visiting notables to the Red Sea. When the Italians were kicked out of East Africa she hastily put to sea to seek sanctuary in Japan. Like all Italian naval ships she was very fast and after eluding the Royal Navy arrived in Tokyo. Rather to their surprise the Japanese were not unduly thrilled to see her and would only allow the crew enough fuel for essential purposes such as to keep the lights on and the galley working. Moreover, not entirely trusting their allies they undid the nuts which held the engines in their beds. The Italian Captain, somewhat irked by these slights decided to do something about it. By careful husbanding of his supplies he managed to save enough fuel to put to sea, which he did, with the engines still loose in their beds. Once off shore they screwed them down then made for Singapore. Arriving there they pointed out that they had done their best to be helpful and resented their shabby treatment. The Japanese then relented and put them on to meeting their submarines and escorting them back to Singapore. This they did quite happily to everybody's satisfaction. Then one day as they were steaming out to meet one they heard that their beloved homeland had changed sides. It seemed to the Captain and crew that it would be only prudent to do the same, and that as quickly as possible. So they opened the taps and headed for Trincomalee where they arrived about two weeks later. It is doubtful if the *Eritrea* affected the strategy of the Naval High Command in the Far East in any way at all but since she was there she could be employed so she was put to escorting British submarines into Trincomalee.

Thus it was that 822 squadron came upon her one day as they were deploying for a practice attack. We had in fact set out to attack a destroyer but some minor navigational error had caused us to miss our intended target by about 50 miles. It so happened that at about the time we should have sighted her the *Eritrea* came into view instead. From 10,000 feet the differences between her and the destroyer were barely noticeable. The sky was blue and clear, the sea was blue and devoid of shipping. The coast of Ceylon was on the horizon in a slight haze and exactly which part of it was visible to check our position was impossible to tell. We stuck our noses down and plummeted on to the *Eritrea* like a gaggle of hungry gannets. The *Eritrea* was on her lawful occasions going out to meet a submarine when suddenly her crew saw six blobs hurtling towards them and another six close behind. Now the crew of the *Eritrea* were no better at aircraft identification than any other ship's crew and the Barracuda was, in any case, like nothing they had ever seen before. However, they had heard about Taranto where British torpedo planes sank many of the pride of Italy's navy and they were in no doubt about what was happening. There was no time to man the guns or even give orders, no time to change course and it seemed to the crew on deck that, things being as they were, it might be best to leave. They began jumping over the side. Whether a moment's reflection would have changed their minds is doubtful but at all events the attack was over before very many had abandoned ship and, finding, much to their surprise, that their ship was still afloat and undamaged their comrades put about and lowered a boat to pick up those members of the crew now swimming strongly, about half a mile astern.

822 squadron flew back to China Bay well pleased with itself. The attack had gone quite well even if it was the wrong ship. It was curious that the crew had started jumping over the side. The usual reaction from a ship accidentally bounced was a hail of bullets. In fact

some ship's captains made a practice of shooting at any aircraft which came within range regardless of which side it was on, so to see the crew behave like this was a welcome change and brightened the day no end.

When we landed the CO was summoned to the presence. He returned a little paler and seemed subdued we thought, however when the *Eritrea* returned to harbour he went on board. He stayed for lunch and came back very much happier than before babbling about spaghetti bolognaise and we felt that he must have resolved the situation. A little later he told us that once the captain realised what the score was he became very friendly and offered to be a target whenever we liked. The CO thanked him for this and fixed a date for another attack. He said that he would send an officer to observe the attack from *Eritrea*'s bridge and take bearings on the attacking aircraft for analysis later and appointed me for the task.

So it was that a few days later 822 once more set off to attack the *Eritrea*. This time the navigation was spot on and they found her cruising about ten miles off Trincomalee, dropped their fish and flew home. Later that day I rolled in, somewhat pie-eyed, with a sheet full of bearings. When I became capable of speech I told all about it.

'They piped me aboard you know, just as if I was an admiral, then gave me breakfast as we put to sea. Then I wandered up to the bridge to wait for you chaps.'

'What were the Eyeties like?'

'Seemed nice enough, very friendly.'

'What's the ship like?'

'Very luxurious — air conditioning — nice mahogany furniture — marble bathrooms — marvellous galley. Do you know I had only been on the bridge about ten minutes when a steward came up with a tray of glasses of wine and handed them round to everybody. Can you beat it. There was the officer of the watch quietly swilling down glasses of wine and the skipper too.'

'Very civilized I call that.'

'Yes, well by the time you chaps turned up I was almost seeing double. However the attack looked most impressive. I've never been on the receiving end before, very professional it looked I thought.'

'Then what?'

'Well, that concluded the business of the day, so to speak, so we went down to the ward room where they have a real slap up meal. You know five courses and wine. After that I rested my legs until we docked.'

We repeated this exercise several times as spotting the attack from on board seemed a very good way of checking our skill, only it was decided that in future two officers should go to *Eritrea* as when the attack came from both sides it was difficult for one person to check all the bearings at once. There was a move to increase this number to three or four in the interest of greater accuracy it was explained, but the CO pointed out that this would have depleted the strength of the attacking force and observers tended to be out of action for a while afterwards.

The Royal Naval Station China Bay was HMS *Bambara*. Like so many 'palm frond' frigates the name was descriptive. The *Bambara* was a beehive, but not your domestic honey-bee type. The bees at China Bay were the size of ink bottles and black. They lived in beehives of their own making. They were about the size of a club arm chair and looked like large stones, so much so that they could easily be mistaken for one especially in the dark. The bees were relatively peaceful unless disturbed but if their bambara was damaged they attacked their aggressor in a large swarm and the only escape was to dive into water. The occasional drunk who fell over one was usually stung to death so I suppose the place was appropriately named except that the enemy was so far away he could never fall over us. Still, if he had we would have been ready for him.

To increase our readiness and put the final touch to the sharp edge before we took off for HMS *Victorious* we had to do a few more deck landings. An escort carrier HMS *Thane* was put at our disposal and so we pilots pushed off for a little practice. It was not considered sporting to carry lookers on what was purely a piece of pilot training so our observers waved us off and returned to the card school. It was a good six months since any of us had seen a deck but the sea was calm the sun shining and there was a nice breeze blowing.

'You don't forget how to deck land Doc do you?' Bill asked.

'I don't think so Bill.' I felt none too sure about it myself but I wasn't sure that I ever really knew how. It was true we had done eight landings on HMS *Ravager* without breaking anything but Cunningham had been an exceptional batsman. The batsman in *Thane* might not be in the same class.

'I'm not sure you ever forget those sort of things.'

'No Doc I don't think you do. It's like riding a bike. Until you can do it it's impossible but once you've done it you cannot ever imagine that you couldn't.'

And so it proved. We were a little nervous, but we each notched up four lovely deck landings before lunch and returned triumphant to the squadron and the secret relief of our observers and gunners.

On our last flight before joining *Victorious* we took off for an ALT. I was too busy keeping my distance from the other aircraft to notice much else as we left the ground and started to climb when suddenly I glanced at the Air Speed Indicator. It was reading *zero*! It couldn't be right of course we were flying. I thought for an awful moment we must have stalled and that I hadn't noticed, a sudden gust of wind perhaps, but that was impossible, in any case we hadn't stalled, how could we have.

'Hey Harry what's your ASI say?' there was a pause.

'Zero.'

'So does mine.' I thought about it. The ASI works on air under pressure, ducted to it from the pitot head — an open tube fitted under the wing. Because the opening is small it is liable to become blocked by spiders or earwigs crawling into it. To prevent this a cover with a long red streamer was used to protect it when on the ground.

'Have a look at the pitot head Harry, is it covered up?' Another pause. 'There's an old starter cartridge stuck over the end.' So that was it, the rigger had lost the cover and used an old cartridge instead. I would have a word in his shell-pink ear when we got back.

'Are we going back Doc?'

'No there's no point. We won't need the ASI for the attack and you won't have to navigate unless we get lost, which seems unlikely.'

'What about landing?'

'We'll have plenty of time to worry about that when the time comes.'

Now it is of course essential to approach to land at the correct speed but after a fair amount of experience in any particular aircraft you get to know what it should feel like on the approach. You can also make an estimate of speed from the artificial horizon, so I was not unduly worried. After the attack we landed without much trouble without the ASI but I think it impressed my crew.

Chapter 14
We Go into Action

In Columbo was the Grand Oriental Hotel, better known as the GOH. A little way out of town, on the sea front, the Galle Face Hotel. The GOH was a pleasant old fashioned hotel with large overhead electric fans to churn the air round. The Galle Face Hotel was a more open sided building with its own swimming pool. From the town it was really too far for anyone to want to walk to it in the tropical sun, so we went either by ricksha or by a horse drawn gharry which would carry four of us. One day as Harry Solly and I were enjoying a gimlet or two on the Galle Face verandah a gharry with a cargo of four young Americans, in our opinion somewhat overpaid gentlemen, drew up. As they dismounted one of them casually handed the driver a bill of generous proportions to pay for the ride. The driver bowed low, thanked them effusively then hurried away. This puzzled the Americans, and us, greatly until it dawned on them with horror that they had unknowingly bought the gharry — complete with horse.

The alternative to a ricksha or a gharry was a taxi. The disadvantage here was the driver. All the taxi drivers were convinced firstly that they were the finest drivers in Ceylon, if not in the world; secondly that no vehicles except the taxi they were driving had any right to the road at all, they ignored pedestrians and cyclists who wisely kept out of the way; and thirdly that it was very undignified, and totally unacceptable, to give way to anyone else — except, if at all, at the last possible moment — and to blow the horn and curse the other driver as they flashed past. The driver always gripped the steering wheel tightly, his knuckles showing white, his whole body tense, in a state of manic concentration as he gazed intently ahead. If they had rear view mirrors they never looked in them. They were good drivers, mind, but they drove to the limit, without really knowing where the limit was.

As we sipped our drinks we chatted. We had got the buzz that we were to fly on board *Victorious* very soon now. Before we did so another convulsion shook the squadron. The CO and over half the crews were suddenly shipped back to England. Those of us left behind joined up with 823 squadron and became a rejuvenated 822 under the command of Lieutenant Commander Lesie Watson — a dynamic fellow. This turned out to be a good move as the pilots left behind were mostly the more junior ones who had been trained initially on Barracudas, brought up on them so to speak, rather than converted from Stringbags, and generally far more enthusiastic about them than the crews who had left for home. Among 823 pilots were Algy Black and Joe Faulkner two old friends from 41 course.

'Got your gear packed Doc?'

'Yes Harry, there seems to be rather a lot of it though.'

We had been having lectures on survival in the jungle among other things and had been provided with machetes about a foot and a half long to hack our way out of it if, by some mischance, we got into it.

'Have you ever heard of anyone who has landed in a tree?'

'No. They say that the best way is to pancake on to the top.'

'That may be so but have you ever heard of anyone who has actually done it?'

'There was a chap who forced landed in the jungle while still on the circuit at China Bay.'

'Yes, and they never found him, but while they were looking for him they found a chap who went in in 1926, still in the cockpit.'

'I reckon we bale out. If you see a flat bit it will probably be a paddy field and, if it's in the East Indies, swarming with Japs.'

'It's a good idea to take razor blades I'm told. I hear the ladies like to shave and razor blades are as good as money to the locals.'

'Yes a few packets don't take up much room in the pockets.'

Very soon our orders came. We were to join *Victorious*. As well as Harry Solly my regular observer, and my regular gunner Petty Officer Wotton, I now had my own aeroplane. Its number was L S 709 and it had a large Q painted on the side. All the aircraft had by now had all their red paint or dope covered. The roundels were simply dark blue with light blue centres, but the letters which were also red had not yet been changed. The Americans had also removed the red from their aircraft. This was simply because the Japanese, who loved red, had in addition to the large red roundels put as much extra red paint on as they could. Recognition was now much easier. Any aircraft with large red spots on it was Japanese.

Q was looked after for me by my fitter LAM Cudworth and my rigger LAF Mellany. They were both excellent chaps. Mellany had spent some time as a cowboy and told me confidently that he could ride anything with two or four legs. Just before we were to fly on board I took them for a trip while I did some ADDLs, after which they went ahead with the advance party to *Victorious*. Sad to say soon after they had gone somebody pushed Q into a hangar door and bent the wing tip. However it was straightened out in time for us to leave in the morning. After breakfast we collected our gear and climbed into the aircraft. We started up, taxied round and roared out of our jungle airstrip at Katukurunda to form up out over the sea to fly to *Victorious*. No sooner had we set off than I noticed that the oil pressure gauge was reading zero. We had only just crossed the coast and were not yet on radio silence so I pressed the transmit button to call the CO and tell him of my plight. As I did so the engine coughed. I hurriedly released the button and the engine picked up again.

'Harry' I said 'We've got no oil pressure.'

'Well the engine sounds all right, only why did it cough just then?'

'I don't know, it did it when I switched on to transmit to tell the CO, I'll try it again.'

I did. Once more the engine coughed and began to splutter as if the ignition had somehow been shorted. I hastily switched off the transmitter again and the engine picked up.

'We'll have to go back and get the spare aircraft.'

We pulled out of the formation and headed back to Katukurunda. It wasn't far and I hoped that whatever was wrong with it would stay in abeyance until we got back. Ten minutes later we landed. The spare aircraft L S 672 had the letter Z on it. It was a brand new aircraft. I had flown it once or twice, it was in fact the one which had given me such an exciting time when it had no oil in its oleos, but I liked it. It had more power than my old Q — also it wasn't flying left wing low as Q had been after being pushed into the hangar door so I didn't mind swapping at all but we had to stay for lunch while it had its daily inspection and was got ready for us and a signal went to *Victorious* telling them to expect us later. We took off again about three that afternoon. The rest of the squadron had of course been struck down into the hangar when we finally caught up with *Victorious*. As we flew past all was calm and peaceful. The flight deck was bare of aircraft. The afternoon snooze had been taken and the watch-keeping officers were pacing the deck before going on watch at eight bells. The flight deck of *Victorious* was a good six hundred feet long and they could have had a brisk walk from end to end, but no, your fishhead has fixed habits. What was done in *Nelson* and *Rodney* was good enough here too, so they paced in pairs briskly along the deck for about thirty paces then turned about smartly, inwards, facing each other, and paced thirty yards in the opposite direction. It was a hallowed ritual and not to be disturbed by anything, except action stations, and certainly not by a lone Barracuda arriving late to land on. We could wait until eight bells, after all what was half an hour.

We circled round and had a good look at her and *Indomitable* and the escorting destroyers. She was impressive as she cut cleanly through the Indian Ocean. She was well armed with sixteen 4.5 inch guns — two pairs in turrets on each corner so to speak and able to fire at high or low angles. The island too was well supplied with multiple pom-poms and Oerlikon guns. Along the walkways on each side of the flight deck we could see Bofors guns too, with clips of shells gleaming in their breeches. The flight deck had a lift either end. These were down when we arrived to allow a breeze to blow along the hangar deck where the mechanics sweated over the aeroplanes.

'She looks very small to land on Doc.'

'Well I tell you Harry she's the biggest one I've had to land on yet. You should see what the little ones look like from up here.' Neither he nor Wotton had ever done a deck landing so they were, to say the least, curious.

'I can't wait.'

'I wish they'd get a move on. It's tempting fate hanging about over all this water although this is a lovely aircraft — I don't expect it will spring a hydraulic leak or anything.'

'Well I don't think anything is going to disturb that routine.'

'Ah the watch must have changed I see some action below.'

'Yes it's 1600 hours according to my clock.'

'The lifts are coming up.'

As we watched the deck was cleared and *Victorious* began to pick up speed and turn into wind. One of the destroyers moved over to take up its position as plane guard as a flutter of bunting broke out from the signal halyards of *Victorious*. The aeroplane flag, a red diamond on a white field, appeared, the barriers went up and the DLCO dressed in his yellow waistcoat went along to his platform. The affirmative signal, a white cross on a red field, appeared on the island.

'Right this is it, tighten your straps and stow any loose gear — we usually stop with a jerk. You know, sixty knots to nothing in about twenty feet.'

I dropped down to 300 feet and opened the cockpit hood. The air rushed in like the blast from a furnace. I circled round about half a mile ahead then turned downwind and flew along to port of the carrier. As midships came abeam I slammed down the wheels and flaps, put the prop into fine pitch, opened the throttle and started my turn. I ran through the vital actions — hook! I'd forgotten the bloody hook — hook down. I had my eyes fixed on the carrier now. I picked up the DLCO standing on his platform just forward of the port side after gun turrets. He had his arms outstretched in the 'Come on in as you are' signal. We seemed to be nicely 'in the groove' so I held it and came on in. As I got nearer he started to wave me lower. I must have been a bit slow responding because I could see him getting more frantic. I put the nose down a bit and closed the throttle a fraction. This brought me down but I was going too fast and I saw one bat go behind his back to tell me so. I pulled up the nose a bit and he went back to giving me come down signals. As we crossed the round down I felt sure we were too high and I would get a wave off, but no, he still waved me down then *cut!*

Well cut it had to be and I pulled the throttle lever back — after all he was in charge. We fell what seemed an awful long way and hit the deck with a resounding crash and bounced up again. However in our brief contact we had caught a wire because we suddenly stopped flying in mid-air and crashed down once more then began to run backwards. I put on the brakes, heard and felt the hook being clipped up then followed the flight deck officer as he beckoned me along the deck. The barriers went down and I taxied past the island with its crowd of goofers on to the forward lift — brakes — came the signal and two of the flight deck party rushed up and put chocks under the wheels.

'Well done Doc — do we always crash when we land on deck?'

'Yes usually — I don't know how she stands up to it.'

I stopped the engine and was about to get out of the cockpit when the wings began to fold as the flight deck party took charge. No sooner had they done this than there was a lurch as the lift started to go down, bells ringing. It reached the bottom with a gentle thud and immediately the hangar party swarmed on to it and surrounded the 'Barra' like a tribe of ants. We began to move backwards off the lift. After a few yards the tail was swung to starboard and we were neatly slotted into place between two other 'Barras'. Brakes! and that was it. Harry Solley, Wotton and I climbed out then walked back to the lift to be carried back to the flight deck. We had just time to grab our hats, the rest of our gear would have to wait. On reaching the flight deck we went over to the island to report to Wings. Our CO was there to greet us.

'What happened Doc?'

'Well Sir first I found I had no oil pressure but when I switched on the transmitter to call you the engine coughed so we went back for the spare aircraft.'

'Good, you found us all right.'

'Yeah, well the ship was almost where she should have been.'

'Come and meet Wings.' Wings was a brisk little man who hadn't flown since they gave up making biplanes but he knew what was what and kept our end up with the fishheads. We were, after all, the point on the sharp end of the spear.

'This is Sub-Lieutenant Hadley and Sub-Lieutenant Solly Sir and Petty Officer Wotton.'

'Welcome aboard, nice landing, glad to have you with us. You'd better go and find your cabins now. I may see you in the ward room later.'

'Thank you Sir.' We took our leave. One of the stewards had materialised and conducted us via the hangar to collect our gear then down three steel ladders, then along a rather narrow corridor, obstructed at intervals by water-tight doors for what seemed a very long way. Eventually, somewhere near the stern, he stopped and opened a door.

'There you are Sir, there are four of you in here.'

We peered inside. Inside were Bill Ringer and "Steve" Stevens.

'Ah G'day Doc, come into the parlour.'

The cabin, if it could be dignified by such a name, was like none I had ever seen before. Six feet wide at the door it tapered to a point. One side was the ship's hull, which sloped up from the narrow piece of deck left to walk on so that the whole thing resembled the inside of a pyramidal box lying on its side with two bunks welded to each side. It was just at the point where the starboard propeller shaft emerged from the hull, a feature made obvious by the vibration felt in the hull and bulkhead and the throb from the propeller blades just the other side of the steel plates. It was hot too. No doubt the forced draught which came from the ventilating trunking was fresh air from outside, but by the time it reached our cabin it was scarcely invigorating.

'My God, the black hole of *Victorious*.'

'Yes, you could say that, still you'll get used to it. It must have been worse in *Victory*.'

'You have a point there Bill.'

'Come on I'll show you the quarter deck.'

He led the way up more ladders until we emerged on to the holy of holies. As we stepped across the threshold we saluted, as every sailor has for almost two thousand years. The quarter deck was an oasis. It covered the last forty feet or so of the stern in spotless holystoned teak planking. *Victorious* being an aircraft carrier, the flight deck formed a fine overhanging shelter which kept off the sun, and a pleasant breeze blew across it in the tropical heat. The paint was fresh, the taffrail smooth, the ship's bell polished. Tiddly bits of rope work covered stanchions and metal hand rails sheathed in painted canvas. As we stood and gazed at the wake, boiling away astern, as the three screws churned through it at 25 knots I felt like an admiral or a king in his royal yacht. We stood there in the cool, revelling in our new home. This was it, we had arrived. A front line squadron in a fleet carrier going into action. We looked at the fleet steaming along with us. *indomitable* with two Barracuda squadrons 815 and 817 and two Hellcat squadrons 1839 and 1844, a battle cruiser, two cruisers and about a dozen destroyers disposed at intervals round the big ships and about a mile or so away. As we were out of range of enemy aircraft, none of our fighters were up, although *Indomitable* had a pair of 'Barras' out on anti-submarine patrol ahead of the fleet. After about an hour:

'Come on' said Bill. 'Lets go down to the ward room for a drink.' It was six-thirty, or the last dog-watch, and one bell had just sounded.

'That's odd isn't it?'

'What is?'

'Six-thirty should be five bells.'

'It was, until 1797.'

'Why, what happened then?'

'The mutiny at the Nore you ignorant Digger. Five bells in the last dog-watch was the signal to start, but someone blew the gaff and so only one bell was struck which signalled betrayal and the mutiny collapsed.'

'A man learns something every day.'

The following day it was our turn to fly patrols. At dawn there were, ranged on the flight deck, two Corsairs from 1834 and 1836 squadrons for the Combat Air Patrol and two Barracudas for the anti-submarine patrol. The CAP would circle high above the fleet to take on any long-range enemy reconnaissance aircraft that came our way. The A/S patrol would range ahead on either side to pick up and either sink or force under any submarines they came across and so they carried depth charges.

The four aircraft were started and, as soon as they were ready to fly off, *Victorious* turned into wind. The chocks were waved away and the Flight Deck Officer beckoned the first Corsair forward and halted it, then swivelled it round to point straight along the deck on the centre line. He raised his green flag and circled it round as the Corsair's powerful engine opened up. The Corsair, an American aircraft, was a tough and rugged fighter with six 0.5 inch machine guns. As the green flag fell the Corsair leaped forward. As soon as he was well down the deck the FDO was bringing the second Corsair to the take off position. His engine roared and no sooner had the first one cleared the deck than the FDO waved him off. He had barely moved when with no warning at all the first Corsair coughed and, as the engine cut, plunged into the sea. Number two just had time to cross the round down and see his colleague dive into the sea when his own motor died and he too ditched.

'Belay flying' The order came from Wings on his bull-horn. The two Barracudas were chocked and stopped as the destroyer on plane guard swung across to the ditched aircraft and called away her sea-boat to pick up the pilots. Only one got out before the aircraft sank. Wings picked up his bull-horn.

'What the Hell's going on?' The FDO went over to the island.

'I don't know Sir.'

'Bad show that.'

'Yes Sir.'

'See if you can find out what the bloody Hell's happening.'

'Aye aye Sir.'

'Are the Barracudas OK?'

'So far as I know — they were all right just now when they were run up.'

'Better get them away, then at least we'll have A/S cover. The last thing we need now is for somebody to get fished.' Wings picked up the bull-horn again.

'Stand by to fly off two Barracudas.'

One of our New Zealand pilots in one of the 'Barras' had watched all this going on. He hadn't actually been able to see the aircraft ditch from where he sat in the cockpit as the island was in the way but he guessed rightly that something was amiss. One of the aircraft handlers went over to him.

'What's up mate?'

'The two Corsairs ditched.'

'Strewth, why?'

'Don't know Sir — is this aircraft all right?'

'Yes — did they get the pilots?'

'Only one Sir.'

The FDO came over and called up

'You OK?'

'Yes.'

'Right start up.'

The two Barracudas again burst into life. The FDO waved the first one forward, centred him and waited for a thumbs up. Then he raised his flag. The Barracuda sounded healthy enough and he sent it on its way, but as it cleared the deck it too spluttered and dived into the sea! The FDO raised his red flag to halt the second one. Wings came on the air again with his bull-horn.

'Belay! Belay! get the air engineer officer up here at the double — I want to know what the Hell's going on.'

The plane guard destroyer which had only just recovered her sea-boat increased speed to pick up the newly ditched crew. The Air Engineer Officer arrived hurriedly on the flight deck.

'One of the 'Barras' has gone in now' said Wings.

'Pull all the stops out I want to know what's wrong, and quick.'

'Aye, aye Sir.' He came down to the after end to find the Chief fitter.

'Most likely the fuel, check the fuel lines. If they're OK then start on the engines.' The Chief was soon back.

'There's sea water in the fuel Sir.'

'Drain all the aircraft and strip the engines.'

'That will take all day and all night Sir.'

'Yes they'll have to work in shifts and go on until it's done. There will be no let up.'

'Aye, aye Sir.'

Wings reported to the Captain.

'Sea water in the fuel Sir.'

'Good God how did that happen?'

'The fuel is raised by pumping sea water into the bottom of the fuel tanks. The change-over from an empty to a full tank was made too late and some water mixed with fuel got into the fuel lines.'

'Find out who's responsible and let me know.'

'Aye, aye Sir.'

The destroyer's sea-boat came alongside and the Corsair pilot and Barracuda crew came up the ladder, but the Barracuda's observer was missing.

'What happened?'

'Don't know Sir.' The pilot was visibly moved 'When the engine cut I had to ditch. My hood jammed and I couldn't get out, my observer climbed out and kicked it open and helped me out, and we all stood on the wing until she went down about twenty seconds later. I think his dinghy lanyard snagged on something because when the sea-boat arrived he just wasn't there. I don't know what happened.'

The loss of two of our number cast a pall over the ship but with the strike only one day away we had to put it behind us and get on with the preparations. As all our aircraft were U/S *Indomitable* had to provide A/S and CAP for the fleet. By early next day, due to incredible efforts by Chief Petty Officer Craig and the fitters, who worked 20 hours non-stop we were operational again and ready to go. The CO recommended Craig for a medal but he never got it. We had been briefed on our target and had been studying photographs taken by a Super Fortress which had flown over a week or so before. We were to attack a railway repair yard at Sigli in North Sumatra. Each aircraft was to carry either three 500 lb bombs or two 500 lb and two 250 lb. The attack was to be at dawn. This would have two advantages. We could fly across the island, about a hundred miles, to our target in the dark for most of the way, attack would not be expected from the landward side and so we should be less likely to attack from enemy fighters. The principal reason for the choice of dawn, however, was that it was hoped that the sheds would be empty of workers. The Japanese had conscripted the local inhabitants into a slave labour force to work in the railway yards and workshops, but they would not have started work when we arrived. Only the Japanese sentries would be on duty. We ought to be in and out in three minutes, or less, then heading out to sea and back to the ship for a deck landing in daylight. The disadvantage was that we should have to take off in the dark. Scrabbling about the flight deck amongst about 30 to 40 aeroplanes with their engines running would be no fun for the flight deck party at 0500 hours.

Without the Barracuda we had lost in the sea and with two kept back for A/S patrol there would be 18 of our aircraft taking part in the attack. We should be escorted by about 15 to 20 Corsairs. *Indomitable* would be putting up a similar number of Barracudas with a Hellcat escort. The aircraft were all brought up from the hangar and ranged on the flight deck in readiness the evening before, as soon as they had been stripped and reassembled and the engines run up and all the equipment tested. Then the armourers started bringing up the bombs from the magazines. They were wheeled to the aircraft on trolleys and winched into place after being fused and the detonators put in. The fighters had their ammunition belts loaded into their tanks. Wotton checked our two Vickers guns and loaded up the rear cockpit with drums of ammunition. Several times in the weeks before we left Katukurunda I had taken him up to practice on a towed drogue target. From time to time he hit it which Solly and I found most encouraging. It was a lot smaller than an attacking fighter would be so we assumed he should do better when faced with the real thing.

'We mustered in the crew room for briefing. The squadron commander addressed us.

We shall take off at 0530. The ship will be dark. The aircraft will carry formation lights only. Form up as soon as you can after take off. We shall fly to the target loosely in three lines astern in a gaggle. Once we take departure we shall climb slowly all the way to cross the coast at 10,000 feet. If we are attacked, close up and stay together. The fighters will be above and come down on our attackers. Once we cross the coast make the bomb switches, or the safety pins won't come out when you drop the bombs, and set the Micky Mouse to drop the stick at one second intervals. When we reach the target area flight leaders each head for your designated targets then pick your aiming points. You should have been studying the photographs so by now you will know what they look like from any approach angle. We shall be coming in from the south east. Release your bombs at 2000 feet and don't forget the altimeter lag in the dive or you will blow yourselves up too. After that fly straight out to sea. When the coast is out of sight head back to the ship. Join up with any other aircraft you see. Radio silence all the way there and back of course. Any questions?

'What if we have to come down Sir?'

It was our belief that the Japs would show us little mercy — a number of captured pilots had been beheaded.

'Ah, the intelligence officer has a few words to say about that.' A bearded officer got up. Before the war he had worked for a Dutch oil company and had a good knowledge of the islands and their people.

If you get into trouble before you have gone very far, jettison the bombs 'safe' and return to the ship. If the engine packs up while you are over the island it would probably be best to bale out. There are very few places where you would be able to put down and it will be dark. Again jettison your bombs safe, you don't want to advertise your presence. Your 'chutes will almost certainly be caught in the tree tops so try to swing to a branch then use the lines to help you down. The natives are neither friendly nor unfriendly. They are oppressed by the Japanese but afraid of them too and of what they might do if they are found helping their enemies. Be careful how you approach them if you have to. The Japs will have no mercy on them or you. Your escape kit contains maps, a fair wad of money, Dutch of course, for compensation for goods or bribery, blood chits — these offer a reward if you are returned to us unharmed. There are also water sterilizing tablets, quinine and a first aid pack. You will have your dinghy and its contents too, as well as your parachute.

Try to find a water course and follow it down stream, it will most likely lead you to the coast but is likely to pass close to villages. If you run into trouble over the target head out to sea. There will be a submarine four or five miles off-shore. She will surface just before you attack and wait on the surface until the attack is over. Ditch as near to her as you can. She will also come back again in two weeks and surface at midnight off the coast five miles North of Sigli to pick up anyone who can reach there.

'What's the recognition signal?'

'Just light a fire, that will not seem too unusual and you may be able to shield it on the landward side. If the sub sees a fire she will send a rubber boat to investigate. Any more questions?'

'Is it best to approach the natives or to avoid them?'

'Only approach them if you have to, or they approach you first. It's better to be independent if you can.' He sat down. The met officer got up.

'Now the weather.' We should only believe half he said but he might be right, sometimes they were right.

'It will be calm but a little misty early, and with isolated rain storms developing later. Over the land there will be early morning mist clearing at dawn just about when you reach the target and no cloud. Wind 065° 15 knots.' The CO got up.

'Now check your aircraft and your gear and then take it easy for the rest of the day. You will be called in the morning at 0400. Breakfast is laid for 0430 — good luck — dismiss.' We went off to do as bid. I checked over my gear. As well as the escape kit and the machetes, we also had commando knives. We had been issued with .38 revolvers. I also had a .45 revolver I had acquired earlier. In addition we were provided with small Winchester machine-guns. How we could bale out with all this stuff I had no idea. The revolvers I had on a webbing belt along with the ammunition. I had no intention of being captured and was determined on escape so I could not leave the machete behind, it would be essential for hacking my way out of the jungle if I had the misfortune to land in it, so it would have to be strapped to my leg. The Winchester machine-gun I decided would have to be left behind if I had to bale out. There were also packets of razor blades and a few extra packets of cigarettes and matches as well. I arranged all this stuff neatly so that I could pick it up easily and stow it about my person when we were called. After supper I wandered up to the quarter deck with Harry to relax in the cool of the evening and contemplate the morrow.

At 0400 I was roused by my steward gently shaking my shoulder.

'Mug of tea for you Sir, it's 0400 hours.'

'Thank you.' I hurriedly dressed and went to breakfast. Breakfast was always a sort of Trappist festival in the Navy and no less so just before going into action, but not knowing how long it might be before we ate again I tucked into the bacon and eggs with a will. Then I went to collect my gear. I had an overall well supplied with pockets which I put on first then distributed the various escape packets and other items about it. Wearing all that stuff I felt like a deep-sea diver. The machete felt most uncomfortable and I was not used to carrying a pair of guns in holsters. I clanked up to the flight deck where the aircraft had been ranged three abreast wings spread, with the outer ones nosed in to form a herringbone pattern on the flight deck. The Corsairs, needing a shorter run, were in front of the 'Barras' and they reached almost as far forward as the Island. We climbed in and settled ourselves and our assorted weapons and other stuff as well as we could. Harry also had packets of leaflets which he and Wotton were to drop on the place, to tell them why they were being bombed and suggesting that they take no notice of the Japanese when they said that they were winning the war.

Each aircraft had two men on its chocks and fitters and riggers and armourers and other types were all hanging about in profusion in case anything went wrong at the last minute. At 0520 the signal was given to start up. The Coffman starters had all been carefully lined up and everybody started. It was still long before dawn, with only starlight to see what was going on. The racket made by forty aircraft all running up to test their engines was indescribable. Signals from illuminated wands carried by the Flight Deck Officers and the DLCO were the only possible way of giving orders. As the ship steadied on her course and opened up to 30 knots the affirmative came from the island. The DLCO waved the chocks away from the leading Corsair with his wands. The two ratings of the flight deck party, with the chocks grasped firmly by their lanyards, slithered across the deck keeping low to miss the propellers and gained the security of the walkway along the edge of the flight deck. The DLCO then, using his wands, beckoned the Corsair forward and lined him up, then, circling one wand above his head he waited while the pilot opened the throttle. As soon as the aircraft was at full power he brought the wand down swiftly and the Corsair roared off. Every 20 seconds he repeated the drill moving steadily aft as the deck park became depleted. When the Corsairs had gone it was the turn of the 'Barras'. The CO went first off the booster, to save time, the rest of us flew off in the normal way. When we had all gone the ship prepared for the patrols. 'Range two Barracudas and two Corsairs. Arm the Barracudas with depth charges.' When dawn broke they would be taking off for CAP and A/S patrols. The fleet was now well within range of shore based aircraft as well as submarines.

Neither I, nor any of the other junior pilots who had recently joined 822 or 823 had ever done a night carrier take off, but with a calm sea there wasn't much to it. When my turn came I taxied out and lined the aircraft up, running forward a little to straighten the tail wheel, then locking the brakes I uncaged the directional gyro compass. 15° of flap, then gradually open the throttle. At full power I waited, then 'go' the wand flashed down. I let go the brakes and kept straight using the gyro compass. The deck lines were invisible in the dark and the island a vague blur. Take off was felt rather than seen — I could not see the sea only a black void. I sensed that I was leaving the deck and once flying got the wheels up and started to search the sky for the formation lights on the aircraft ahead. The formation lights were small lights fixed on the wing tips and tail and designed to shine dimly astern and be just visible to an aircraft not too far behind. It was easy in the dark to confuse them with a star and many a pilot had formated on a star in the belief that it was his flight leader. We circled round the fleet until everyone had joined up then headed off towards our target.

Now the great worry in the mind of any ship's captain and especially in the mind of the captain of an aircraft carrier, was that somebody might know where his ship was, more so even when he was operating Barracudas, which had only a short range, which meant that he had to come closer than he liked to the enemy's shore. So to try and confuse our enemies and keep the captain's blood pressure down, we set a course which took us away from the carrier and past the northern end of the island of Sumatra where our target lay. Once out of sight and on the far side we turned to fly across the island. Whether this really confused anybody we never knew. We flew steadily on for an hour or so altering course a couple of times until the coast came into view just before the sun began to rise. It came up magnificently beyond our starboard wing tips with a purplish red haze in the early morning mist. It was still dark on the ground but rapidly got lighter as the sun inched its way up. We flew on. No one shot at us and we could see no sign of activity on the ground. As it got lighter the reason became obvious. Sumatra was covered with thick jungle. Here and there a paddy field was visible, much like Ceylon. We droned on wondering how long it would be before someone objected to our presence, thirty or forty Barracudas and as many fighters could hardly be unnoticed. Looking down I could see an airfield almost directly underneath us.

'Do you see that airfield Harry?'

'Yes, quite a lot of aircraft on it too.'

'They don't seem to be taking any notice of us.' I had been watching carefully for any sign of movement.

'No, I think they are bombers — they all have two engines.'

'Don't the Japs have any twin engined fighters?'

'I don't think so, not that I've heard of anyway.'

'What could they bomb from here?'

'Us I suppose, if they knew where the fleet was.'

'Anyway there's no sign of anything happening.'

We flew on. After twenty minutes more of unmolested flying we reached the other side of the island and there was our target, just like the photographs, dead ahead. 'Good show skipper' I thought 'You got us here right on time.'

'Target ahead' I said. The sun was just beginning to light up the sheds in the railway yard as we got the signal to deploy for the attack. I set the 'Mickey Mouse' to drop bombs at one second intervals then made the switch to hold on to the safety pins as the bombs dropped so that the little propellers on them would spin off as they fell, to render them live.

'Got your leaflets ready?'

'Yes'

'Right here we go.' I had picked out the shed I had been detailed to bomb. At 10,000 feet I watched it carefully as we appeared to creep across the ground towards it. As we crossed the estuary of the river running out past the town I peeled over into my dive. I pushed the nose down and aimed for that shed. As we plummeted down I could feel the pressure of the rudder bar building up under my left foot as the speed increased. I gently wound on a bit of left rudder trim to ease the pressure and prevent us skidding, which would upset the fall of the bombs. Half way down I could see that I had started my dive a bit too early and was undershooting. I eased back the stick a fraction and let the nose come up a shade, to make a little headway. The target disappeared under the nose. After about half a second I pushed over into the dive again. We had drifted off to starboard a little so I banked round to bring the target back into line. The shed was getting rapidly bigger and taking up more of the windscreen as we hurtled down. The altimeter was unwinding like a clock with a broken escape movement. I made another little correction to the line then with the altimeter reading 2500 feet I pressed the tit.

'Bombs gone Doc.' I started to pull out then heard a yell from behind.

'What the Bloody Hell — Oh God, they're all over the place. Shut the flare shoot Wotton.' I pulled the 'Barra' into a steep turn away from the target which was now erupting, and in a shallow dive headed for the sea at full throttle. What ever was going on in the back would have to wait. Then at last:

'What's going on Harry?'

'It's these bloody leaflets. We pushed them down the flare chute and they all came back and now they're all over the place — hundreds of them. We're collecting them up and pushing them out as fast as we can. With an on shore breeze some of them might drift over the town.'

At 250 knots I roared down to the sea and swept along just above the surface. Looking back I could see the bombs still going off as the rest of the chaps came in and dropped theirs, and a thick cloud of smoke was rising up. We had given the Japs a good pasting. As we tore along I spotted the submarine. She had surfaced just as promised. 'Well at least we won't need that' I thought. Then I saw a Barra going down.

'Someone ditching there Harry — can you see who it is?'

'No — there's smoke coming from his engine though. I think it's one of 817's.'

We watched as he dropped it skilfully into the oggin just beside the submarine. The crew of the submarine quickly had a rubber boat in the water and the 'Barra's' crew were aboard the submarine in less than five minutes. Then suddenly!

'Look at that!' One of the fighters came down and sprayed the submarine with machine gun fire.

'What the blazes is that stupid prick doing! Is he out of his mind!'

'He must have gone to sleep during the briefing and thinks it's a Jap sub.'

'It's certainly made the chaps on the sub hop about a bit. They won't be too pleased about that.'

'I think he's realised his mistake now. He's circling round.'

'He's pressing his luck hanging about. It wouldn't surprise me if the sub loosed off a few rounds at him.'

As the rest of the planes finished their attack and flew off the submarine closed its hatches and dived. We turned and flew after the rest of the squadron heading back to the ship.

'Well they won't be mending any railway engines for a time.'

'No, I think we have put them out of business for a while. I hope they enjoy the leaflets.' We droned on.

Now the Indian Ocean is prone to conjuring up little isolated rain storms. You find them dotted about here and there in otherwise clear weather. Heavy little lumps of cloud about five miles across and underneath them there is a tropical storm raining down like Niagara falls. As we straggled up to the fleet there was one of these little jokers just waiting. So what does the fleet do? Well no doubt the Admiral had his reasons. No doubt he thought 'Just the place. Once in there and I shall not be torpedoed by a lurking submarine just as I steam into wind to land this lot on, because he won't be able to see me' Maybe that's what he thought, or maybe he didn't think at all. Or maybe, just at that moment, he had his admiral's finger well and truly in, because he turned the fleet straight into it. A few moments more on the old course and he would have missed it.

We joined the circuit just as *Victorious* plunged into the murk. The rain was lashing down and we could see about a hundred yards as we played follow-my-leader round the ship. The CO peeled off and made for the deck as the rest of us queued up to do the same, barely able to see the aircraft in front, or the ship. As we staggered round I picked up the batsman just before we got to the round-down. I suppose he must have seen me because he had his arms in the 'Come on in' position and I just saw the 'cut' as we flashed past. We landed with a bit of a thump but all was well and we hurriedly taxied forward over the barrier which sprang up as soon as we had passed and the next aircraft roared in behind. The handlers leaped upon us and folded the wings as I was directed into my parking spot. I climbed out and my fitter took my place in the cockpit for it to be struck down into the hangar.

'How'd it go Sir?'

'All right thanks we knocked 'em for six I think.'

'Good oh!'

Harry, Wotton and I headed for the crew room and a cool drink and got buttonholed by a reporter from the Daily Express or Telegraph I think. No sooner had the last aircraft landed on than the fleet steamed out into blue skies again and the sun blazed down again with oriental force.

822 Squadron on Sigli Raid — 18 Sep 1944

Pilots.

Watson, Leslie (CO)
Moore (Mumble, senior P)
Ringer, Bill
Hadley (Doc)
Black, Algy
Faulkner, Joe (Butch)
Bower
Prentice

TAGs

Mc Cullogh
Boddy
Challinor
Wotton
Martin
Smart
Kerr
Feltoe
Bailey
Dimmock
Skeldon
Stevens

Observers

Burbidge (Hiram)
Siddle
Stevens (Steve)
Solly, Harry
Hardcastle
Hogarth
Bramwell
Jackson
Lea
Cowie
Jameson

One Barracuda hit the barrier.
18 crews took part. This list is compiled from memory. Any information to complete or correct would be welcome.

Squadrons taking part in Sigli Raid — 18 Sep 1944.

Victorious

822 Lt Cdr Watson, Fairey Barracudas.
1834 Lt Cdr Charlton, Chance Vought Corsairs.
1836 Lt Cdr Tomkinson, Chance Vought Corsairs.

Indomitable

815 Lt Cdr Lawson, Fairey Barracudas.
817 Lt Cdr May, Fairey Barracudas.
1839 Lt Cdr Shotton, Grumman Hellcats.
1844 Lt Cdr Godson, Grumman Hellcats.

Chapter 15

The Rug is Pulled From Under Us

In cricketing terms we had 'broken our duck'. Not only was 822 a front line squadron, we were welded together under a first class commander and we had been in action. We hadn't done very much perhaps but we had done it well. It was a start and we looked forward to bigger things. There was a good spirit in the squadron. There was nothing to do on the way back to Katukurunda except fly A/S patrols and in the evenings we sang songs and played liar's dice. The night before we were to fly off back to Kat we played another game.

The ward room tables in *Victorious* were long and smooth and, after a few gins, began to resemble a flight deck. It occurred to somebody that they could be used to provide the thrilling experience of uninhibited flight, which had not been experienced since we left Tain.

One of the smaller observers was seized and put under the table for safe keeping while a chair was put on its back beyond the end of the table. One of our pilots put another chair beside the table and stood on it.

'I shall be wings' he said 'and this is the island. Flight deck party ready? right — range one observer.' His conniving mess mates dragged the protesting observer from 'the hangar deck' and put him on top of the table. Three of them stood either side, firmly clutching his arms and legs.

'Stand by to boost off one observer' called our pilot as he stood up.

'Right he's run up and ready.'

'I'm not — I'm U/S — my plugs need changing.'

'Rubbish he's just had a major overhaul, he's serviceable and he's just been refuelled.'

'Boost one observer!' Another pilot raised a table napkin in his right hand and waved it round.

'Right I'm the DLCO.' As he said this the boosting party made engine noises. As the roar rose to a crescendo the DLCO dropped his arm, the boosting party rushed the helpless observer feet first along the table. Half way along they released him. Uttering a loud yell he flew off the end of the table into the chair. We collapsed laughing.

'Who's next!'

'This man!' He had been quietly sipping gin, an air of amused tolerance on his face. He hurriedly downed his gin and made for the door. Too late. He was intercepted by the recently boosted observer who had by this time recovered, and finding that, after all, nothing was broken now determined to be part of the boosting party himself.

'Put him in the hangar, put him in the hangar!' he yelled, and under the table went the victim protesting loudly.

'Stand by to boost off the flyer' called our self-appointed 'wings'.

'Flyer serviceable Sir.' said the DLCO.

'Right — range one flyer.' The flyer was transferred struggling to the table top.

'Flyer ranged and ready Sir.'

'Boost off one flyer.' And off he went, flying along the table and into the chair.

We all stopped for a drink.

'You know' said a voice, 'I think we should spread the word. It is most unfair that only the Fleet Air Arm should experience the pleasures of flying. We must share our joy with the fishheads.' As he said this the speaker turned and grabbed the nearest watchkeeper who was enjoying a peaceful drink. He was boosted off amid loud protest and cheers. Thereafter he was always considered an honorary member of the Fleet Air Arm. The next morning we all felt a little worn as we flew back to Kat to recover and wait for our next job.

Now the Barracuda was an excellent torpedo bomber. It could come down vertically, like a guided stone, from any height without exceeding a safe speed, drop its fish and be away. The Grumman Avenger could not dive like this and it could not carry a British torpedo. American torpedos were prone to destruction before they ever reached the enemy. Even as a dive bomber the Barracuda was superior to the Avenger, but it lacked one thing and that was range. With a more powerful motor it could have carried more fuel and performed much better. It had, too, a hydraulic system which worked at enormous pressure and which periodically ruptured and either half asphyxiated the pilot or removed most of the paint from the fuselage. The Avenger was easier to fly, faster, had a longer range, power folding wings and more guns. It was an excellent anti-submarine aircraft. It was a pity that as a torpedo strike aircraft its performance was so poor.

But as it was, when operating Barracudas, the carrier had to come within range of the enemy aircraft to get its aircraft into action. For some reason this never appealed to the fishheads very much except in the North Sea, where they were always within range of enemy aircraft anyway, so the ludo-players decided to withdraw the Barracudas from the Far East, this decision floored everyone, except one pilot of my acquaintance who decided that he didn't want to fly Barracudas anymore anyway in case something fell off, so some of us were amalgamated into 831 squadron and banished to a place called Minneriya until it was decided what could be done with us. This was a dismal failure.

Minneriya was another jungle airstrip, lurking deep in the Garden of Eden. Apart from a few local Adam and Eve type inhabitants with pet elephants and numerous serpents the place had been taken over entirely by plant life of dense and prolific proportions. Not too far away was the capital, the Holy city of Kandy. One day Harry, Steve, his pilot and I were returning to camp from a weekend on leave there, after seeing the sights and visiting the temple of Buddha's Tooth, in the squadron 15 cwt truck. Harry was driving with Steve beside him. I and the other pilot were standing in the back of the truck holding on to the metal support, put there to take a canvas cover, which it didn't appear to have, probably stolen.

As we lurched along a man suddenly leaped out of the jungle into the road in front of the truck. At least, ever afterwards, Harry swore that this was so. My friend, the other pilot, and I on the other hand attributed what followed to finger trouble on Harry's part, which was not unexpected amongst observers in control of mechanical contrivances which, properly in our opinion, should only be in the control of pilots who understood these things. This ghost, for such we assumed it must be, or figment of Harry's imagination, had not materialised to us as he did to Harry. It was therefore, we felt, somewhat vulgar of Harry to suggest, as he later did, that we should get our eyes tested.

At all events what happened was that the truck suddenly swerved across the road and its right hand front wheel went into the ditch. It must have hit a large stone for it jumped out of the ditch again. The truck then crossed the road at high speed, doubtless Harry still had his foot on the throttle because it ran off the other side demolishing an ant-hill five feet high, containing about thirty million fit and hungry ants as it did so, before turning over. As it rolled in a graceful manner Steve's head came through the canvas roof of the cab. My friend the other pilot and I, four suit-cases and the spare wheel, which was loose in the back, revolved in a fairly dignified manner until the truck was inverted and then I fell out. The truck rolled on until it came back on to its wheels again, with Steve sticking up through the roof.

As I sat on the ground I felt no pain but felt that perhaps I should not move in case something fell off. I tried moving one finger and all seemed to be well. I was about to experiment further when I noticed that the top of the ant-hill was missing and the inhabitants were just starting their banquet. I deferred further experiment and regardless of the consequences sprang to my feet and knocked off the ant vanguard. As I did so the other pilot emerged from the truck nursing his shoulder which had been dislocated. Harry came out rubbing his chest and Steve his head. His brains didn't appear to be more than slightly scrambled, as he was able to utter a few meaningless phrases.

We gathered glumly with our cases at the side of the road when along came an ambulance. I thought that I must have been concussed because at this point I expected to wake up and find I had fallen out of my bunk, but to my surprise it stopped. It really existed and just happened to be passing, which, in the middle of nowhere seemed very odd. We got in and back to Kandy we went. On the way we stopped at a doctor's house and my friend the other pilot was taken in to have his shoulder relocated, we then continued on our way. In Kandy we were unloaded in hospital and, I hoped, time for some lunch.

'Sorry Sir, lunch has just finished.'

'Is that so, well what would you suggest we might give to our craving innards until the next bun fight is due?'

'I'll go and see if there's anything left Sir.'

After a while he came back.

'Cook says you can have this Sir'

He put on the table an enormous dish of asparagus, and that was it. I must be in a dream after all. It was very good though.

By the time a breakdown truck arrived from camp to remove our truck the wheels had been removed and there was a small army of the local inhabitants all armed with spanners at work on it. Another two hours and it would have disappeared without trace.

A week or so later we were back at camp. The CO called us together.

'We are going home. Their Lordships have decided to recall us all to the UK and withdraw Barracudas from the far east. We are to return the 'Barras' to store in Coimbatore then we shall be going home in *Atheling*. Here endeth 822 and 831 squadrons.' And that is what we did. In almost my last flight in Ceylon before flying off to

Coimbatore I was attacked by a playful Spitfire pilot who wanted to practice his dog fighting. I think he thought I would be easy meat, but I found that if I put down a bit of flap I could turn inside him, which doubtless gave him cause for thought. Full marks to the 'Barra'. Pity we had no front gun, it might have come in useful sometimes.

Chapter 16

I Go in to Bat for England

Promotion in the Royal Navy goes by time and to a variable extent ability, especially in wartime, when a chap might be appointed to an acting rank well above his actual rank. I, as a Sub-Lieutenant, had another year to do before getting my second ring. So I was much surprised when, back home in England enjoying some leave with Patsie, I got a telegram addressed to Acting Lieutenant (A) D.L. Hadley. Even more surprising was the order to report to RNAS East Haven, to train as a Deck Landing Control Officer. 'It is quite plain to me,' I said to Patsie, 'that the ludo players have flipped — gone berserk.'

'Why?'

'It is well known that DLCOs are carefully chosen from very experienced pilots who volunteer for the job when Admiralty Fleet Orders announce that volunteers may apply. I am a very junior pilot and I have not volunteered and I am not a Lieutenant — someone has blundered.'

'Well you'd better do something about it.'

'I shall have to acknowledge this telegram and do what it says but I will point out that a mistake has been made.' So I wrote to the Captain at East Haven accepting the appointment but added a PS pointing out that I had not volunteered to be a DLCO and did not want to be one, and that I wished to continue flying and that the appointment must be a mistake. Then I set out for Scotland once more. I arrived at the main gate in the evening and was greeted by the duty officer:

'Lieutenant Hadley?'

'Yes.'

'Sorry chum, you're under arrest.'

'Arrest! whatever for?'

'Seems you've upset the Captain somehow.'

'Well — what happens now?'

'It's only open arrest so nothing much. It means you are confined to camp and have to go before the Captain at 0900 tomorrow — oh and you can't buy any drinks in the bar.'

'No drinks?'

'Well it's OK if someone else buys you one.'

'Thanks' I was escorted by a Petty Officer of the regulating branch to find my cabin feeling a little confused. I dumped my gear and went over to the ward room. There I found a subdued bunch of new arrivals looking a bit lost but there was one familiar face, from my pilot's course and 822.

'Algy Black!'

'Hello Doc what are you doing here?'

'I've been sent here to do a DLCO course, but I'm under arrest.'

'Under arrest! whatever for?'

'I don't know. I have to see the Old Man in the morning.'

'Well, have a drink.'

'Thanks — I'm not allowed to buy one though.'

'Oh that's OK.'

'What are you doing here Algy?'

'I'm on a DLCO course too'

'Did you volunteer?'

'No of course not. No more did these other fellows. Here fellers — this is Doc.' He introduced me to three other pilots.

'I always thought you had to volunteer to be a DLCO'

'Seems not — none of us have.' We passed the evening quietly although I noticed a number of the resident officers eyeing me with interest from time to time. In the morning I went before the Captain.

'Lieutenant Hadley, you replied quite correctly to your letter of appointment then added this curious postscript. What is the meaning of this?' He was a stern man, but not a pilot, and he seemed to be genuinely puzzled.

'Well Sir, I want to go on flying. I thought you had to volunteer for this course.'

'Lieutenant Hadley, in the Royal Navy you don't do what you want, you do what you are told. Leave and wine bill stopped for the duration of the course — dismiss.'

I retired from the presence, tried, convicted and sentenced. The course was to last three weeks. I had thought of getting Patsie up to East Haven but my punishment put the kibosh on that. We assembled in the class room for the first lecture. Our instructor addressed us thus:

Now, you chaps have all been selected to train as DLCOs. I know that you thought that a person had to volunteer but there aren't enough volunteers so some people get drafted. Not too many people want to do this job but it is essential, and has to be done, so you might as well assume you volunteered. We look upon all people on this course as volunteers. Right, well this is the latest gent's natty batting outfit, complete in handy carrying case.

He produced a flat fibre case from which he withdrew a pair of 'bats' consisting of round metal frames with glowing fabric stretched across them, and wooden handles.

This is day-glow cloth, it is fluorescent and you can see it for miles. The bats come supplied with handles eighteen inches long for some obscure dockyard reason, so we cut them down to about six inches as soon as we get them.

He went on to demonstrate the signals for: Come on in as you are: Turn left: Turn right: Go up: Come down: Too slow: Too fast: Put your wheels down, you prune: Hook — you clot: You've forgotten your flaps — idiot: You've made a complete balls-up of it — go round again: Cut — you're OK to land.

You are in charge of the landing he said and, no matter who they are, they have to do what you tell them, although you will find that the more experienced pilots may ignore you. If they crash when they have disobeyed you, you will not be blamed, but they seldom do. Now you will find that every aeroplane has a certain look about it when it is coming in right. After a time you will be able to spot this a long way off and you know at once if a chap is going to make it. The other thing you have to watch is the movement of the ship. If the deck is coming up give them the cut a bit earlier, or if it is going down — later, although sometimes you have to cut early when the ship is pitching fast. When it is rough you will have to be more careful, but even on the roughest days you will find that every now and again it will settle down between periods of severe pitching and stay level for about half a minute before the pitching starts again, and that's when you can get them on. You can't land them on when the deck is moving a lot without a good chance of a prang. If it's very bad and they must be brought on because they're low on fuel or for some other reason then land them further along the deck where the movement is less, say the fifth or sixth wire or even later, rather than trying for the first wire, although you risk a barrier prang, but it's better than the cold cold oggin. Now we'd better go out and do some ADDLEs.

There were some station pilots who earned their daily bread flying round and round to give us practice. Known as clockwork mice they would take off, fly round and land in the space of about three minutes or less. With three of them circling round at once we got plenty of practice. They were so good at it that they didn't need our signals but they obeyed them within reason and after a time we learned what their aircraft looked like when they were 'in the groove'. At the proper speed and attitude the leading edge of the tail plane was just visible below the port wing and this was the same with all the different aircraft we batted. We practised on Swordfish, Barracudas, Wildcats and Avengers.

We had been at it for about an hour, taking turns when 'Wings' Cdr R.N. Everett RN himself came out to watch. His piercing eyes fixed us from under bushy eyebrows and he watched us in action until he could bear it no longer then he seized the bats off Algy, whose turn it happened to be. Algy had been giving all the correct signals but, to the critical eye of wings, in a mechanical sort of way, devoid of any emotion. Now batting was Wing's passion.

'You must *take charge*' said Wings '*Make them do what you want them to do*. Look, I'll show you.' He whirled into action. His signals were firm and filled with fire. The pilots immediately noticed, even half a mile away, that a human dynamo was now in command and all their approaches became impeccable. As they neared the runway the maestro went into a frenzy of activity edging further and further on to the runway himself, until, as he gave the cut he had to duck low as the wing flashed over his head and the wheels hit the runway not ten feet from him. He handed back the bats to Algy.

'There, that's how to do it — now you do it.'
Algy emulated the great man's style as best he could.

'That's better — you see you're in control now, that's what you have to do.' We all did our best. We didn't leap out on to the runway as that seemed to need more panache than we had yet acquired, but we improved, and no doubt more dash would come with experience.

We shared the aerodrome of course with the pupil pilots who were learning to deck land and when they were flying we had lectures on ranging aircraft on deck, parking them safely, striking them down into the hangar and the other tasks of a flight deck officer. With a party of aircraft handlers, also under training, we practised pushing the aircraft about and ranging them in patterns on the marked out runway, spreading and folding wings as would have to be done on board ship. We learnt how to move wrecks. We also had to learn how to put out fires. We tried on the fireproof asbestos suit and walked through flames to prove that it worked. As the course went on and our batting got better we were allowed to bat in the pupils some of the time, to give us a real chance to try our skill. In the evenings we relaxed in the usual way. My punishment in fact proved no punishment at all. From East Haven there was nowhere to go except Dundee. There was not much in Dundee to attract many people to make the trip so those on course mostly stayed in the mess anyway. It was true I could not buy drinks but someone would always get one for me, to be refunded later. We noticed however that the whisky always seemed to disappear from the bar very fast. The bar was rationed to one bottle a night and by the time the Commander and his cronies had each had a couple of doubles before dinner there was nothing left for the riff-raff.

'You know' said someone one evening 'I reckon we should teach these fishheads a lesson.'

'Hear, hear. How?'

'Tomorrow we'll come in at five past six, before the brass hats get here and we'll order three doubles each, that should stir things up a little.' So next night:

'Yes Sir, what'll it be?'

'I'll have three double scotch please — oh and put it in a half pint tankard. What about you Doc?'

'Same for me please.'

'And you Freddy?'

'Yes, same here Algy.'

'Right Sir — all in tankards?'

'Yes please.' We topped them up with soda then retired to a quiet corner of the ante-room to sip them gently and await results. The ante-room soon filled with officers ordering their drinks as the mood took them. At twenty five past six the Commander, who was a regular man, came in for his usual pre-prandial drink and joined the First Lieutenant at the bar.

'What'll you have number one?'

'Scotch please Sir.'

'Two scotches Barman, make mine a double.'

'Sorry Sir, no scotch.'

'No scotch!' The Commander was taken aback.

'It's all gone Sir.'

'Gone! it can't have!'

'Yes Sir, we only get one bottle a night Sir, and it's gone.'

'The whisky's all gone number one!'

'Gone Sir?'

'Yes gone.'

'But the bar hasn't been open half an hour yet.'

They looked around in bewilderment to see who was drinking whisky. Their malevolant glances rested briefly on one or two officers drinking their evening tipples but they were all the usual whisky drinking station fishheads together with the Paymaster and the Principal Medical Officer. They glared at us innocently holding our half pints and taking no notice of the atmospheric disturbance near the bar.

'Well — have to make it double pink gin then.'

'Yes Sir.' The barman obliged with a straight face. He had been a willing party to our ruse. Naturally as we consumed our hijacked whisky at the speed of our usual half pints we became a little pickled so it was not surprising when Algy announced that he had had a letter from home which he found upsetting. While we were on leave Algy had got married to a girl in Paddington. We had all been surprised at this. He was a first rate fellow but he didn't seem to be the marrying type. He was a big strong ugly chap. His face looked as though it had been hit with a hot frying pan. He had huge hands like legs of mutton and a figure like a boxer a little out of training, but he was a charming man and had won this girl's heart. He had been married about three weeks when he arrived at East Haven and this was only about the second letter he had had. He was downcast.

'I'm a pipless orange' he said.

'No, no, give it a chance.'

'A pipless orange, a seedless grape.'

'That can't be true.'

'It is.'

'Lots of people don't ring the bell the first time.'

'Ah well we shall see.' he said not really comforted. However, after a good dinner he brightened up. We all played liar's dice and sang a few songs and he eventually turned in content.

The course rolled smoothly on. One day they decided we could have a break. There was an old Fairey Fulmar on the station.

'Who'd like to fly the Fulmar today — all right don't all rush. They are repainting some of the runway lines and we can't use the one into wind. There's no point in doing ADDLs in a cross-wind which you will never have to do in a carrier so you may take turns to go flying.'

We had a quick rush through the pilot's notes for the Fulmar then started queueing up to get it into the air before it went U/S. When my turn came I had watched a couple of the others.

'It's a lovely kite — easy to fly — nice wide undercart — you won't have any bother.'

I strapped myself in, taxied round and took off. They were right, she was a lovely aircraft. The wheels snapped up fast and she climbed easily. I flew around for a bit then did a slow roll. She rolled smoothly and easily. Why wasn't the 'Barra' like this? When I came in to land she glided so well I overshot slightly so that I missed the first turn off point on the runway and had to use the next, where the runways crossed. This brought me on to the freshly painted one which I had entirely forgotten about in the thrill of flying the Fulmar. The wheels rolled over the newly painted lines picking up paint which they deposited as little white squares in a random and untidy pattern all over the runway as I taxied along. I pulled up at the dispersal point and got out feeling pleased with myself — unaware of the brewing storm.

'Lieutenant Hadley.'

'Yes.'

'You're wanted in the control tower — Wings wants to see you.'
I went over to him, oblivious, and thinking that perhaps he was going to tell me what a nice landing I had made.

'Hadley — what the devil do you mean by it?'

'By what Sir?'

'Those filthy marks all over the runway. It's only just been painted. Now it's covered with filthy little marks — look.' My heart sank as I looked out of the window.

'I'm sorry Sir. I completely forgot about it being painted.'

'Forgot — you're not paid to forget.' He seethed almost in silence for a moment.

'Well you'd better go out and expunge them.'

'Aye, aye Sir' I left hurriedly. We discussed it.

'You know I think he's serious.'

'You really think so?'

'Yes I'm sure of it' I said 'Somehow I've got to get those marks off the runway.'

'How are you going to do that?'

'I don't know, yet. Get some turps off the painter I suppose.' I sought out the Chief.

'Chief can you tell me where the paint shop is?'

'Yes Sir — Hangar four.'

'Thanks Chief.' I began to wander thoughtfully over there. There must be an easier way. Then in a flash I knew what to do. I quickened my step. At the paint shop I found an old sailor clad in a paint spattered overall stirring a pot of paint.

'Yes Sir.' he said.

'May I have some black paint please?'

'Black paint Sir, what for?' I explained my crime.

'Ah I see Sir — well don't worry about it Sir, you just leave it to me.'

'I think perhaps I should do it myself, Wings might see you. He told me to do it.'

'Don't you worry Sir. I'll wait until he's busy somewhere else.'

'Well thank you.' He smiled benignly and I walked back to the crew room.

By the time the course came to an end we were all considered competent to send to do our carrier training. I don't think they would have allowed us to fail. If we hadn't been good enough we should have been kept there until we were. The Navy it seemed was very short of batsmen. So off we went to join HMS *Trouncer* an escort carrier like *Ravager*. Lt Cdr Howard was there to greet us. We were still pupils, but no longer pupil pilots, so that he looked upon us more as equals. We were all experienced pilots, not very experienced perhaps, but none the less we had survived the perils of operational flying and he wanted to teach us as much as he could in the short time we should be with him. Up on the flight deck the wind was thirty knots. The ship was only doing ten but there was a brisk wind coming up the Clyde which made the sea choppy but with no real swell so the ship was not pitching. We were going to start the easy way with Swordfish.

Algy was the first to try his hand. He stood on the batsman's platform with the instructor standing behind him to coach him in the art, as three Stringbags which had flown over from Machrihanish buzzed round like bees round a honey pot. The rest of us stood in the walkway to watch the fun. The pilots of these Stringbags — all full time clockwork mice — spent most of their lives training batsmen. They could do deck landings in all the Naval aircraft there were, day or night, winter or summer, with a smooth precision which left us in awe. As we watched, the first one peeled off and came round into the groove. He made a perfect approach. At a word from the instructor Algy began to bring him down then — cut. The Stringbag, with his hook still up, flopped gently on to the deck then opened his throttle and went round again. As he left the deck he jinked to starboard then flew in a circle round to port to start a new circuit. Meanwhile Algy turned his attention to the next one, about thirty seconds behind him, he was already well into the approach. He too came in, smooth as a duck to a pond, bounced gently and went on his way, to be followed by the third. By this time the first one had come round to make his second run. They came in steadily at regular intervals. They were so practised that they didn't really need a batsman, at any rate on a calm day. But Algy was going through the motions. He was learning what to do and learning the feel of it. After about a dozen landings his arms began to ache. He came down and I went up for a go.

On the airfield there had never been much wind but as soon as I held the bats out here on the flight deck I knew what it was all about. Those bats were the size of dinner plates and as the wind caught them I was almost blown off the platform until I steadied myself and leaned back into it. There was a windscreen, which folded flat on the deck when not in use, but we were not using it partly to help strengthen our back muscles for this unaccustomed exercise, but also because it left more room for the instructor to stand behind us.

As I watched the Stringbag plodding in I got a firm picture in my mind of what it looked like in the correct approach attitude. I made the signals which seemed to me appropriate, much harder to do in a stiff breeze, and the aircraft seemed to comply in a vague sort of way and I guessed that the pilot would have done what I was telling him to do anyway. I gave him the cut and he flopped down nicely near the first wire and took off again. After a few more my back began to ache and I realised that with a whole squadron or two to bat in, especially if some of them had to go round again, I would have to be fairly fit, and today the sea was calm. After about ten landings I handed the bats over to the next man.

After we'd all had several goes the Stringbags put down their hooks and landed on. As each one landed it taxied forward of the barriers, which were raised behind it. When all three were on, the barriers were lowered again and the flight deck party ranged them back on the stern ready for the next session. The pilots climbed out and we all went to lunch while the aircraft were refuelled.

After lunch we had an encore then they flew back to Machrihanish. Next day we had Wildcats. They were much friskier than the Swordfish but good deck landers, as also were the Avengers we had on the third day. After that came the Barracudas. At the end of the week we had each batted about a hundred landings. In between the deck landings we had practice in ranging aircraft on deck as they were handled by the flight deck party, not so easy on a moving deck, you wait for the roll and pitch and take care that they don't run away from you. After that we practised flying them off the deck at the correct moment as the ship pitched.

And that was that. We were now qualified Deck Landing Control Officers. A sticker was put in our flying log books to prove it to anyone who might doubt it and we were sent on leave again to await our appointments as Flight Deck Officers. I didn't have to wait long. In February 1945 I was again on my way to Scotland to join HMS *Queen* as Flight Deck Officer.

Chapter 17
The 'Old Queen' and After

The 'Old Queen' was of course brand new. HMS *Queen*, one of Henry Kaiser's escort carriers, was also sister ship to *Ravager*. She had been in commission about six or eight months when I joined her at Rosyth. I must have been about the last crew member to join and we promptly set sail for Scapa Flow as soon as I stepped aboard. She carried 853 Squadron, under Lt Cdr Glaser, twelve Avengers and four Wildcats. We were going North to join a small fleet of carriers and cruisers under the command of Admiral Sir Roderick McGrigor to harass the Germans in the North Sea and protect convoys on their way to Russia. The 'Wee McGrigor' was in fact a submariner, but it was not unusual for their Lordships to appoint submariners to command aircraft carriers and fleets. Submariners were highly competent sailors and well liked but many of them didn't really understand aircraft.

The DLCO was Dusty Miller. He was an experienced batsman and ex-Stringbag pilot who had previously been in Nirana. I didn't discover until long after the war was over that he had never done a deck landing himself, but of course you don't have to be a chicken to know if an egg is bad, in fact chickens are notoriously stupid in this respect and will happily sit on a bad one or even a china one. They don't know much about flying either. Dusty was a first rate batsman. Part of my duty was to help out with the batting and otherwise organise the flight deck party of aircraft handlers.

'Come and meet Wings.' he said to me when we met. Wings, was Lieutenant Commander Derek Malcolm-Brown one of the very few RNVR officers to achieve this exalted position. Wings, or Commander Flying, was responsible for the entire operation of aircraft. He had previously been DLCO in *Indomitable*. He was a cheery soul but seemed to me very fierce when I first met him, although after a few weeks we became firm friends and remained so until he died in 1985.

Life aboard *Queen* was routine with episodes of activity interspersed with periods of swinging round the anchor in Scapa Flow. There seemed to be very little attraction about Scapa Flow in February 1945. It was cold and bleak and the attractions ashore were minimal, and a cold boat ride away, so we mostly stayed on board.

Among my responsibilities were a couple of derricks. They were placed one either side of the flight deck just aft of the funnels and folded flat lying beside the flight deck when not in use. They were used for bringing stores aboard also ammunition and sometimes aircraft, but they had been carelessly used. The wire on the starboard one was badly kinked and was liable to raise or lower loads with sickening jerks as the kinks came round the drum and this made the derrick's jib shudder like the string of a one stringed fiddle whenever it happened. The wire on the port derrick had been so badly kinked that it had been replaced with a new wire but the new wire was too short, so that when the hook was lowered to the water there were less than three turns on the drum and so it could not be used to lift anything very heavy in case the wire came off. New wires had been demanded, but never arrived.

On the way up from Rosyth I had been encouraged to try my hand at batting the squadron. This was my first experience of the real thing. It went quite well except that I found that one pilot, Harry Beeston, the leader of the fighter flight was difficult to bat. He liked to approach by drifting over to starboard then crabbing in to port as he reached the deck. I never felt very comfortable with this so after a while Dusty always used to bat him in so that he could do it the way he wanted. As Harry and I shared a cabin this made for a little coolness, but he was a nice guy and I liked him and I don't think he bore me any grudge.

I was also introduced to the booster. The booster, or catapult, was a necessity in *Queen*. The flight deck was only just over 400 feet long and it simply was not long enough to fly off a squadron of fully loaded aircraft, especially if the wind was light. *Queen*'s flat out maximum speed was 18 knots. The booster could whack them off at 95 knots even at anchor. A metal strop, hooked on to the aircraft, was looped round a metal stud which ran along a slot in the deck. The stud was connected by cables to a fearsome hydraulic engine somewhere in the bowels of the ship. The aircraft's tail was held by a wrap-over hook held in place by a metal ring designed to break when the power was put into the booster. Once the aircraft was in place the launching officer, either Dusty or myself, circled a green flag to tell the pilot to open the throttle. Once the engine was going full bore the pilot signalled with his hand. We dropped the green flag. The flight deck engineer pulled a lever and the aircraft was on its way. As the aircraft left the deck the strop fell off and should have been caught by a special retrieving hook but it never was. It just went into the sea. This didn't matter too much because we had hundreds of strops on board. The chief ERA who had ordered them in the first place had estimated how many he would need then doubled the number expecting to get only half of what he ordered, as usually happened. The engineer officer who signed and passed the order on doubled the number again for the same reason, as also did the supply officer and possibly the captain too, all for the same reason. Such is the way of life in RN ships.

We could boost them off about every 90 seconds or so which pleased the Captain who didn't like being on a straight course into wind for longer than necessary. Captain D'Arcy was a charming man. I don't know how ever he got promoted, he seemed much too nice. It always seemed to me that he got too much stick from Sir Roderick for not keeping station to Sir Roderick's satisfaction, but I always thought Sir Roderick a trifle bumptious in these matters.

The flight deck party composed of aircraft handlers was divided into port and starboard watches. Petty Officer McLeod led the starboard watch and Petty Officer Pearson the port. PO McLeod came from Skye I believe and was a fisherman, PO Pearson was a destroyer coxon somewhat irked to be in a flight deck party, much as I was. On duty on the flight deck they all wore special Foul Weather clothing with red linen helmets for the port watch and green for the starboard. The fitters and riggers wore white or blue helmets. Dusty and I wore yellow waistcoats over our flying suits, which were the warmest things we had, and of course everybody had lifebelts.

One of the first bits of excitement I had was loading some mines on board. The ariel mines were long canisters weighing about a ton each. They were ferried out to us in lighters which tied up under the derrick. The day they came was rough and windy. We sent down the hook and the first mine was hooked on. The lighter was heaving in the swell so of course as soon as the derrick wire tightened the lighter fell away and the sudden weight twanged the wire like a banjo string. No sooner had this happened than the next wave lifted the lighter and gave the mine a tremendous blow from underneath. They were not fused of course but they were stuffed full of Amatol or some such powerful explosive.

'Full speed on the winch Chief' I yelled, hoping to get the mine clear of the lighter before the next wave. The lighter had by now drifted under the curved side of the ship to some extent so that when the mine whizzed up clear it swung out like a pendulum increasing the violence of its oscillations as the wire grew shorter.

'Vast heaving.' I waited with bated breath as this dreadful object swung to and fro. It didn't quite hit the ship neither did the wire fracture at one of its kinks and drop the mine into the sea. Eventually we hauled it up and gratefully deposited it on the deck to be carried away to the magazine. There were still eleven more to come up. With much banging and twanging we got them all up eventually, then happily stowed the derricks and put to sea.

The weather in the North Sea is mostly bad. It is usually windy, the sea a bit rough and with short waves because it is fairly shallow, and the sky is usually grey. Such a day it was as 853 Squadron under Lt Cdr Glaser set out to lay mines off the coast of Norway. We got all the aircraft up and ranged them along the deck then up came the mines on trolleys. Lt Ken Terry the Air Gunnery Officer appeared, gingerly holding a box of detonators and went round arming the mines as they were loaded into the Avengers. The crews then came up from the briefing room and climbed in. The engines were started. Aircraft engines are all unsilenced and the din made by 12 Avengers and 4 wildcats each of well over a thousand horsepower is much the same as about two dozen pneumatic road drills all going at once in a space the size of a tennis court. The spoken word is of course inaudible, only sign language is of any use. Lying beside each main wheel of each aircraft an aircraft handler held grimly on to the wheel chocks as the pilot ran up his engine and a freezing hundred mile an hour or more gale tried to blow him away. Once everyone was ready the ship turned into wind, the plane guard destroyer moved into place astern to rescue anyone who went into the sea and Dusty and I waved the aircraft handlers away. Taking their chocks they scuttled away to the walkways dodging the whirling propellers as they went. If they fell over they were bowled along the deck like bits of rag until they were able to catch hold of something solid, or were blown over the edge. Meanwhile we coaxed the aircraft on to the booster in succession and sent them on their way. After a busy twenty minutes we had got them all away. From then on we were at 'flying stations' for the next few hours, there was nothing to do but wait. Dusty and I usually climbed up the ladder to keep Wings company on the island while the aircraft handlers cowered away from the weather in the various holes used as stores under the flight deck or behind the guns. When the aircraft were sighted returning Wings picked up his electric bull-horn:

'Stand by to receive aircraft.' The flight deck party emerged to stand poised in the walkways. Dusty went down to the batsman's platform and I went up to the forward end of the flight deck to marshal the aircraft after they landed. As the first one came in the ship turned into wind and anyone not otherwise engaged came out on the island or walkways to watch the fun. Had it been possible to build a grandstand on the edge of the flight deck and charge admission I could have made a fortune.

As the aircraft came in and landed with a crump I watched them pick up a wire, which pulled out with an agonized squeal. The handlers rushed out, unhooked the wire, and the pilot taxied his Avenger along the deck folding his wings as he came. The Flight Deck Engineer dropped the barriers and the pilot taxied up towards me at the forward round down. I beckoned him on and parked him as near the round-down as I dared on the port side as two men rushed up with chocks for the wheels. As I did this the barriers went up and the next aircraft was on his way in. So long as they came in at intervals of about half a minute to a minute we could get them on and parked. The Wildcats had hand folding wings but the flight deck party could usually get them folded as fast as the Avengers with their power folding wings. When they were all down the ship resumed her course and chased after the rest of the fleet, the plane guard destroyer resumed her station and we started striking the aircraft down into the hangar deck. There was a lift at each end of the flight deck. A fitter jumped into the cockpit and the handlers pushed the aircraft on to the lift. If the ship was moving much they waited for the roll then the fitter let off the brakes and the aircraft swooped along the deck guided by a man with a dolly on the tail wheel and restrained by the handlers if it charged the side. Once in the hangar the process was repeated somewhat more perilously by the hangar party, as there was less room, which became even more restricted as the hangar filled up. Once in their places they were securely lashed down.

One of the more humorous episodes concerned the soot. From time to time the funnels were swept. When this occurred the Flight Deck Engineer used to collect the soot and store it in sacks in one of the spaces under the flight deck. I asked him about this.

'It's for use when the flight deck is covered with ice and snow.'

'Go on!'

'Yes we have to mix it with sand and spread it on the flight deck — it melts the ice you see.'

Well maybe it did and maybe it didn't but it seemed to me that it would make a ghastly mess, especially when the aircraft started their engines — I could picture lumps of black mess being hurled about in a hellish blizzard. I discussed this with Wings and the engineer and we decided that the idea had probably been thought up by some featherheaded boffin who had never been within a mile of an aircraft carrier nor probably even an aeroplane and that we would ignore this piece of advice. I asked if I might dispose of the soot before anybody changed their minds. You never know whether some fishhead might have decided that we ought to try it, after all, they would not be wallowing in it themselves. Permission was granted.

I called out part of the flight deck party and started to heave the bags of soot over the side. We were anchored in Scapa Flow at the time but the bags didn't sink as I expected. They began to float slowly away from the ship. Word must have got round because Wings soon appeared.

'You can't do that.'

'Why not Sir?'

'Those bags will float ashore on the Orkneys, and then what would the Commander say?'

'We'll punch holes in them then they will sink.' We did, but they didn't sink. They continued to float away dismally into the distance. There was only one thing to do.

'Just tip the soot out of the bags.' It was so simple really, but of course it just blew away in a black cloud and hit the side of the ship. We had forgotten the golden rule — never spit to windward. So what to do? Well there was only one thing. The bags of soot were lifted on to the flight deck then humped along to the after lift. Then we took them down to the hangar deck, then carried them astern to what the Americans called 'The Fantail', it would have been the quarter deck if we had built it. We untied the bags again and quietly tipped the soot into the sea. And that was the end of that bright idea. I wished we could have thrown the boffin in with it.

The fantail held two other interesting features. One was the rubbish machine. Rubbish could not be jettisoned at sea in wartime as enemy submarines finding a trial of floating cabbage leaves, tins bottles and so forth only had to follow it to find the ship or convoy chucking it out so it was the practice to stow it all in dozens of dustbins. Owing to the number and the pong, they rapidly made the stern of the ship uninhabitable. The Yanks had devised a machine to compress the rubbish into cubes which would occupy much less space and pong less until they could be dumped when we got to port. By chance it was discovered that the compacting machine made the rubbish so dense that it sank and could then be thrown into the sea.

The other feature of the fantail was a pair of 4.5 inch guns. I suppose it being a warship they felt that we should have some guns and the flight deck was equipped with a number of Bofors and Oerlikon guns for anti-aircraft defence. The two naval guns on the fantail were designed for use against ships. On a ship that, flat out, only did 18 knots bow chasers would have been useless but it was thought that a couple of pop guns on the stern might be useful in case anyone chased us, and from time to time the First Lieutenant who was also the gunnery officer used to let them off to see if he could hit anything. I do not recall now if he ever did; we used to tow a target for him, but the first time he fired them the blast blew the perspex windows out of the aircraft ranged on the flight deck overhead, making them unserviceable for a day or two, so that in future whenever he wanted to play with his guns we always put the aircraft safely in the hangar and hoped that we would not be attacked by enemy aircraft or submarines until gunnery practice was over.

Towards the end of April we set off one day for a raid on Kilbolton in Norway. The squadron had been ashore at Hatston in the Orkneys and, as soon as we had put to sea, flew over in formation to land on. Dusty was batting and I, as usual, was standing at the forward end of the flight deck doing the parking. The sea was calm the sun was shining and the Avengers came trundling in in a steady stream. Cut — land — unhook — down barriers — taxi forward to be parked — up barriers —

'Suck back' calls the Flight Deck Engineer and the wire is reset ready for the next aircraft. Cut — land — unhook — and so it went on as smooth as silk. I had got five of them neatly parked when number six landed. His hook caught a late wire and as he lurched forward the engineer dropped the barrier so that his propeller would not catch it, as sometimes happened with late wires. At that precise moment the hook pulled out of the Avenger. Gathering speed it raced up the deck towards me straight into the space between the two previous aircraft to land, now parked either side of the deck, with their wings folded. Its outstretched wings demolished their rudders and then hit the gun turret bubbles. The three aircraft, now locked together, surged forward and rammed the tails of the three aircraft which had landed before them. I just had time to shout a warning to the handlers and disembarking aircrews before it hit.

We had instantly lost six aircraft, damaged beyond any repair we could do on board, but nobody had been hurt, and there was no fire. The rest of the squadron returned to Hatston and we returned to Scapa. Now the maximum load our derricks could take was about six tons. An Avenger with no fuel, crew or ammunition weighed just a fraction less than that. The pile of junk on the flight deck was hurriedly separated into its component parts, the fuel and ammunition taken out and when the lighters came alongside we started to lift the aircraft up and lower them over the side. Lifting them was simple enough. The derrick then had to swing out over the lighter. This was accomplished by teams of the flight deck party heaving on blocks and tackles as the aircraft swung crazily about in the wind on the end of that dreadful kinked wire. At last we could lower it down. It went down with a series of sickening jerks. Each time the wire twanged and the jib of the derrick vibrated like one of the long-bows at Agincourt. At any moment I expected the wire to part and the Avenger to make a crash landing on the lighter sinking it and going down with it and its crew. Even worse, I thought the derrick would fracture and be driven through the side of the ship and out through the bottom, sinking the old *Queen* as well. This was not so far fetched as it might sound. The old *Queen*'s sides were very thin. We had been rammed by a drifter coming alongside a few days before, because the skipper had been a bit late going full astern before he hit us, probably drunk, and had left a large dent in the hull. However all went well and we got rid of our six wrecks.

They scoured Britain for Avengers and gathering one here and another there managed to re-equip the squadron, which arrived back on board a few days later and went off on its raid to Kilbolton, which turned out to be most successful. A good time was had by all and one or two of them got gongs.

One day when we had four Avengers up, the wind suddenly dropped to nothing. When they returned to land on board again the most we could get over the deck was 17½ knots. Now a six ton aircraft flying at about 60 — 65 knots really needed a bit more than that for a safe landing but it's Hobson's choice in the middle of the North Sea. I was batting at the time so I decided the best thing would be to bring them in a bit lower and flatter than usual hanging more on the propeller so that when I gave the cut they would sink more quickly on to the deck. The first Avenger was the CO piloted by Tiny Sailes the senior pilot. He made a beautiful approach but I brought him a bit too near the port side. He landed fast with a dreadful bump and I had to duck under the wing as the radar aerial, which stuck down underneath the wing, buried itself in the screen behind my back and knocked it over. Still, it missed me. The wire pulled out a long way and pulled him up with his propeller about two feet from the island. We got him out of the way and the next one came in. He too made a hard but good landing followed by a prolonged screech as the wire pulled out about as far as it would go. Dusty who had heard these goings on from below the flight deck then came up to try his hand at what he called 'This low-wind larky' and batted in the other two.

Sometimes we had a high wind. One day during a gale the wind was a steady 60 knots on the flight deck gusting up to 90 knots. I know this because I borrowed the meteorologist's portable anemometer to measure it myself. The Wee McGrigor in one of his more switched off moods had decided that we needed a fighter cover overhead despite the fact that nobody but us in the whole of Europe would be flying in the weather we had that day, so two Wildcats were scrambled much against our will. One flown by Harry Beeston and the other by Bob Parker. The flight deck was going up and down a good 50 feet. When they came back Dusty did his best but they both broke their undercarriages landing, though neither pilot was hurt. My thoughts about the Wee McGrigor were most uncharitable.

Although I was a DLCO it seemed to me a good idea if I went flying occasionally just to show the chaps in the squadron that I really did know what it was all about. I had the feeling that they might have forgotten that I really did appreciate their problems. So one day when we were in Scapa I went ashore to Hatston and borrowed a Barracuda for a flight. They all came out to watch me take off and cheered me on so I felt it was worth while. I just flew around for a while looking at the countryside then came back and made a perfect landing. A fluke of course but it earned me approving nods.

The old *Queen*, like the others of her class, was a remarkable ship in many ways. For one thing she had a single screw, unheard of in a warship. For another the engine room was automatic. We always carried a full engine room crew in case anything went wrong but in fact two men were all that the engine room required. Another feature of the ship was her huge fuel capacity. She carried enough fuel oil and aviation spirit to stay at sea at least three months and could have stayed longer except that the food ran out. She carried so much oil that she could refuel our escorting destroyers, which ran out after 10 days, and we often did so. They would plod away astern taking it green over the bows and half drowning the crew as they hooked up the oil pipe we trailed astern for them.

She had also been designed to be fireproof. She had been built with no internal wood, we had glass fibre curtains instead of cabin doors, which of course could not jam if the ship became distorted either, metal furniture and fittings and only two coats of paint. The Royal Navy however jibbed a bit at this austerity, put on an extra coat of paint, covered all the decks with acres of corticine — a sort of thick and luxurious linoleum which burns beautifully — built a wooden bar or two — the US Navy is totally dry of course, and generally made the ships as comfortable and tiddly as possible with plenty of gin, painted canvas, and rope turk's heads and such like. The only wood the Americans supplied was the flight deck which was four inch thick oregon pine. British carriers usually had four inch thick armoured steel flight decks.

One day we had a man overboard. He had been quietly minding his own business at the edge of the flight deck when the folded wing of a nearby Wildcat unfolded itself and knocked him into the sea. I heard a yell and saw him go.

'Man overboard!' I looked over the side and saw him emerge, after a while, from the waves. Where his head should have been was a red blob. For a moment I was stunned then I realised that being a member of the port watch he was wearing a red helmet. The destroyer picked him up and he returned to us a few days later when we got back to Scapa.

Once I had a mutiny. Usually we only had either the port or starboard watch of the flight deck party on duty, unless we were at action stations, but sometimes, if things got busy, I had to keep the off duty watch on deck longer than usual. On this occasion I had kept them up so that I could move some aircraft faster than could be done with only one watch. I cannot remember why they felt so irked about this, maybe they missed lunch, but the off duty watch just sat down on the deck and refused to help. Whether I had been right to keep them on duty I don't know but I felt that my authority was being challenged and I was livid, mainly because it was wartime I think, and I felt that in wartime people should work when they were told to even if they were off duty. So I stormed up to them and addressed them thus:

'Listen you lot I don't care whether you are on watch or off watch you damn well do as I tell you or I'll run the whole lot of you before the Captain. We can sort out your troubles later. Now get on with it.' And they did.

Finally on 8 May '45 came the end of the war in Europe. VE day it was called and was one of the busiest days we ever spent. There might be, it was thought, German U boats which had not heard that the war was over. There might be German U boats, with fanatical Nazi crews, who would decide that even if the war in Europe was over they would go on sinking anything they could find. We were, after all, still at war with the Japanese. So off we went escorting official landing parties to

Norway. We approached the Skagerack in the dark and at 0430 flew off two anti-submarine Avengers, and two Wildcat Combat Air Patrol fighters. Thereafter we flew off two Wildcats and landed on two every hour and a half. And every two and a half hours flew off two Avengers and landed on two Avengers. This went on continuously until 2300 hours when the last two landed on. We struck them down into the hangar and gratefully turned in. No fanatical Germans were seen at all, and we returned to Scapa.

A convoy of ships was due to set sail for Russia and so, for the same reasons, we set off to escort the last Russian convoy to Murmansk. We didn't really expect to see any fanatical U boats or be attacked by fanatical Luftwaffe pilots off North Cape, which hadn't yet been reoccupied after the German invasion, but you never knew. Still, after an uneventful voyage we arrived at Kola inlet, just East of where the coast lines of Norway and Russia meet. As we sailed into the port we were greeted by USSR ship *Archangel*. She had once been HMS *Royal Sovereign* but we had sold her. She was very rusty but otherwise in good working order and trained her fifteen inch guns on us to prove it. We thought this a little unfriendly towards an ally but after checking the range the guns were returned to their normal fore and aft position. Thereafter she did this once every morning as long as we remained in Kola.

Still the war was over, at any rate in these waters, everybody felt very friendly so we invited a party of Russian officers from the Russian Naval Air Base ashore to come and dine with us. They were glad to accept and about two dozen arrived. We showed them the ship, wined them and dined them and exchanged cigarettes. Russian cigarettes were small cardboard tubes with what looked like fag ends attached to them. Some of the Russian officers spoke a little english and we got on well. There was also a serious little man with spectacles. He was not an aviator and he did a lot of listening as well as talking. He was, one of the english speaking officers told us, a member of the KGB and had really come with them to see that they curbed their tongues. I have a photograph of him and I think now that he was probably Yuri Andropov later to become general secretary of the communist party, who was in the Murmansk area in 1945. At all events they all enjoyed themselves and invited us to dine with them.

Kola is North of the Arctic Circle and at that time of the year the midnight sun went round and round the horizon without ever setting. We set off in broad daylight at midnight in the liberty boat and stepped ashore to be greeted by a somewhat stern looking lady wearing a quilted jacket and holding a machine gun. She gave us the once over then directed us along the road to the camp. As we walked we passed a work party of other young ladies, wearing quilted jackets, engaged in digging, and laying drain pipes, beside the road. We also passed a number of gibbets. They were not in use but had rusted wires dangling from them testifying to the fact that war is a serious business. After a while we reached the camp to be greeted by our erstwhile friends of the shipboard party. There was a difference though. We noticed that those who spoke the best english were unavoidably on duty and a number of less well endowed officers had taken their places. The KGB man was still very busy helping out with translations when needed. They showed us the aircraft. There was a primary trainer, some fighters and a captured Messerschmit 109 but the most interesting aeroplane was the Iluyshin II or Stormovik. This was a tank-buster, and designed to take heavy punishment. It was a single engined plane slightly like a Fairey Battle to look at, there the similarity ended. The whole nose from the propeller boss to the cockpit was covered with steel plate a quarter of an inch thick. There was a thick steel bulkhead, about an inch thick between the pilot and the engine and more armour plate behind and under his seat. The windscreen was three inches thick bullet proof glass and the rest of the cockpit glass one inch thick. The wings were wooden and the bomb doors underneath them simply wooden doors on springs which opened by the weight of the bombs falling on them as they left the aircraft and closed automatically after they had gone. It was very heavy and rather slow. Anti-aircraft fire either bounced off the armoured parts or passed harmlessly through the soft wood of the wings. It was an extremely successful anti-tank weapon.

Even in June there was ice and snow about so we were glad to get into the mess hall. Built of wood it resembled a church hall with a trestle table down the middle, literally bending under the weight of food. We had whitebait, pots of caviar, huge dishes of salmon and salad to go with it. Beside each place was a carafe with a glass inverted over it. It seemed to me very thoughtful to put a carafe of water beside each place as the meal looked salty and thirst making so I poured myself a tumbler full and took a swig to find that each of us had a carafe of neat Vodka. Naturally we had a very good party and returned to the old *Queen* about 0400. We never saw the Russians again but I've no doubt they remember the party as well as we do. We sailed for Scapa again soon after. On the way home we had a few sing songs and games of liar's dice of course and when things seemed too dull boosted a few mess mates off along the ward room tables. We had to give this up however because the boostee sometimes hit the bulkhead, and on the other side of the bulkhead was a rating asleep in his bunk, US built ships did not have hammocks, and when this happened he fell out.

When we got back to Scapa 853 left us. The plan then was for us to take on a squadron of Barracudas and sail for the Far East. I think the ludo players had decided by this time that since they still had a few hundred Barracudas left over they might as well use them up on the Japs even if they did need heavily escorting, so I was sent off to Machrihanish to meet the new squadron and give them some deck landing practice on the aerodrome before they came to *Queen*.

Well nobody was very enthusiastic about all this; the war was over in Europe and Japan seemed a long way off. The squadron was 810. They had been shore based for some time and were a little rusty on deck landings. I spent some time coaxing them down but the wind was seldon along the runway and proper training was difficult. One pilot landed a bit heavily and as he bounced up I noticed that his wheels were not spinning as they normally would have been. When he came down again the port undercarriage leg collapsed and he slewed off the runway. I think he had probably put on the brakes as the wheels were retracted after take off, as he should have done, to stop the wheels spinning as they entered their housings. This was to prevent the tyres being cut on any sharp edges, and he had forgotten to release them again before landing. However for this and other reasons I decided that they were not yet ready for the deck, made a report to that effect and went on some leave which had become due to me, leaving behind, as it turned out, a time bomb. Somehow my report reached the ears of Commander R.N. Everett RN. 'How dare I criticise pilots he had trained? Of course they were good enough to go to the deck.'

He arrived hot foot in Machrihanish, breathing fire and put the squadron through their paces. With the maestro leaping about the runway, and doubtless a nice steady breeze straight along it, they came in to land like billiard balls rolling out of a tube. The first I knew of this was a message from *Queen* telling me not to return. I had been relieved of my job. The next thing was an appointment as Flight Deck Officer to HMS *Ocean*.

It was a curious fact that whenever my path crossed that of Cdr. R.N. Everett RN I always put up a black. To begin with he didn't like my ADDLs much when I was still under training. About the same time I borrowed one of his station flight aeroplanes one day and brought it back after dark which irked him considerably. Then there was the business of being arrested and also of taxying over his newly painted lines and finally my batting of 810. Perhaps eventually I would have done something that he approved of but the war ended before I had the chance.

Ocean was also waiting to take aircraft on board before setting out for the far east and I joined her in Liverpool docks. My first job was to work out a plan for parking the aircraft in the hangar and another for arranging them in a deck park prior to flying off, using cardboard cut outs of the aircraft with their wings folded and spread on a large chart.

One day I was sitting alone in the wardroom listening to the radio when I heard the BBC announce that an atom bomb had been dropped on Hiroshima. It sounded so incredible I couldn't really believe it. I hurriedly spread the news but naturally enough nobody believed me. Nobody had ever heard of Hiroshima nor an atom bomb. The whole thing was preposterous and I must be mistaken. Five days later the war ended and shortly after that I was sent on leave to await demobilisation.

Index